The history of the Kingdom of Kongo during the era of the civil wars is a major theme in precolonial African history that has, until now, eluded full explication.

Utilizing contemporaneous written records, Thornton has produced not only a highly reliable history of events and trends, but a history alive with details of everyday life and ordinary people. The faithfulness of the reconstruction gives depth and cogency to Thornton's analysis of the decline of Kongo's centralized political system and the radical transformation of its society. His work offers to scholars a sophisticated interpretation of Kongo in the seventeenth century, for the first time bringing order to this difficult area of precolonial history.

The Kingdom of Kongo

The
Kingdom
of Kongo

Civil War and Transition
1641–1718

John K. Thornton

The University of Wisconsin Press

Published 1983

The University of Wisconsin Press
114 North Murray Street
Madison, Wisconsin 53715

The University of Wisconsin Press, Ltd.
1 Gower Street
London WC1E 6HA, England

First printing

Printed in the United States of America

For LC CIP information see the colophon

ISBN 0–299–09290–9

Contents

Maps

Preface

THE KINGDOM of Kongo has had a fascination for historians on two counts. First of all, its flirtation with Christianity and with the outward trappings of European culture has made it a model of early acculturation for some, while for others it has been an example of the effects, for good or ill, of "foreign aid." Secondly, and also as a result of its conversion to Christianity, Kongo is described by a wealth of contemporary documents, some from missionaries who served long terms in the country, some from merchants, and others from literate Kongo themselves. The result of this documentary abundance is that Kongo history can be studied in detail from a much earlier date than is possible for most other major, independent African states.

For myself, the possibilities opened up by the extensive documentation provided the initial attraction to Kongo history. I hoped to undertake a study which would combine two very different approaches to history: the newly revived Marxist historical and anthropological approaches, and "total history" of the kind preached, and usually practiced, by Fernand Braudel and the "Annales school." Both approaches, to be utilized effectively, require extensive documentary material. In addition to the advantages of abundant source material, Kongo had also undergone rapid change in the period of greatest documentary abundance, allowing me to undertake an interesting case study in historical change.

The two approaches I envisioned are far from incompatible. In fact, not a few "Annalistes" use Marxist methodology, and the Marxist theoreticians of today are full of praise for the "Annalistes." If readers feel that Braudel is better served in the pages that follow than Marx, it is probably because I have avoided Marxist terminology and the theoretical hairsplitting that so often encumber attempts at Marxist history.

This work is nevertheless an ambitious one. I hope to do no less than to explain as well as describe the major changes that occurred in Kongo in the seventeenth and early eighteenth centuries in the context of the civil wars. Furthermore, I hope to place this explanation in a theoretical framework that will make it applicable beyond a few hundred thousand square kilometers of central Africa. I will pose, and attempt to answer, important questions about continuity, change, and development in history. To succeed in this, I must do more than simply describe one central African polity in the process of change—I must explain that change as well.

At the same time as I have tried this rather charged attempt at the philosophy of history, I have tried to preserve the human side of history in Kongo. The seventeenth-century documentation provides the historian with an unusual number of humans whose lives are well enough described to emerge as real, many-sided personalities. I have tried to capture that flavor without drifting too far into simple anecdote. This desire to always keep the human beings of Kongo in mind has also played a role in my decision to keep heavy theoretical discussion out of the text, which will at least prevent jargon and abstraction from interfering with our appreciation of the people of Kongo.

Ultimately, the whole attempt rests on the careful reading of a fairly large group of sources. Much of the considerable time that I spent preparing this book was simply in collecting the huge body of written documents and working with it, over and over, until I felt that I knew Kongo personally. The whole project therefore took rather a long time. I began it in earnest in the fall of 1973, while serving in the U.S. Air Force, and completed it as a Ph.D. dissertation for the University of California (Los Angeles) in the summer of 1979. Two more years spent teaching in Zambia and reworking the text and rereading the documents have brought it to its present form.

In many ways this long period of collection, even though much of it was spent outside formal academic institutions—indeed completely away from a scholarly environment—was worthwhile. I collected the material slowly, using interlibrary loans for published material not available locally and ordering the unpublished material on microfilm. By far most of the unpublished manuscript material mentioned in the footnotes of this book was gathered by mail while I was living in Denver and Los Angeles. In that way I was able to read each new set of material as it reached me, and work through it carefully over the long period between shipments of microfilm from Europe. When, in 1978, I finally visited the Arquivo Histórico Ultramarino in Lisbon, the Archives of the Propaganda Fide in Rome, and other archives of Europe on a six-week grant, I discovered to my surprise and delight that I had collected nearly everything of relevance by mail. Moreover, I had learned much, much more about the problems of the material, its paleography, its classification, and the like than does the average graduate student setting foot in the archives for the first time. I had learned where to look, what to expect, and generally how to use what I found during the five years of collection by mail.

Since the completion of the dissertation, the process of collection has continued, for even while living in Zambia I was able to gather a few more bits and pieces of information through the mails. My living in Zambia was more important for me, however, in a more personal sense. Living and working on the soil of central Africa brought many problems into focus which I had hitherto not encountered in person, but instead only through the oblique medium of the written texts. My visit to Luanda in July of 1981 had a similar personal and inspirational effect, which, while it has not changed either the theoretical perspective of the work or its historical reconstruction, has put me more intimately in touch with central African cultures. I believe this personal feeling is reflected in the rewriting of the text for this book.

I owe a tremendous debt of gratitude to the researchers who pioneered the study of Kongo history. Through guides to source material, bibliographies, and footnotes, they have made it possible for me to collect a great deal of material "from an armchair" in the United States. Kongo's documentation has been worked over for many years by many people, from early pioneers such as the Conde de Paiva Manso, through the diligent researchers of the '40s and '50s such as Jean Cuvelier, Hildebrand de Hooglede, or Louis Jadin, to modern scholars like Teobaldo Filesi, François Bontinck, and António Brásio. Their thoroughness in tracking down material and their scrupulous recording of its location has made my research possible. Without their efforts, I could never have gathered as much material as I did.

Along with this scholarly help, I must thank the staffs of the libraries and archives of Europe, who helped me to locate documents and provided me with microfilmed and Xeroxed copies. The whole staff of the Archives of the "Propaganda Fide" in Rome, and especially the archivist, Father Metzler, have been very prompt and helpful not only with my many mail requests, but also when I worked in their archive in person in 1978. I must also mention Father Giacomo Carlini of the Capuchin Archives of the Province of Tuscany for his help in mail requests. The Jesuit Generalte Archives in Rome and the Overseas Archive in Lisbon also provided help for me during my visit and allowed me to carry away many feet of microfilm. In fact, I must say that the staff of every archive I wrote to or visited helped me considerably, although not all were quite as willing as these to provide service from a distance.

Several other scholars have helped me as well, both in research and in writing, not to mention inspiration and even debate. My Ph.D. thesis committee, headed by Edward Alpers and including Geoffrey Simcox, Agnes Aidoo, and James Lockhart, all contributed to the original thesis version of this book. In addition, Linda Heywood provided fine theoretical criticisms as well as patient reading of all my drafts, on top of many hours of discussion and correspondence. Wyatt MacGaffey shared some of his intimate knowledge of the modern Kongo people with me during several intense hours of discussion and in correspondence. Comparing my documents with his firsthand knowledge convinced me that we were both talking about the same people.

Joseph C. Miller read the draft of the thesis and commented on it, and our correspondence on a wide range of topics has proven inspirational. Jan Vansina provided me with a detailed list of criticisms which have been most helpful in revision. Others who assisted me in revision by their critical readings of the dissertation were François Bontinck and David Henige. I also benefitted from lengthy discussions of Kongo history with Emmanuel Esteves in Luanda and through discussion and correspondence with Henrique Abranches and Simão Souindoula of the National Anthropology Laboratory in Luanda. These discussions and correspondence were especially helpful in clarifying the relationship of Kongo's history to the history of Angola.

Finally, I must give hearty thanks to the institutions that allowed me to continue to eat while doing this work. Much of my graduate study was financed by the Veterans Administration through Veterans' Educational Benefits and part-time work-study employment at the Veterans' Administration Hospital, Brentwood. I also received financial support from a National Defense Foreign Language Title VI grant. My research in Portugal and Italy was financed by the Regents' Patent Fund and the Center for the Study of Portuguese-speaking Africa at U.C.L.A., and by the Fundação Calouste Gulbenkian of Lisbon. I must also thank my parents for consistently supplementing my income when I needed it most. With the exception of my parents, none of my financial benefactors influenced my work in any way, and they cannot be held responsible for any errors or misinterpretations arising from it.

Introduction

IN LATE February, 1641, Álvaro VI Afonso, Nimi a Lukeni, "Defender of the Faith, King of the most ancient Kingdom of Kongo and Lord of all the Ambundos,"[1] died suddenly after a short illness. The illness was so short, in fact, that it was rumored at the time that he had been poisoned.[2] Since Kongo's system of succession was elective rather than hereditary, the royal electors met soon afterwards to choose a successor, and chose a certain Dom Álvaro to succeed Álvaro VI in office. But the electors had not counted on Álvaro VI's ambitious brother Garcia, the Duke of Mbamba and Captain General of Kongo, a military hero who had once saved a Kongo king from rebels and who had important friends and relatives in the capital. Warned of his brother's death by a canon of the cathedral of São Salvador in the capital, Garcia quickly raised an army, marched on the capital, and in the confusion reigning in the city, turned the electors out and proclaimed himself King Garcia II of Kongo.[3]

Garcia's violent seizure of the throne was not unusual in Kongo in the period before 1641. If anything, violence and bloodshed were typical of it, as the Jesuit priest Matheus Cordoso wrote in 1622:

> In this kingdom there are certain to be great revolts upon the death of the king by the fidalgos [nobility] and the common people, the commoners to steal and the fidalgos to make a king who conforms to their pretentions and to avenge themselves upon each other, therefore paying more attention to their own particular good than to that of the common, general good.[4]

In fact, the seventeenth century had witnessed a number of kings who had occupied the throne only briefly, ruling for a few weeks after an election and then succumbing to revolts of ambitious relatives. The reigns of Garcia II and his son António I, however, marked the high point of the Kingdom of Kongo's history—the culmination of nearly 250 years of development, and the turning point as well. The succession disputes that would follow Garcia II and António's reigns would be entirely different, never resulting in the successful choice of a king and ultimately laying waste to the entire kingdom. The form of struggle for the throne would change from short, sometimes bloody but ultimately decisive contests, to an era of civil war. During the chaotic era of the civil wars, which stretched until the restoration of King Pedro IV in 1709, not only did the form of succession struggle change, but the entire social, economic, and political base of the kingdom altered. The civil wars were decisive, not just for the small and contentious group of nobles who ran the country, but for everyone, from the king to the humble peasants in their rural villages.

The kingdom that Garcia II took over in 1641 occupied the south bank of the Zaire River in what is now northern Angola and western Zaire. In his day, the population was somewhat over half a million people living in an area of some 130,000 square kilometers, although Kongo's claims extended to a larger area than did its effective rule.[5] Today Kikongo-speaking people extend over a still larger area, including sections of Congo-Brazzaville, and they number about one and a half million. Founded in the late fourteenth century, Kongo had expanded from a nucleus in the territories a short distance north and west of its capital, Mbanza Kongo, later to be renamed São Salvador when it became an episcopal see. By the time the first Portuguese navigators reached its Atlantic shores in 1483, Kongo encompassed much of the territory that it would hold at its height, although major conquests and incorporations of territory were undertaken in the sixteenth century. The Portuguese and other Europeans saw "Manicongo" as the most powerful kingdom in the whole Gulf of Guinea region.[6] The sixteenth century, which saw the end of Kongo's expansion by the 1590s, also saw consolidation of the main core of the Kingdom and the finalizing of Kongo's political system.[7]

The Europeans who reached Kongo in the late fifteenth century brought Christianity and contact with a host of regions hitherto unknown to the Kongo. In 1491 Nzinga a Nkuwu was baptized as João I, and his son, Afonso Mvemba a Nzinga, established Christianity as a religion of state. After a somewhat turbulent beginning, during which Christianity was challenged, Kongo became a firm convert to the new religion, retaining it right up to the present day.[8] As a result of its early conversion, Kongo enjoyed friendly diplomatic relations with several European countries, including Portugal, Spain, the Low Countries, and the Holy See in Rome.[9] Kongo kings corresponded with members of the French court, and in 1617, working through channels in Rome, tried to establish diplomatic relations with Ethiopia, the other Christian country of the African continent.[10]

Foreign contact also brought foreign trade. In the sixteenth century this trade was largely in slaves, copper, and ivory.[11] Kongo's expansive wars to the south and east fueled the slave trade, and Portuguese settled in Mbanza Kongo and the Atlantic coastal port of Mpinda. They provided military assistance in wars, and bought the salves netted in the expeditions.[12] Other Portuguese, concerned with restrictions on their activity by royal officials both of Kongo and of Portugal, sought their fortunes in Kongo's powerful but nominally subordinate southern neighbor, the Kingdom of Ndongo. Attempts to control a trade that was considered contraband along the Kwanza River eventually led to the founding of the Portuguese colony in Angola, a development that the rulers of Kongo at first supported but later resisted when it conflicted with their interests.[13] By the time Garcia II came to Kongo's throne in 1641, Kongo and the Portuguese of Angola had fought several border wars and were generally on unfriendly terms officially, although considerable trade and settlement continued to link the two states.

Although many historians have seen the development of the slave trade and settlement of Angola by the Portuguese as prime causes of a decline in Kongo, these probably did not have any long-lasting effects on the Kingdom's stability. Much of the literature of complaint of the sixteenth century about Portuguese settlement in Kongo and the slave trade concerned either the interest of Kongo kings in the internal affairs of the Portuguese community or their concern about the support that some Portuguese gave to Ndongo.[14] The slave trade was almost always confined to the borders of the country, and even by mid-century slaves bought by Kongo or Portuguese merchants from neighboring countries to the east were an important source of slaves for São Tomé and the Americas.[15] When Kongo's expansionary wars of the sixteenth century stopped, so did Kongo's direct participation in the slave trade.[16] Garcia II's Kongo was primarily an exporter of cloth to Angola, ivory and re-exported slaves originating from beyond her eastern boundaries.[17] The export of copper was on the decline, although Portuguese beliefs that rich deposits of copper lay in the country fueled their interest in control of Kongo's commerce and mining.[18]

The quarter century when Garcia II and António I ruled marked the high point in Kongo's long course of development. At the same time, it marked the beginning of the long period of transition, the violent era of the civil wars. The civil wars gave birth to a different Kongo, which retained its new characteristics throughout the rest of the precolonial period. The era that began with the reign of Garcia II in 1641 and ended with the death of Kongo's restorer king, Pedro IV, in 1718, marks a crucial period in Kongo history, setting a pattern that would hold for the next two centuries.

The period opens with the Kongo of the sixteenth and seventeenth centuries, the powerful centralized state that was well known not only in Africa, but to the rest of the world as well. It was the crowning period of centralized control, when Garcia's word in the capital was obeyed by everyone in the country. It was at the same time the period of Kongo's maximum prestige, when Kongo's diplomats were active in Europe and Brazil, and when it seemed quite possible that Garcia's diplomacy would break the Portuguese stranglehold on Kongo's ecclesiastical establishment as it had already done to Portuguese control of its diplomatic and commercial activity. Moreover, it was a continuation and maximization of the work of Afonso I (1506–43) in the Christianization of Kongo, when the Capuchin mission to Kongo began to reach, for the first time, beyond the courts of the king and the great nobility to the ordinary peasants of the countryside.

The end of this turbulent sixty-year period saw the establishment of a new Kongo, decentralized, internationally forgotten, and, in time, even without missionaries. The tiny impoverished courts of the local nobles, independent of each other but cognizant of their past glories and recognizing a token king in a depopulated capital, represented the new order of Kongo. This order was already visible when Pedro IV restored the Kingdom in 1709, after defeating the forces of his rival, Pedro Constantinho da Silva. It was the period in which the modern Kongo society so well known to anthropologists and ethnographers of the present century was formed, as well as those of modern northern Angola and western Zaire.

It is quite correctly, then, that Jan Vansina has described the period 1665–1718 as a "mutation process," in which one political system was replaced by another. Of special relevance to historians and ethnographers, though, is the existence of immense documentation covering the whole period. Vansina notes: "The mutation process itself is one of the very few instances where such a phenomenon is documented in Africa and therefore should be fascinating to historians and anthropologists alike."[19] This period of Kongo history, then, is of interest not only to those concerned with the history of a small area of west central Africa, but to all students of African history, or of the historical study of social change. While for most African societies the study of social change can only be seen in detail in the nineteenth century, for Kongo this process can be witnessed over the past four centuries. Furthermore, for most of Africa the period of the best documentation coincides with the last precolonial years and the colonial era, when Africa was subjected to immense external impacts wrought both by the implantation of European colonialism and by the worldwide consequences of the Industrial Revolution. While Europeans were present in Kongo throughout the years 1641–1718, their influence was not as pervasive as that of the Europeans of the colonial era, nor was an economy anywhere based on industrial power. As a result, the changes that occurred in Kongo were much more the product of internal dynamic than simply reaction to external pressure. As such, Kongo's history in the seventeenth and eighteenth centuries helps to illustrate the possibilities for and limits of change in an African society.

The documentation that makes this close study possible is unlike the type of documentation normally encountered for relatively remote periods of African history. It was made by observers (missionaries) who knew the language of the country,[20] lived there for a considerable time, and were assisted by a large and important staff of bicultural Kongo.[21] Despite their origins as upper-class European missionaries, the Capuchins (whose writing makes up the bulk of our material on Kongo) took an interest not only in the lives of the social and political elite of the towns, but also in the daily life of the rural villagers.[22] This unusual quality of eyewitness documents, at least by the standards of European documentation for precolonial Africa, allows for a detailed social and economic history of all social strata in Kongo.

However unusual and good the missionary documentation may be when compared with the documentation for equivalent time periods in other African regions, it is sadly lacking for a full-scale social history on Kongo. For one thing, it is entirely the observations of outsiders, and while the outsiders were well informed, they were still foreign in outlook. Second, it is general rather than specific. With the exception of baptismal statistics, there is little quantitative data, and moreover, social institutions are presented in the data as averages—that is, the ideal situation is depicted. There are not the specific data for the day-to-day operations of single households, villages, or other units that might fill this ideal depiction with life. We do not possess those tax lists, estate records, wills and testaments and inventories that enliven the social history of other regions.

Nevertheless, it is still possible to penetrate beneath the political events which were visible even to casual observers and discuss the deeper structures of the kingdom which gave direction and sense to those events. The documentation permits examination in some detail of the effect of political structures on the settlement pattern of the kingdom and on the distribution of surplus. The political events which form the starting and ending points of this study are themselves no more than reflections of deeper changes going on within Kongo society, changes in the relationship between rulers and ruled, workers and consumers, masters and slaves. At the same time, the acute eyes of the missionaries reveal the ideological structures of the country—its traditional religion, the newly introduced Christian religion, and their alteration with changes in other sectors of Kongo society. What the French historians of the "Annales school" call "total history" is therefore allowed: the interactions between humans and the natural environment, between town and country, between rulers and ruled are visible, and, moreover, visible in the process of change.

The very fact that great changes occurred during the period requires that the documents be used to discuss not only the events of the time, but also the underlying structures that caused the changes. This study is intended, then, to be more than simply another one of several attempts to reconstruct the confused period that followed the battle of Mbwila in 1665 by making use of a more careful study of the documents. Instead, it will focus on the causes of this process of mutation, in the hope that the examination in depth of such a process in one central African kingdom can contribute to the understanding of social change in general, and not simply present a parade of political events that make up what historians of the "Annales school" scornfully call "l'histoire événementelle."

The process of discerning social change solely through present-day observation requires care in the use of the material. Africanists, used to inferring past structures by use of contemporary material, oral tradition, and perhaps a few documents, have developed, over the past twenty years, a whole historiography for reconstructing past societies with limited material. Such techniques have resulted in important contributions to African history, but when adequate contemporary material in the form of written documents does exist, more traditional types of historical work are preferable. In the case of the Kingdom of Kongo, the documentation does exist, and it does more harm than good to make use of modern materials, ethnographic analogy, or other techniques, since these techniques all rely on an assumption that the society under examination has not changed in any fundamental way. When one posits that change has occurred, as indeed it has in Kongo, then the only allowable approach is to reconstruct the social, economic, and political baselines of the society from the contemporary evidence. Thus, in the early stages of this work, only documentation drawn from a tightly defined time period—roughly 1620 to 1740—was used. While this procedure did not produce as full a picture of daily life in Kongo as Georges Balandier was able to draw using material taken from modern ethnology, oral traditions, and documents from all time periods of Kongo history,[23] it did reveal a different social and economic structure in Kongo from that described in later documents or modern ethnography. Understanding how this earlier structure evolved into the later structure makes a genuinely historical picture of Kongo's development possible.

The tendency to mix modern and older sources together to produce a uniform description of Kongo is perhaps the greatest fault in modern research on the history of the region. It is especially noticeable since the most ambitious attempts to produce analysis as well as description of the country and its history have generally suffered from it. Historical descriptions and analyses of Kongo pioneered by Joseph van Wing in 1921 and Alexander Ihle in 1929 were oriented by modern anthropological research work in the region and have left their mark on most subsequent work.[24] More recent attempts at an anthropologically oriented history of Kongo by Georges Balandier (1965), W. G. L. Randles (1968), and Kajsa Ekholm (1972) have continued this tradition.[25] Because their methodology necessarily assumed a static social structure, they could not explain the changes in the kingdom by means of any sort of internal development. As a result, all have looked, to a greater or lesser degree, to Kongo's involvement in foreign trade and contact for the source of change. Much of their historical orientation came from Afonso de Albuquerque Felner, probably the leading early Portuguese researcher into Kongo history, to whom they were heavily indebted not only for his documents but for his interpretations. Felner, like other Portuguese historians, was quick to emphasize the revolutionary nature of European contact in order to give Portugal pride of place in the history of the region.[26] Later historians of the Portuguese in Africa, James Duffy and Basil Davidson, writing in the late 1950s and early '60s, reinterpreted Felner without changing the supposition that Europeans were fundamental movers in Kongo's history.[27] Even though they saw the Portuguese as destroyers rather than builders in Kongo, they still maintained that European contact was the prime cause of change in Kongo society. The anthropologically oriented scholars, such as Balandier, Randles, and Ekholm, by recognizing that European activity operated within an already functioning and independent social structure, assigned it a more balanced role than did either Felner or Duffy and Davidson; but even they looked to the Portuguese to supply the lost dynamic that made Kongo change.

Although all the anthropologically oriented students of Kongo's history have made use of a fair sample of material available, their description and analysis have often suffered because they were not close critics of the documents. Those whose reading was more careful have had more doubts about the specific effects and the general importance of European influence. Jean Cuvelier, who published his history of sixteenth-century Kongo in Flemish in 1941, was perhaps the most erudite early scholar to deal with Kongo.[28] While Cuvelier read a vast quantity of documents very carefully, for his anthropology he relied on Ihle (as well as on his own knowledge of modern Kongo society gained while serving as a missionary in the Belgian Congo). In general, the faults of Cuvelier can be said to apply to most of the large number of missionary and clerical scholars who have studied Kongo, drawn by its early conversion to Christianity. Most never attempted to write a general history of the country, instead restrict-

ing their activity to close studies of a small group of documents, or relying
on their theoretically oriented anthropologist colleagues for major interpretation. Their greatest contribution has been in the publication and
annotation of documents, and in studies of fairly restricted episodes in
Kongo's history. Louis Jadin, for example, wrote articles on the Antonian
movement as a preface to the publication of a dossier of documents from
Roman archives on the subject; and discussed Luso-Dutch rivalry in Nsoyo,
the organization of the Kongo church, and the Jesuit missions to Kongo
in similar contexts in a series of major articles published by the *Bulletin
de l'Institut Historique Belge de Rome*.[29] Teobaldo Filesi limited the focus
of his work to diplomatic activity in the sixteenth and seventeenth centuries, and François Bontinck has edited several contemporary texts, and
done detailed studies concerned with events of the early sixteenth century.[30]

Valuable as their work has been in building up thoroughly documented
studies, publishing documents, and establishing a chronicle of events,
this group of historians have not made the major contribution to the
understanding of society and social change in Kongo that their knowledge
of the documentary material might have allowed them. When they made
comments on Kongo history as a whole, they turned to Ihle, van Wing,
or, more recently, Balandier. The irony of the situation is that the anthropologists were relying on an earlier generation of clerical and missionary
scholars to write their history.

Ultimately, however, the exchange between scholarly and erudite priests
and theoretical anthropologists has paid off in creating a large and full
historiography of Kongo. In 1965, Jan Vansina wrote what was probably
the best summary to that date of Kongo history as a whole in the first,
French, edition of *Kingdoms of the Savanna*.[31] Vansina, trained as both
an anthropologist and a historian, was careful to make use of the documents critically as well as to dwell on the major themes and to ask the
questions fundamental to understanding Kongo history. His work was not
free from the tendency to mix modern and older source material,[32] but it
was conscious of the need to approach the matter critically, and his criticism of Georges Balandier's book, published the same year, was quick to
demand a more rigid use of documentary material.[33] Likewise, David
Birmingham dealt with Kongo largely from contemporary documents,
and although never going much beyond a summary treatment of the
country, broke new ground in the use of documents.[34] Finally, Anne
Hilton's Ph.D. thesis (1977), a major study of Kongo in the sixteenth and
seventeenth centuries, took the work initiated by Birmingham to its log-
ical conclusion. Although the analysis of the present book differs substantially from Hilton's findings, its methodology is not substantially different.[35]

Note on Orthography

I HAVE used modern orthography for all proper names in Spanish, French, Dutch, Portuguese, and Italian, and for Kikongo as much as is possible. In Kikongo I have generally followed established forms for all provinces of Kongo except Nsoyo (which has been variously spelled *Sonho, Sonyo, Soyo, Sonhio,* etc.). *Kongo* has been used in both a nominal and an adjectival form. That is, I have spoken of the Kingdom of Kongo, a Kongo custom, the Kongo people. I have used the class prefix only in referring to the language (Kikongo).

In reference to political titles of the Kingdom of Kongo, I have used the "feudal" terminology (King, Duke, Count, Marquis, etc.), as this was the terminology officially in use in Kongo after 1596. It replaced a more general system of titles which used only the Kikongo word *mwene* (*mani* in contemporary texts) for all major positions, although at some levels of administration the *mani* form continued in use (i.e., for districts of Nsoyo, administrative titles in the capital, etc.). The same administrative decrees altered the name of the capital city of Kongo from Mbanza Kongo to São Salvador, and for this period I have retained the name of São Salvador. In 1975 this city was renamed Mbanza Kongo.

When referring to Kongo people in the text, I have preferred the baptismal name (a "European" saint's name) even when other (Kikongo) names are known—hence my choice of "Pedro II," rather than "Nkanga a Mvika"—except where reference to the additional names is necessary for clarity. Moreover, I have given these names in their modern, European orthographic form rather than using modern Kikongo orthography for them, which would have made *Dom João* into *Ndozau* or *Dom Afonso* into *Ndofunsu,* etc.

The Kingdom of Kongo

1

The Natural Setting

THERE WAS a constant interplay between the people and the natural environment in the Kongo of the seventeenth century. This interplay was not always obvious in the visible social interactions of its people, the interactions that make up what are usually considered history and society. Yet the natural environment in Kongo, as in any nation, was always quietly active as a backdrop, always taken into consideration—for making war, collecting taxes, or trade and travel—even if its presence was such a commonplace that the considerations were almost unconscious. Often this natural environment which was taken for granted or only unconsciously considered would suddenly emerge from the background and impose itself on Kongo's inhabitants, as it did when hordes of locusts appeared suddenly and inexplicably over the eastern mountains. Nature provided Kongo with a number of possibilities in the various gifts it had bestowed upon the country, in minerals, soil, water, and so on, and at the same time it imposed certain limitations on the speed and direction of travel, absolute amount of water from rivers or rainfall, or seasons when one could plant or fight.

Although the human inhabitants of Kongo did not control their environment to the same degree that is possible today, human decisions often had long-term and significant effects upon nature, and much of the environment of Kongo was a product of human activity. In some places, the planting of trees or the building of towns reduced wild vegetation and placed large regions directly under human supervision—some species were permitted access, others were not. People would burn large vegetated areas, sometimes as a prelude to planting, at other times simply to frighten animals that were worrying travellers. This activity, like the gradual reduction of the forests and their replacement by grassland as a result

3

of agricultural activity, had permanent effects on humanity's interaction with nature.[1]

Kongo's geological map can provide a starting point. Geological events determined the shape of the land, the direction of the rivers, and the fertility of the soil, and they influenced the distribution of rainfall. These effects were ancient and for practical purposes unchanging. The rocks of the eastern escarpment that rose up abruptly from a plain of 500 meters elevation to another, more rugged plain of 1,000 to 1,500 meters elevation were ancient indeed, some over 2,500 million years old. The sedimentary material that covered the lower and flatter western regions was younger, but the tectonic movements that had created Kongo's base had already finished some 450 million years before Garcia II began to rule in Kongo.[2] People could scarcely change their land's topography and human will had to bend to it, and accept it as it was.

The great escarpment of eastern and southeastern Kongo that formed the border between the coastal lowlands and the central African high plateau was the central and most important feature of Kongo, a feature that had considerable influence on its history and politics. In the east of the country this escarpment formed a range of mountains which Matheus Cordoso, a well-travelled Jesuit of the 1620s, rightly called the "backbone" of the country.[3] Merchants or travellers going east to the slave markets of Mpumbu had to bypass the mountains to the north along the plain cut by the Zaire River, or thread their way through steep and narrow passes, such as the one the Italian Capuchin Lorenzo da Lucca negotiated in 1706 on his way from Luanda to Nkusu in the east.[4] The eastern edge of this escarpment was a series of steep mountain slopes, cut into ridges by streams, while east of the immediate break the land levelled off, but river action made the land into a series of mountains varying from 1,200 meters on their peaks to 500–700 meters in the beds of the deeper river valleys.[5] Thus the flat plains of the west and the low, undulating hills of the center of the country gave way to sharp and sudden mountain barrier, which, when crossed, opened to a district of great parallel ridges, aligned north to south, with rivers running between them. It was because of this feature of the geography of eastern Kongo that the Capuchin priest Luca da Caltanisetta, crossing the eastern province of Nsonso from west to east, believed he was endlessly climbing mountains and then crossing rivers, only to be confronted with still another mountain on the other side.[6] The rivers that formed the low and level land in the east were the seat of human life and activity there. The Nkisi River running from the mountains of southern Kongo into the Zaire River on the north was the most important of these eastern river valleys, and the capitals of three major provinces of the east, Mbata, Mpangu, and Nsundi, all lay on it.[7]

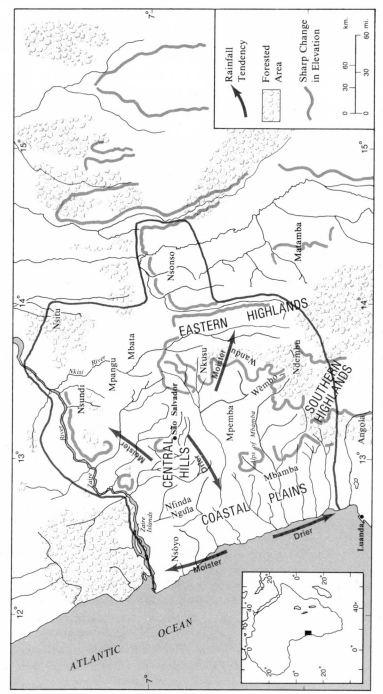

Geography of Kongo

Map labels:

Rainfall Tendency

Forested Area

Sharp Change in Elevation

km.
mi.
60
60
30
30
0
0

7°

15°
15°

14°
14°

13°
13°

12°

7°

Matamba

Nsonso

EASTERN   HIGHLANDS

Nsitu

Mbata

Nkusu

Moister

Wandu

Ndemba

SOUTHERN HIGHLANDS

Nkisi   River

Mpangu

Wembo

Nsundi   River

Mpemba

Mbamba

Alps of Mbamba

Angola

São Salvador

Moister

CENTRAL HILLS

Drier

COASTAL   PLAINS

Mbamba

Luanda

Zaïre   River

Nfinda
Ngula

Drier

Zaïre
Islands

Nsóyo

Moister

ATLANTIC   OCEAN

20°

0°

20°

40°

0°

20°

0°

20°

5

This great eastern escarpment was curved, so that in its northern area the coastal plain and hills of the center were some 150 kilometers across, while in the southern parts they were only seventy-five kilometers across. Because of the extension of the escarpment into the southeast and south central part of the country, the mountains formed a considerable length of Kongo's boundary on the south as well as the east. Rivers likewise cut into this region north and south, and like the parallel ridges and valleys of the east, the southern region was divided into inhabited valleys separated from each other by uncultivated and wild ridges.[8]

In addition to forming a barrier and an inconvenience to travellers, these two mountain complexes had a considerable effect on political sovereignty and military activities in Kongo. The mountains were formidable military barriers, and the narrow settled valleys, isolated from each other and the outside world, were ideal areas for local, independent polities to establish themselves and to defy the centralizing military efforts of the lowland kings. In the east of Kongo the mountain provinces, Nkusu, Wandu, and Wembo, for example, were all more independent than those in the lowlands, for they preserved the right, even in the middle of the seventeenth century at the height of Kongo's centralization, to elect their own rulers.[9] Peoples of the mountains of the south were similarly independent; the Ndembu region that lay in these mountains defied both the kings of Kongo and the rulers of Angola, and despite many treaties and military expeditions, preserved the reality of their independence throughout the seventeenth century.[10]

The mountains themselves were often military objects of considerable utility and political importance in Kongo history. Mount Kimbangu, an imposing flat-topped formation on the front of the eastern range, was the refuge of a whole line of Kongo's kings. Rising up from the 600-meter plain, its peak was a large, triangular plain some thirty kilometers on a side and uniformly 1,000 meters high, while its steep sides were thickly wooded. Small wonder that its very name (missionaries said) meant "fortress."[11] Its well-cultivated top guaranteed at least enough food to support any pretenders for as long as they desired.[12] Not just kings, but more ordinary rebels, often sought refuge in the flat-topped mountains of the east. When Pedro IV successfully drove the rebel pretender Pedro Constantinho da Silva from São Salvador in 1709 his forces fled to Nfinda Kongo and Ntadi a Nzundu, locations whose names indicate mountainous, wooded areas.[13] Matheus Cordoso, author of an important seventeenth-century description of Kongo, reported the similar use that rebels occasionally made of "Mofindas" (*Nfinda*—woody, mountainous areas) in his time.[14] Even the government occasionally made use of these natural fortresses; in 1651 the official candidate for the office of count of Wandu was driven from his office by his brother and fled to the mountains, where, with the king's consent, he established a rival government, which some years later took back the county.[15]

It was not just the rich, noble, or famous who made use of the mountains as fortresses—peasants and villagers did, too. When the troops of Queen Nzinga of Matamba invaded Wandu in 1648, all the women, children, and old people were sent to the hills to hide.[16] On another occasion, Antonio de Teruel and Joseph de Pernambuco, two Spanish Capuchins, were travelling across Nkusu when the ruler of Nsonso threatened war. On their way back to Mbanza Nkusu they came across a large, flat-topped mountain where the women, elderly, and children of all the surrounding villages were establishing a settlement and planting crops.[17] During the great disruptions of the civil wars there was a general movement of the population from the valleys of the east into the mountains to avoid the constant ravages of passing military forces. Lorenzo da Lucca passed a whole series of mountain fortress-villages in Wandu, each buried deep in the forests of the highlands to escape the constant struggles of the valleys.[18] Security was so important to the inhabitants that they sacrificed convenience for safety in travel, with roads that were no more than tortuous paths through the mountains.[19]

The rugged terrain and independent will of the eastern regions contrasted with the flatter central and western parts of the country. The land gained elevation as one moved inland from the coast, so that rolling hills eventually dominated the terrain of the central regions. But nowhere in central Kongo could fortresses rivalling those of the east and south be found. São Salvador, the capital of Kongo, was the center of this central region. It was perched on some of its highest hills, but its elevation was only some 600 meters, and it was reached by a fairly mild climb.[20] The flat, open country that surrounded the capital, as well as the abundance of rain, made agriculture easy and productive there, and travellers usually described the capital region as if it were a continuous garden, with houses and trees everywhere.[21] It was the great productivity of this region that helped to make São Salvador the social as well as geographical center of the country.

The hills of the lowlands began quite near the coast. In fact, along the coast villages were regularly built on the highest ground (which rarely exceeded 150 meters, however) to catch the sea breeze and reduce the sweltering heat of the plain.[22] On the Atlantic coast the immediate shore was low-lying beach, while on the bank of the mouth of the Zaire River it was a tangled mangrove swamp which was often difficult to traverse but which was used for the culture of rice.[23] Inland the hills became higher, but although São Salvador stood on ground over 600 meters, nowhere did

these hills provide the shelter and inaccessibility that the eastern mountains did. Only the areas immediately south of the Zaire, where the action
of that river and its major tributaries made some of the lower land into
steep-sided, flat-topped formations that proved to be reasonable natural
redoubts, did the terrain allow regions to attain local defensibility. Indeed, Mbula, a district in this region, became the safe refuge of another
line of Kongo kings, just as had Kimbangu in the east.[24] The flat-topped
formations south of the Zaire were not mountains in the same sense that
the lands of the great escarpment of the east were, but they did insure a
certain independence to the region due to their military inaccessibility.[25]

The Zaire River, which made land on its south bank into potential
fortresses, had a similar effect for another unrelated formation, the islands
of the river's mouth. These islands never truly fell under Kongo's sovereignty, and the inhabitants could not be counted upon to render tribute.
But they were skilled agriculturists and canoeists, and they engaged in
considerable trade with the states on the north bank of the river.[26] The
small size of the islands made them often densely populated, and according to baptismal statistics left by the Italian priest Serafino da Cortona for
Mboma, one of the islands, the density there was about eighteen per
square kilometer, greater than anywhere else in Kongo save the centers
of the towns.[27]

Long-past geologic episodes conditioned the soil of the country, just as
it shaped the contours of the rocks from which the soils were derived.
Contemporary witnesses distinguished three soil zones. First, there was
the sandy soil of the coast, which was so free of stones that when the
people of Nsoyo decided to abuse the missionaries they had to content
themselves with throwing sand.[28] In the hilly and mountainous central
regions, on the other hand, wash from the mountainsides that enriched
the soil of the valleys made the higher ground stony, so stony that Lorenzo
da Lucca noted the entry into this region was hard going for barefooted
travellers.[29] On the other hand, once one passed this region of hill and
dale or mountain and valley, the land again became sandy; indeed, Matheus
Cordoso wrote that this region was "so denuded of stones that it is impossible to find a single one."[30] However, Kongo's agriculture and low population density required little of the soil. Even in sandy Mbamba province,
the Capuchin priest Dionigio Carli thought the soil exceedingly rich, and
"black like the people of the land."[31] In the end, it was rainfall that
counted more than soil type in deciding settlement pattern.

The shape of the land and the nature of its rivers were factors over
which the Kongo had no control, save for the long-range effect of their
agriculture in changing the pattern of erosion.[32] They were similarly quite
helpless in the face of the climate. The rhythm of the seasons imposed its

tempo on them, and they could do little to change it. But unlike the shape of the land and the direction of the rivers, the climate was not itself unchanging, and therefore not predictable.

A normal agricultural year was divided into six seasons, according to Kongo usage, which corresponded to the pattern of rainy and dry spells encountered. *Mapanza*, the first, was the season of rain that began in September and lasted until November, when the first crop was planted. In November *Mapanza* gave way to *Nsatu*, a period of much heavier rain which guaranteed the germination of the seeds. The crops were harvested in *Ekundi*, from late January to early March, when the rains let up. The rains began again in *Kintumbu*, another maximum rainy season which lasted until about the end of April, when a season of lighter rains called *Kibisu* marked both the end of the rains and the harvest of the second crop. The remaining five months of the year, from May to September, were the long, cool, and often hungry dry season called *Kimbangala*.[33]

The fundamental rhythm of life and history was strictly governed by this seasonal cycle. During the rainy periods people did not travel, but stayed close to their homes to work their fields. The dry season was a time for travel, trade, warfare, and social activity. The liturgical calendar of Kongo's Christians shows this well—most of the major feast days are concentrated in the long dry season or during the short dry period between the two rainy seasons (*Ekundi*).[34] Only Christmas was celebrated during the rains, and then it was usually celebrated close to the hospice or parish church, and was not a greatly significant occasion. The major celebration of the year was Saint James' Day on 25 July, in the height of the dry season. It was then that Kongo took in its annual tribute, and in the late seventeenth century the festival in Nsoyo was truly extensive, people travelling many miles to attend the festivities, which might last for three days.[35]

While the rainy season was of critical importance for the continued cycle of life in Kongo, life was not easy during the rains. The torrential rains which regularly struck could wash buildings away, and one storm in 1666 tore the roofs off every church in São Salvador.[36] In the east, the runoff from the hills would turn valleys into lakes and small streams into dangerous torrents. The well-traveled Florentine priest, Girolamo da Montesarchio, en route from Nsundi to Luanda in the rainy season of 1655, described some of the difficulties encountered by travelers during this season, including walking for entire days in waist-deep water, crossing rivers on bridges where the water was completely covering them, and being stranded on "islands" in what was dry land during the dry season.[37] The rising waters generated great hordes of mosquitos—Lorenzo da Lucca found that their bites had left him with permanent scars[38]—and Antonio de Teruel noted that the higher water marks increased the range of crocodiles.[39] Under these conditions, it is easy to see that the rainy season, as much as it was necessary for the agricultural cycle, severely restricted a wide range of social activities, and enforced a more or less local life pattern on the people.

As inconvenient as the rainy season was, of course, its absence was nothing short of disastrous. Indeed, some regions of Kongo suffered greatly from recurrent droughts that ruined crops and greatly increased social tensions. Generally the rainfall followed an east–west gradient, the dry lands being on the western part of the country along the Atlantic coast, and the areas inland being moister. In addition, there was a lesser north–south gradient, so that the southern areas received less rainfall, while those to the north got more. Thus Mbamba in the extreme southwest was the driest province, while Nsundi, in the extreme northeast, was the wettest. Antonio de Teruel noted that rain seldom lacked in the highland regions of the east, although Girolamo da Montesarchio did observe that in both 1651 and 1653 rain was somewhat late-coming in Nsundi, much to the dismay and concern of the people.[40] Similarly, Garcia Mendes de Castello Branco, an Angolan resident, noted that within the dry coastal lands, Nsoyo was much better provided (being on the north) than Mbamba.[41] But drought did indeed strike even in Nsoyo. Throughout the period 1640–1720 there was at least one major drought each decade.[42] Normally, droughts were caused by the late arrival of rain, rarely by its failure. The month of December seems to have been the breaking point, for in 1673 the drought let up on 23 December and saved the crops, while the drought of 1692 lifted only on 25 Fanuary, and by that time the first crop was completely lost.[43]

The droughts caused considerable hardship, as can be well imagined, and appear to have significantly increased mortality in the years they struck.[44] And this was an aspect of the natural environment over which the people of Kongo had no control, nor even any sure way of prediction. The droughts therefore caused general crises, and in their helplessness people turned to supernatural means to relieve their sufferings. In the traditional Kongo religion the role of rainmaker was very important; during the late rains of 1651, Girolamo da Montesarchio intervened to put a stop to the activities of one of these rainmakers, who were called *nganga nsandi,* in southern Nsundi.[45] The Christian community had their own supernatural way of dealing with the droughts. Every time the rains were late in Nsoyo the missionaries organized a penitent procession in which the whole society prayed for forgiveness for whatever sins had caused the Divine Powers to hold back the rains.[46] Nor was scapegoating unknown, especially for those held to have some sort of power in the religious sphere. In 1673, for example, during one of Nsoyo's droughts, the Prince of Nsoyo blamed the Capuchin missionaries for the lack of rain, saying they had delayed it as a part of their preaching against the Prince's sins, and he roughly expelled two of the Capuchins from his domain.[47] Shortly afterwards, however, this same prince was expelled by a rival, who, like the Capuchins, blamed his predecessor's sinful life for unfavorable natural events.[48]

The natural environment of Kongo did not just include the inorganic forces of rocks, wind, and rain—Kongo's people shared their land with a host of living forms. Some of these forms they controlled directly, like their domestic animals and their grain crops; others, like many species of predatory insects, wild animals, and forest and grassland vegetation, were beyond their control, or at least beyond their total control. In some cases, human control was no more effective than it would be for the wind and rain. Such a case was that of the locusts, born somewhere far to the east, which would suddenly and catastrophically appear in Kongo, devouring everything in their path. Serafino da Cortona described the terror that these insects inspired when they invaded southern Mbamba in 1653: "This same year in the month of January, many locusts and grasshoppers appeared here and covered the sky for eight days continuously, hiding the sun and frightening the people, who believed they had destroyed their seed and the crops."[49] Lack of control was evident, and the solutions proposed were the same as with the uncontrollable forces of the climate. Penitent processions were organized, and Girolamo da Montesarchio found that such processions were already a time-honored tradition when locusts invaded his post in Nsundi in 1649, for the secular clergy had organized them long before his arrival.[50] In the mid-seventeenth century the locust invasions seemed a constant scourge on the kingdom, and King Garcia II begged the Pope to provide him with supernatural assistance. The Pope complied, issuing an edict lifting all excommunications and interdictions that had been previously pronounced in Kongo.[51]

Microbes were another living form that was beyond human control or comprehension in seventeenth-century Kongo. The Kongo tended to blame the everyday diseases that affected them on social forces, especially witchcraft, and devised means of dealing with them in daily life. The country was not unhealthy by seventeenth-century standards, in any case. Giovanni Antonio Cavazzi da Montecuccolo, a Capuchin with many years' experience in central Africa, believed the Kongo suffered from fewer diseases than Europeans did at home, although European mortality in

Kongo was very high due to the change in disease environment.[52] At any rate, mortality in Kongo was not abnormally high by standards of the time.[53] It was not the average incidence of disease that seemed to fall out of human control, but the devastating epidemics that struck from time to time. It is impossible to identify the diseases involved, usually called simply "peste" (plague) in the texts. Da Montesarchio survived and described the effects of one such epidemic, which struck Nsundi in 1654–55. He was appalled by the mortality; in Mbanza Nsundi alone (whose population could not have exceeded 2,000) he gave the last rites to as many as twenty people a day for weeks. When he travelled he found whole families dead in their homes, and the production of food was so disrupted that he could get nothing to eat along the way. Further, his own porters died one by one, and he was eventually left, alone and sick, with no one to care for him. His illness lasted a year, and although he finally recovered, his companion died.[54] The relatively low population densities of rural Kongo probably provided the people with their best defense, for it inhibited the spread of epidemic disease, as during the epidemic of 1659, which hit hard in Mbata, but missed Nsundi, less than seventy-five kilometers to the north.[55]

In their interactions with larger life forms, the Kongo had more control. The lands around the villages were more or less totally under human control, forming a landscape of trees and fields and fallows set against a backdrop of savanna grasses. Thus, Lorenzo da Lucca noted, one could always tell a village from a distance, standing out as it did as an island of cultivation in a sea of grass.[56] But between the villages was land which fell only intermittently under human control, although the long-term pattern of Kongo agriculture had probably altered it quite a bit from its pristine state. Centuries of burning grass to clear fields partly determined which species of grass survived in the savannas, and inhibited the growth of certain species of trees.[57]

The effects of human cultivation were most obvious in the mountains, where the forests had been pressed to the tops of the ridges, In some areas—Mpemba, for example—grass covered the whole area, hills as well as valleys.[58] Where forests remained, they provided a natural defense against would-be conquerors. *Nfinda Ngula* was a great forested and deserted region that separated Kongo from Nsoyo, and it was the presence of this wilderness, as much as the valor of Nsoyo's inhabitants, that allowed them to retain their independence in the year 1636 and after, when Kongo repeatedly attacked them.[59] A similar situation permitted Nsanga, straddling the Zaire River, and Kinsitu in the extreme northeast of Kongo to maintain considerable independence from their nominal overlord, the Duke of Nsundi.[60] We have already seen how the combination of forest and mountains contributed to the great defensibility of many eastern areas, permitting them relative autonomy.

The vast land areas outside the villages and towns remained largely unaffected by humans, who crossed them for trade, travel, or warfare. When Giacinto Brugiotti da Vetralla, prefect of the Capuchin mission, decided to travel from Luanda to São Salvador, the King of Kongo ordered the Duke of Mbamba to set to work a large number of people to clear a road for him, so that his party could travel without delay.[61] But the difficulty of travel through the uncontrolled areas went beyond the inconvenience occasioned by the grasses, which stood higher than a man's head, and whose sharp edges cut the legs of travellers and left them painfully wounded.[62] The grasslands were also a source of danger. They provided food for a great variety of wild grazing animals like antelopes, zebras, and buffalo, which in turn furnished prey for predators like lions and leopards. Wild spaces held large food resources,[63] for not only wild animals but also a variety of edible roots and grasses figured in the average Mukongo's diet; but they were also areas of danger, because the predators might attack people as well as animals. The fear that predators inspired was probably much greater than their real danger. For example, Cavazzi never failed to record stories of deaths due to animal attack in Angola in the 1650s and 1660s, even though such deaths were not numerous.[64] The same danger was present in Kongo, where one year even the son of the Marquis of Mpemba was killed by a lion.[65] Night was especially dangerous. In the south of the country, where there were few people and the villages were located far apart, each village was strongly stockaded to keep wild animals out at night, and travellers might even build stockades on the spot when they settled for the night away from a village.[66] Similarly, stockades were built in the rivers to protect the women who washed or drew water there from being devoured by crocodiles.[67]

At times, the relations between Kongo's human and animal inhabitants even assumed the aspect of a war. Travellers might light fires in open country to frighten dangerous animals away from the road, as a group travelling with Dionigio Carli did in Mbamba in 1667.[68] Elephants, although a source of economic bounty, also caused considerable trouble for Kongo's people. They abounded in the seventeenth century; often herds of thirty or forty beasts would travel together, and at times as many as 200 could be counted in a single valley.[69] They provided ivory and a number of other products as well as meat and were thus valuable, but they might trample crops and destroy houses if they wandered unchecked. When Mbanza Nsundi was temporarily abandoned in a war, the elephants invaded the spot, ruining buildings and uprooting crops, and were only driven out by what Girolamo da Montesarchio called a "war" against them.[70] Even the great town of São Salvador was not exempt. Elephants moved in to eat the bananas of the city's trees when warfare forced its abandonment in 1678.[71]

The human interaction with the natural environment in Kongo was a varied one, ranging from total helplessness to more or less full control. It was a background that was easily forgotten when it followed its normal, regular pattern, but difficult to ignore when it varied. It conditioned political and economic life, forcing them into its rhythms, and at once limiting them and providing them with possibilities. Subject in some ways and at some times to human control, and even in some cases subtly changed by human activities, nature nevertheless was an influential shaping force in the playing out of Kongo's history.

2

The Social Environment of Kongo

IF KONGO'S natural environment defined, broadly, the choices open to human beings, it was Kongo's society, the relationships among people and their institutions, that determined what choices were made. The natural barriers to travel in Kongo had much to do with the country's linguistic division into coastal, central, and eastern dialects, and blocked the spread of Kikongo beyond the southern mountains where Kimbundu prevailed.[1] It was society, however, that decided how each of these semi-isolated communities would be linked. It was society, rather than nature, which formed the real divisions of Kongo: divisions into classes, occupational groups, households, or kin groups.

The fundamental division which transcended all others in Kongo was its division into those unnucleated population clusters called *mbanza* (towns) and the tiny villages of the rural countryside. This division was represented by Kongo tradition as an ethnic one. According to notions of the seventeenth century, "it is necessary to know that two peoples are found in this kingdom: one outsiders and the other natives (*paesani*), the latter the subjects and the former the rulers."[2] The intrusive rulers, according to the Portuguese Angolan, António de Oliveira de Cadornega, were "always regarded as foreigners, outsiders who had come from the interior to dominate this kingdom,"[3] a contention with which contemporary Kongo oral tradition was in full agreement.[4] These outsiders, the Ashikongo, were "the nobility and people of the capital," and they ruled not only in areas where their dialect prevailed, but in the highest positions of the kingdom.[5] In the end, though, it was more than just dialect or supposed ethnic origin that set the Ashikongo off from the rest of the people of the country. Rather, this distinction was a social and economic one, a reflection of the way in which Kongo's production system and social

15

relations were organized in the seventeenth century. Modern research
has suggested that the story of the Ashikongo's invasion, rather than being
an instance of "pure" oral history, may serve as a structural part of the
Kongo's traditions, according to which those who rule are expected for
religious reasons to demonstrate superior force and to maintain an opu-
lent way of life.[6]

The social dimension of the supposed ethnic division is clearly visible
in the account of Kongo oral traditions given by Bernardo da Gallo, an
Italian Capuchin who worked in Kongo:

> The rulers are those who came from Coimba with the first king Muttinu à
> Lucheni and they are called Essicongo or Congolese nobles and citizens of
> the royal city. The others, the subjects, are those found in the countryside
> and provinces of the kingdom, and are called Abhata, Abumba, which means
> villeins and rustics.[7]

The *abata* (da Gallo's "Abhata") were the residents of *mabata*, the Kikongo
word for villages, while their rulers, the Ashikongo ("Essicongo" to da
Gallo), resided in the towns, the *mbanza*. In the seventeenth century,
Kongo used these words to make fine social distinctions, and thus "barbarian" was rendered as *mubata* (literally any inhabitant of a *lubata*).[8] Da
Gallo's other word for the rural villagers, "Abumba," today means any
simple, ignorant, and naive people.[9]

The two worlds indicated by these two words, *mbanza* and *lubata*, did
not represent a simple class division any more than they represented an
ethnic one. Rather, each of these two sectors of Kongo society was a
complete social system, with its own pattern of production, distribution,
and exchange, its own structure of status and power, relations of domination and subordination, means of control and continuity, and to some
extent, even its own ideology. Yet, although they might appear independent of each other, they were never equal. The towns dominated the
country. Though the towns produced a surplus and the villages their own,
smaller, surplus, the town residents were able to demand a portion of the
surplus from the villages. The *nkuluntu*, rulers of Kongo villages and the
dominant social class within that world, were the link between sectors,
for while they drew their subsistence from the villagers whom they ruled,
they passed on a part of this surplus to the representatives of the towns,
whom they recognized as political superiors.

Each of the two sectors possessed its own economy and each was thus
ruled by different economic forces. In the villages, production was regulated by kinship, and the surplus was obtained by the transfer of a part of
the production of the village to the local rulers or their allies. In the

towns, on the other hand, most of the production rested on slave labor, and slaves worked on the land controlled by the nobility or rendered service in their homes as domestics. The nobility, who consumed the surplus of this labor, directed its production to fit their needs and the needs of the large sector of nonproducers who served them. Not surprisingly, town and country possessed different outlooks on life. Giovanni Francesco da Roma, a Capuchin observer, noted the different outlooks on life that characterized the two sectors in 1648. While in the villages an easygoing life prevailed, the nobles of the towns seemed to him preoccupied with the troubles of management in a slave society, such as how best to produce the surplus and especially how to manage its occasionally unruly producers. [10]

Each of Kongo's two sectors produced a surplus: a portion of the production of those who engaged in the labor of the society was turned over to other members who did not labor at all. The mechanism for this appropriation was one or another form of rent, and the form of this rent is a key indicator of the different economic processes that set the two sectors apart from each other. [11] In the villages, this rent was collected either in money or in kind by a variety of assessments levied by nonproducers. The *nkuluntu*, for example, was given a share of the harvest at the point when it was taken in, [12] while the *kitomi*, a religious leader in the village, obtained the first fruits that were sown in a religious ceremony, or in other cases was supplied from the share taken by the *nkuluntu*. [13] Other levies, tolls, and taxes contributed to the subsistence of a small class of village rulers. [14] Thus, although the village rulers did not guide or control the process of production, they were able to share in it through their position in the political and ideological structure of the village.

Since their claim to a share of production did not originate in their playing a part in production, either as workers or as directors, the village rulers relied on othe forms of justification. The *kitomi*'s share was based on his power to mediate with the supernatural, while the *nkuluntu*'s was based on a claim of being an elder. Anne Hilton has suggested that the term *nkuluntu* ultimately derives from *nkulu*, meaning age. [15] In Kongo, as in many other societies, older persons enjoyed not only respect, but a share in production even if they no longer worked. This amounted to a sort of retirement pension accorded an elder worker who had spent his productive life in the service of the community, and was often paid to him by younger relatives. The *nkuluntu* apparently was accorded such status by his people even when he was young, and he extended it to his own and some other households who acted as "assistants." [16] In short, a whole class had taken up the privileges normally only extended to the aged. [17]

While the production of a surplus through the assessment of rent in money or in kind was relatively easy and straightforward, it had certain difficulties which permanently prevented it from yielding a very great surplus. For one thing, the nonproducers had no control over the type of product they got, since they exercised no control over the process of production. Thus they could ask for little more than the food and other goods that the villagers produced for their own lives. This was equally true when the rent was taken in money, for the markets in the rural areas where the money would be spent contained no more than what the rural producers taken as a whole had decided to produce and exchange. The position of the nonproducers entitled them to enjoy a life of leisure, but otherwise they were scarcely distinguishable from the villagers they ruled. Eyewitness testimony of Dionigio Carli da Piacenza, who left detailed accounts of rural life in Mbamba province in 1667–68, show the *nkuluntu* and people dependent upon the *nkuluntu* as having little to show for themselves—a few pieces of extra clothing, a certain distinctiveness, a somewhat larger home (but occupied by more people), and some personal service rendered by dependents.[18] Greater prosperity would have required a more vigorous policy of intervention in the lives of the villagers than a system based on rent in kind would permit. Finally, the rural population was scattered about in small villages—total population density rarely exceeded four persons per square kilometer in 1650—and the accumulation of a sizable surplus through simple rents in kind would have had to involve costly and difficult transportation from outlying villages. Such a system could not have paid for the costs of operating it.

As long as the producers controlled the process of production in the rural countryside, rent in kind was the only way to extract surplus after the process of production was complete. In the towns, on the other hand, the nonproducers played a direct role in the production process, and the actual producers did not control the entire system of production. Instead, the nobility of the towns extracted a rent in labor on land whose product they controlled. This was managed through the enslavement of the producers. The importance of slavery in the towns was not so much that it enabled their masters to command more labor, but that it permitted concentration of the population and it allowed (or rather required) management of production. It was these two elements—management of production and concentration of population—that permitted Kongo's two towns, São Salvador in the center of the country and Mbanza Nsoyo on the Atlantic coast, to enjoy the relatively high level of luxury that set them off decisively from the villages.

Concentration was the first feature of the town economy, as both São Salvador and Mbanza Nsoyo were surrounded by a countryside supporting at least ten times the population density of the rural districts.[19] Even so, these towns were no more than "clumps" of population; Mbanza Nsoyo, especially, was really just a large agglomeration of villages, packed together in a dense settlement pattern, the palace and living quarters of the Prince being only a slightly larger village than the rest.[20] In the case of São Salvador at its height in about 1650, there was certainly more nucleation, for the central settlement there was very large, and due to the availability of stone, it was built with more permanence and stability than the plank construction that characterized even the richest homes of Mbanza Nsoyo.[21] In both cases, however, the town was little more than an agricultural center, in which the combined surpluses of hundreds of villages were consumed by a class of residents and their servants who engaged in no productive activity.

Slavery had been necessary to build up and maintain this centralized agriculture. Slaves, removed from the productive arrangements of their earlier lives, were integrated into a new society in a new location. In early periods of Kongo history the slaves were obtained by wars of conquest—no doubt many were obtained when Kongo's hero-founder Nimi Lukeni conquered the provinces of the country, and the Portuguese records of the early sixteenth century mention slaves being brought from the southern regions of what was to become Angola under Portuguese role to São Salvador.[22] By the seventeenth century wars of conquest had stopped; Kongo still imported some slaves to the central town, no doubt, although a large number were then being simply re-exported via European slave traders to the Americas. Giacinto Brugiotti, the Capuchin prefect of the Kongo mission, remarked in horror that when he was resident in Kongo between 1652 and 1657, Kongo nobles often would raid within the country for slaves, and that it was common for villagers to assign themselves to a noble patron rather than risk being captured.[23] These people were normally not exported, but remained within the country, often leaving the village sector for the town sector.[24]

Still other slaves were obtained by nonmilitary means. Not a few fell victim to a system of fines for minor offenses which involved the poor (especially travellers) in debts which they could not pay, or required kinsmen to pay a slave to the offended party as restitution.[25] Pawnship for debt might result in slavery and eventual transportation to a town. Giuseppe Maria da Busseto, a missionary in Nsoyo in the 1680s, denounced the practice of pawnship and spent considerable time redeeming pawns. But his efforts only reinforced the essential process, as these freed slaves ended up concentrated around the Capuchin hospice in Mbanza Nsoyo. Although these slaves ended up in the service of the Church rather than the nobility, they still conformed to the general process of concentration and rendering surplus through labor services.[26]

Concentration was not only important in assembling a large labor force in one area; it was also required to render the slaves' surplus accessible to the surplus-consuming groups in the towns, for Kongo did not possess the transportation facilities, either in navigable rivers, roads, or wheeled and animal-drawn vehicles, to move bulk commodities very far. At any rate, as long as simple concentration of the producers was possible, there was no need to invest time, effort, and resources to erect a transportation infrastructure or to move commodities long distances by human porterage. The nature of tax and tribute collection around Mbanza Nsoyo in the 1680s can illustrate the situation. There, Andrea da Pavia, an Italian Capuchin who served many years in Nsoyo, noted that the annual tax collection day, Saint James' Day, brought the prince grain and animals from the nearby districts, but that a separate collection of these products was necessary in the province of Kiova, some sixty to seventy kilometers to the east, as the distance was too great for these commodities to be brought to Mbanza Nsoyo.[27] A distance of thirty-five to fifty kilometers probably represented the practical limit of transportation of surpluses in agricultural products. It was because "food cannot be transported, the kingdom being large," Álvaro II explained to the Pope, that he could not feed the secular clergy directly, but had to pay them in money so that they could purchase food on local markets.[28] This critical distance, thirty-five kilometers, beyond which it was not practical to transport food, formed the limit of concentration in Kongo: in both Nsoyo and São Salvador the region of dense settlement extended to about thirty-five kilometers from the town's center.[29]

While the institution of slavery was necessary to strip producers of their former relations to production and to concentrate them in new locations and productive arrangements, the masters did not totally control either the slaves' lives or their labor. Thus slavery in Kongo differed from systems of slavery such as were practiced in Roman estates or in the contemporary European plantations in the New World.[30] In these systems, the slaves' only function was to labor for their masters, and they were in turn housed, clothed, and fed. In Kongo, on the other hand, the surplus was rendered as labor rent. The slaves fed themselves and their families on land which they planted on their own account; they then would render their surplus not as a portion of their own production, but in labor. This labor was used on fields belonging to the state or nobility, the entire product being taken by the owner.

There is little information on the structure of production around the towns and the life and routine of the slaves. The best information comes from Nsoyo in the closing years of the seventeenth century. There, ac-

cording to the Capuchin priest, Girolamo Merolla, the state owned uncultivated land, local villages apparently having considerable rights over
the land they cultivated. The prince could alienate this uncultivated land
to his sons or favorites; he was also sometimes successfully petitioned for
lands by missionaries.[31] The nobles (*mani*) and missionaries to whom state
lands were granted then saw to it that they were cultivated, presumably
through slaves' labor rent in the case of *mani* and through the labor of
freed slaves in the case of the mission churches. The *mani* then transmitted a portion of the harvest to the prince and his court, while they
retained a portion to support their own households.[32] Slaves were certainly used to cultivate the royal estate called *Matto Cortado* (cleared
wasteland) which Lorenzo da Lucca visited and described in 1705.[33]

Less detail is available for São Salvador at its height, but some evidence
is provided by a letter from King Pedro II to the Pope explaining the
support he planned to give the clergy of his royal chapel in 1622. In this
letter, he specified that 100 of the 440 *kofu* he set aside for the chapel
would come from the "stati di Amballa" and these would be paid by the
"Cabatas of Emballa."[34] In Kikongo, the term *mbala* applies to the court
and land pertaining to it, and he must therefore have meant estates
located near the palace or in the immediate vicinity of São Salvador.[35]
The "Cabatas" (*Kabata*) were titled nobility, whose function here was
clearly the same as that of the *mani* in Nsoyo as described above by
Girolamo Merolla.[36] It was perhaps to these nobles that Giovanni Francesco da Roma referred in 1648 when he spoke of the cares that seemed
to burden them, including "how to cultivate their lands, how to sell their
harvests, how to recapture fugitive slaves."[37] That at least some of the
harvest of these royal estates was sold to the other residents of the town
is suggested by the existence of a large and active market there called
"Polangola" and the fact that the Kabata were expected to render their
support to Pedro II's royal chapel in money.[38]

The slaves themselves seem to have been allowed a fair amount of
freedom. Once the act of enslavement and transportation had been completed, their lives were otherwise very much the same as that of their
rural counterparts, save for the requirement of rendering surplus in labor
and not in money or in kind. The terminology of slavery in Kikongo
suggests that it was possible for a slave to move from a relatively degraded
status to a freer one, as is found in many African societies.[39] The lowest
condition of slavery seemed to be that of the *mbika*, for the Catechism of
1624 rendered those unfortunates who were "slaves of the Devil" as *mbika*.[40]
Another term was *mwai*, which was used to render "prisoner" as well as
"slave", and ultimately derived from the verb "to capture."[41] A more

liberal status, however, was that of the *nleke*, literally "child", but used regularly in missionary literature to describe slaves whom the church had formally set free.[42]

Thus after a time, the captured people, *abika* or *awai*, were freed, but integrated into their new society as junior relatives, with the same duties and obligations as junior relatives, in the families of their masters. Such a status would not free them from labor dues, though it probably did free them from the possibility of resale to another master or overseas transportation. Slaves were encouraged to form households—at times even forced, for missionaries noted that masters often directed their slaves' marriages.[43] Creating such a household organization among the slaves insured that, like the villagers, they could engage in a complete set of subsistence activities on their own account.

Thus the economics of slavery in Kongo rested on granting slaves considerable rights in land and some personal freedom, which made them more like medieval serfs in Europe than the slaves of ancient Roman estates or the plantations of Brazil and the Caribbean of the seventeenth century. It was this difference which probably led missionaries to remark that Kongo's slaves were "slaves in name only."[44] The institution of slavery only insured a concentration of laborers and conferred the ability to direct production on the master class; it did not necessarily require that slaves work much harder than the rural peasants. In fact, the system of Kongo could have functioned well if the slaves rendered no more surplus than the rural villagers rendered to the *nkuluntu* of the village. Taking the village in Mbamba observed by Dionigio Carli in 1667 as an example, it would appear that about five households out of fifty lived on the surplus—and granting these households a larger average size than the peasant household, we can guess that the rate of surplus extraction was about 15–20 percent, so that 100 villagers produced enough surplus to support fifteen to twenty nonproducers.[45] In the villages, as we have seen, due to the low population density and inability of the Kongo to transport bulk goods over a long distance, this did not result in a high standard of living. But in São Salvador and Mbanza Nsoyo population density was much greater, so that the 60,000 residents of the region around São Salvador, for example, could produce enough surplus to leave 9,000–12,000 people free from the task of producing. The concentration of this many people freed from productive activity in one region could naturally lead to a high standard of living, as the relatively small number of nobles in the area could thus be served by many domestic servants, retainers, military personnel, and other low-status, but surplus-consuming, dependents.

Of course, the system of labor on common fields and rent in labor instead of rent in kind could have yielded a higher rate of surplus, but not necessarily much higher. There is no evidence to suggest that any advanced agricultural techniques were employed on the great fields of the nobility, and the density of population (which, even in the regions around the town, did not exceed fifty per square kilometer) was not so great as to require more efficient agriculture. What the use of labor rent did allow, however, was better control over exactly what was produced, and that, in the end, allowed the townspeople a more luxurious life-style.

One important indication of this is that Kongo nobility enjoyed special food, which was deemed to be more palatable than that of the common villagers. Although maize was the main crop of rural Kongo in the mid-seventeenth century,[46] it was considered a somewhat inferior crop, for the Kongo believed that the millets and sorghums that had occupied its place in Kongo's previous crop inventory tasted better.[47] Earlier in the history of the conquest of Kongo by maize, it had been considered fit only for pigs.[48] Thus, by 1640, the rural people and the commoners and slaves of the towns were eating maize, or cassava in the coastal regions, while the nobility continued to eat their traditional millets. One such millet, called *masa ma luku*, had become a royal monopoly, and in 1705 Lorenzo da Lucca found whole fields given over to the cultivation of this grain near Mbanza Nsoyo.[49] The nobility's persistence in this culinary habit, which besides reflecting an honest preference had something of snobbery in it, parallels the case of seventeenth-century European nobility, who insisted on eating white bread made from wheat and leaving the "inferior" grains to the poor, despite the nutritional superiority of the despised grains.[50]

Direction of production, made possible by the existence of slavery and the system of labor rent, was the single most important aspect that differentiated the system of surplus appropriation of the town sector from that of the village sector.[51] However, the slave-worked estates around the towns were not the only source of surplus for the nobility or the town sector. The rural regions played a role in the town's economy, and it was this role that made Kongo a unified state with a single economy and not simply a pair of city-states surrounded by an indifferent countryside.

No matter how independent from the towns the village sector might seem, the two sectors were interwoven in a single, noble-directed economy. The rural areas produced items that were not available in the towns, but which could be transported more readily than foodstuffs, and were thus obtained even in the towns through the exaction of rent in kind. Metal goods, cloth produced by rural Kongo from special trees, wild animal products, and the shells (*nzimbu*) that served in Kongo as money were among the important items produced in the rural districts and transported to São Salvador in the form of taxes.[52] In addition, the rural regions were a source of slaves, either directly in that some nobles raided villages in their own districts for slaves, or indirectly in that the products of the villagers were used to purchase slaves from foreigners in the east.[53] Thus, while the town systematically extracted surplus from its own producers, the slaves, it obtained additional surplus from the rural regions, in the forms of their specialized production and the supply of new slaves needed to fuel the town sector's economy. The specialized production of the rural regions left the slaves of the towns free to concentrate their efforts on the production of foodstuffs which were more difficult to transport, so that in the end the economy of Kongo taken as a whole produced efficiently what the directing nobility desired.[54]

In addition to the rent in money or kind due to the *nkuluntu* and other rural notables, the entire country was subject to a head tax.[55] This tax was apparently payable in money (forming a second rent on rural people). Andrea da Pavia gave its level in Nsoyo in 1690 as two *mabongo* per person.[56] The seventeenth-century Dutch geographer Olifert Dapper, probably using accounts of the Dutch embassies to Kongo in the 1640s, noted that the king of Kongo received a total equal to 7,000 *kofu*, (at 20,000 *nzimbu* per *kofu*) from the annual head tax.[57] This sum, a modest, though still substantial one by European standards, figured as only a relatively small portion of the total income in goods the king received from slaves and specialized producers.[58] In any case, the income so derived was not unimportant.

Collection of this tax was one of the prime duties of the nobles from the towns who were posted in rural areas as governors. Special tax collectors, called *mani mbembo*, collected the tax and transmitted it to the town, and often a good deal of force was used to insure payment.[59] More than one rural revolt was specifically to drive the tax collectors out of the province, and in provinces where the nobility sprung from local roots, these revolts might include noble reactions against royal collectors as well.[60] In the end, however, a noble's performance, and his worthiness to continue in his office, were judged by his ability to collect the tax.[61]

In addition to the head tax there were some other taxes whose total revenue contribution cannot be judged but which were also assessed in money. One such tax, designed to provide subsistence for the king's wife, at one time was paid by tribute in Mbata province, but became generalized in the seventeenth century, Likewise, the Kongo were subject to a number of arbitrary taxes—Dapper mentions a tax that was collected whenever the king's beret fell off.[62] The king and his court seemed to have substantial powers to tax the population at will, both with fixed fees such as the head tax, and with other assessments as the need arose.

Money taxation gave the town sector power to collect revenue from the provinces without interfering in the process of rural production. All rural producers were forced to engage in some activity that would earn them money to pay the tax. This might include paid service to nobles, or sale of goods to them, or sales and services for money within the village sector. Seventeenth-century sources indicate that there was a wide range of specialized activities and local trade within the village sector and that money was widely available in it. When the Portuguese decided to invade Kongo in 1670, the commander of the force deemed it sufficent to supply the army with a large sum of *nzimbu* shells, so that they could purchase food without alienating the people of southern Kongo.[63] Rural people paid in money to marry and paid priests to perform services.[64] The head tax of two *mabongo* in Nsoyo was in any case not a crushing burden; it is safe to say that even poor families would have been able to raise it, since they would have needed anywhere from 80 to 120 *mabongo* to marry.[65]

In any case, the peasants were left to figure out how to raise this money, and there appear to have been many ways of doing so. Since the nobility who received the tax could spend it freely, they were able to avail themselves of the country's surplus at any time, any place, and for any goods or services available in the commodities or labor markets of the country. Their choice was limited only by the availability of the goods or services in the village sector (if they lived there) or in the town—and money gained in one sector could easily be spent in the other. Money formed the bridge between the different economic activities of the two sectors. It allowed the rulers of the country to tap surplus from the entire kingdom, while still allowing for the different productive and surplus-generating activities of the country.

The goods produced in rural regions ultimately allowed the rulers of Kongo to participate in international trade and to obtain goods and services completely unavailable in Kongo. Slaves and cloth from the eastern regions allowed Kongo to trade with Europeans, while the salt and *nzimbu* shells of coastal regions permitted her to trade beyond her eastern borders for other slaves and other types of cloth.[66] Europeans brought in a number of luxury goods—munitions, certain types of alcoholic beverages, European cloth, iron, and the services of missionaries.[67] Trade both with the east and with the Europeans allowed the nobility of Kongo to live in what they perceived as grand style, something which could not have been obtained to the same degree simply by making use of the products of the slaves or the rural villagers of Kongo. Cavazzi noted in the 1660s that it was the possession of European goods that marked the difference between being merely leisured and being really wealthy to the Kongo upper classes.[68]

The existence of extensive markets, international trade, and a fully developed monetary system made it possible for a merchant group to develop. In fact, however, according to seventeenth-century sources, Kongo was not a nation devoted to trade, and most merchants were non-Kongo. Those nobles who did trade sent trusted slaves out to the markets to secure goods for them, and raised their capital not so much from trade as from rental income.[69] Although some of the resident Portuguese did live by trade, a certain number also acquired money incomes in Kongo which acted as trading capital; some of these settled in Kongo and married into Kongo families. One such merchant was Tomas Robrerdo, who married Dona Eva, daughter of King Álvaro V.[70]

The real professional merchants were real foreigners, like Portuguese who lived outside of Kongo, in Angola or São Tomé, or, by the middle of the seventeenth century, the Dutch who had established a network or posts from Nsoyo to São Salvador and Ngongo Mbata in the east.[71] Europeans were not the only foreign merchants in the country, for by 1650 Vili from Loango had established themselves in São Salvador. They formed their own community there and developed a trade network stretching from Loango north of Kongo across the country to Matamba in the south, where Portuguese complained in 1655 that "Mubilis, vassals of the King of Kongo" were ruining their trade.[72] Both the Protestant Dutch and the non-Christian Vili had to compromise to remain in the area—both groups converted to Catholicism to trade smoothly in a Catholic country.[73] Not only that, but they had an eventual interest in settling down and perhaps even forgetting trade, a risky occupation in any case. The fact that the Vili of whom the Portuguese complained in 1655 were noted to be vassals of the King of Kongo shows that they were becoming naturalized. Similarly, the Portuguese general Salvador de Sá recorded that the Dutch in Kongo were consistently loyal to Kongo even when their fellows in Angola were quick to declare loyalty to the king of Portugal.[74]

Thus, despite its seeming independence, the village sector in Kongo was an important part of its total economy, providing the upper-class Kongo with vital goods for luxury and trade, and in the end giving the country a substantial surplus. And because of a peculiar set of circumstances, the relative poverty of the village sector (in contrast to the towns), which was part of this one-way economic arrangement, was self-perpetuating. Although the nobility who were posted in the countryside to collect taxes took a substantial share of the tax collection for themselves,[75] the only way that a member of the nobility could hope to enjoy a relatively luxurious life in Kongo was to locate in the town. The nobles' inability to invest in building an independent economy in the provincial districts meant that as long as they resided there they would be condemned to relative poverty. In these reduced circumstances they anxiously awaited the moment when they could return to the town. They thus perpetuated the separate sectors of Kongo, for their continued inability to invest productively in the provinces insured that their successors in the same location would face a similarly undeveloped base, and would be moved by the same desire to return to the city.

Understanding the basic social and economic structures in seventeenth-century Kongo is an essential preliminary for understanding Kongo history of that time. How essential it is will become clearer as we examine the accelerated pace of events, and the attendant profound changes in Kongo's political, social, and economic life, that followed the battle of Mbwila in 1665.

3

Villages and Production in Kongo

IF THE towns dominated Kongo politically and economically, the villages were dominant demographically. Between two-thirds and four-fifths of all Kongo lived in rural villages, and if we take northern Nsoyo to be representative, there were as many as ten or even fifteen *mabata* for every *mbanza*.[1] Kongo's villagers lived scattered throughout the country in relatively small settlements—a *lubata* (rural village) would normally only number some 150–300 people in the second half of the seventeenth century, settled in anywhere from thirty to fifty housing compounds.[2] In the south and southwest of the country, where the low population density made for an abundance of wild animals, the villages were closed in with a hedge or a stout palisade for protection at night, while elsewhere in the country the pattern was more sprawling.[3] Even in the closed villages of the south, however, the houses were widely spread out within the *lubata*, for the dominant building materials—grass, dried leaves, and wood—created a considerable fire hazard.[4]

More important even than the technical predominance of the villages as a settlement pattern was the dominance of the village as the productive unit in all of Kongo. While we have defined a *lubata* as a rural village, and set it aside from an *mbanza*, or town, in fact this distinction cannot be so clearly made when speaking of production. In seventeenth-century Kikongo, *lubata* meant not only "village," but also "quarter of a town."[5] Although rural *mbanza* were socially distinct from the rural villages (and somewhat larger), economically they functioned in very much the same way, the most important difference lying in the career possibilities of the surplus-consuming classes of the rural *mbanza*. The major towns, Mbanza Nsoyo and São Salvador, the real operating centers of the town sector, were nothing more than a profusion of *lubata*. In Mbanza Nsoyo, missionaries enumerated over one hundred such settlements within a day's walk of the hospice.[6] The most significant difference between the rural village and these town settlements was the fact that most of the inhabitants in the town settlements were slaves or their descendents as opposed to free villagers, and the town sector inhabitants owed labor rent on fields in the vicinity. Otherwise, production and distribution were organized in much the same way in both types of settlement.

Each of the two dozen or so housing compounds of these small settlements sheltered a household, the basic social unit of Kongo society. While the village inhabitants collectively owned the surrounding land, the food harvested from this land was divided by household, "according to the number of people in each."[7] On the average, these households seem to have numbered about five or six people each, centered on a married couple whose dependents, whether young or old, relied on them for food, clothing, shelter, and social support.[8]

Since a sexual division of labor was one of the most fundamental divisions of labor in the village, marriage, by uniting men and women, provided the household with the products of each of the two halves of the productive economy. The contributions of the two partners to the evening meal, which was consumed by the household together in their home,[9] were the basis for Lorenzo da Lucca's somewhat tongue-in-cheek depiction of the division of labor in eighteenth-century Nsoyo: "The women have the duty of providing the food, and the men that of obtaining the wine. If the men do not give the women anything to drink, the women will not give the men anything to eat, and vice-versa."[10] Girolamo Merolla, who lived in the same area twenty years earlier, described this division more specifically:

> The manner in which the man and his wife regulate the household is this: the man is obliged to build a house, to clothe his wife according to her status, to care for the trees, to help pull up roots in the fields when needed, and to bring the wine which he gets every day from the palm trees; and if any of this lacks, he will not live in peace in his home. The woman is supposed to provide food for her husband and children.[11]

In order to meet these mutual obligations, the women worked the fields and raised the crops, which provided the bulk of the food for the evening meal, and the men labored in an intensive arboriculture which provided not only palm wine, but cloth, utensils, medicines, and building materials.

From a strictly economic viewpoint it appears that both of the two partners put in a full day's work at their respective tasks, and each stopped work at the same time. For the women, the day commenced at sunrise, when they all went out together to work the fields. Returning at noon when the sun became too hot for further heavy work, they engaged in more work during the afternoon to prepare the evening meal, which normally took place about two hours before sundown. Other meals during the day were light, normally consisting of some peanuts or snacks made from manioc meal, washed down with palm wine.[12] This work of food preparation involved pounding the grain down to make flour, and then boiling the flour for *nfundi*, the starchy gruel whose name Christians used to translate "our daily bread" in the Lord's Prayer.[13] The pot of boiling *nfundi*, which sat on three stones over the fire in each house, became the center of a meal to which side dishes were added: *mwamba* (the gravy that invariably accompanied *nfundi*), fruits, raw vegetables, and finally wine.[14] For their part, the men spent the day tending the tree crops, and their contribution to the evening meal was not only the wine, but also the fruit that accompanied the meal, and the oil (derived from palm trees) that made the base for the *mwamba*. In addition to the production of garnishes to the main meal, the men, in their work with Kongo's bewildering variety of useful tree crops, also built and repaired homes, and produced the cloth that everyone wore from pounded fibers of tree bark or leaves.[15] Thus, although at first glance women's agricultural work appears to have been more important (and the missionaries, used to thinking of this heavy work as a male obligation, often criticized the Kongo division of labor in this regard),[16] in fact, husband and wife spent equal hours of the day in socially necessary labor.[17]

The worlds of the men and women were separate, so that women never even ate their meals with the men,[18] yet they were so interdependent that no one could have lived successfully without combining both in a household. In this aspect of the economy, the joining of the two separate branches of production, the household was the center of economic activity as well as a unit for child raising. Because of the households' central economic function, no one could live outside them. Thus it often happened that when a woman outlived her husband she was forthwith remarried by one of his kin—prompting complaints from the missionaries that men would at times "inherit" the wives of their relatives.[19]

A marriage not only created one household, it necessarily bound two other households together. Thus marriage not only established the domestic economy's fundamental unit, it also bound the members of the village together, in one way or another, through a complex web of kinship. Bridewealth was the tangible representation of this bond, and it formed a debt which linked one household to another. Because Kongo bridewealth was payable in money (which could be put to any use) and not in special marriage goods, it was technically possible for a young man to marry

without recourse to elders or others who might control the circulation of
such goods.[20] For the most part, however, the freedom from control by
others was illusory. The amount of bridewealth normally demanded was
high—in early eighteenth-century Nsoyo it amounted to eighty *mabongo;*
by comparison, missionaries charged only one *lubongo* for a baptism, and
even that small fee was foregone when the parents could not afford it.[21]
Therefore a young man would have had considerable difficulty raising
such a sum by himself, and in the end would have had to rely on his kin.
Since this assistance might come from his own and other related households each marriage in fact involved several households. However, the
relative openness of the system showed that in Kongo there was not the
elder control of women that has characterized some African societies, and
that has led some observers to speak of the conflict between youth and
age as a central one.[22]

The union of two households in a marriage was clearly an important
matter. Considerable negotiations accompanied it, between the man (who
apparently approached his respective in-laws directly) and a representative of the woman's household.[23] There was a period of trial marriage,
which was sometimes a long one, before the formal wedding occurred.
This trial period allowed the young couple to see if they were compatible,
and allowed the lengthy negotiations over bridewealth to be carried out.[24]

The complex group of intermarried households, and the descendents
of such groups, made up the various *dikanda,* or lineages, of the village.
These lineages dominated the village socially and made it into something
of a "republic," as seventeenth-century catechists defined *dikanda.*[25] This
"republic" of kin regulated the activities of the village and established life
patterns for the inhabitants. It regulated not only the internal structure
of each village, but even relations between villages. Although the upper
levels of the provincial pattern of Kongo were probably imposed from
above, at lower levels the districts probably grew out of the village economy. Mountain valleys, rivers, forests, and other natural obstacles formed
boundaries between these social regions, as did local patterns of surplus
creation. These units, the largest natural political and economic units of
the village world, preceded the founding of Kongo and outlasted its demise, surviving down to the present day.[26] Even among the tightly packed
villages of the Mbanza Nsoyo, a district organization had grown up, so
that each group of twelve to fifteen villages formed a district, whose
boundaries were known at the end of the seventeenth century to the
Capuchin missionaries who worked there.[27]

The economy of the household, and its extension to the lineage and
district, formed the core of almost all productive activity in Kongo. It
accounted for all productivity in the rural areas, and in the towns allowed

workers who gave their surplus time to the cultivation of the fields for the
nobility to meet the subsistence needs of themselves and their dependents.

While the household was responsible for most of the distribution of
production, this activity was also affected by other forces. Of course the
most obvious outside force was that of the dominant social classes who
appropriated a portion of the product. In the case of the village *nkuluntu*
in rural areas, it is possible that manipulations of surplus reserved to
support elders who had retired let the dominant class claim a part of it.
Such a situation would amount to the virtual control of the economy by
the *nkuluntu*, as discussed recently by a number of anthropologists.[28] In
the towns, on the other hand, the appropriation clearly stood outside of
the village economy. No justification in terms of the household or lineage
was provided for the town sector's appropriation of village surpluses or
the labor of slaves. Here, the right of conquest, whether applied to the
legendary conquest of the country by Nimi a Lukeni or to the forcible
seizure of villagers for enslavement, was the only justification given.[29] As
for the fields which the slaves worked on behalf of the nobility, the distribution of their product was governed through the separate kinship system
of the ruling class.[30]

Another force affecting distribution independently of the household
was the market system. Markets existed all over the countryside, in "neutral" country outside the control of villages and households. They fit into
a cycle so that within any given region there would be several markets at
different locations within a week.[31] Luca da Caltanisetta described one
such market cycle as he found it in 1697 in northeastern Nsundi province.
The first market, *nsona*, was held on the western side of the district; the
second, *nkanda*, on the southern side; the third, *konzo*, near the *mbanza*
in the center; and the last one, *nkenge*, on the eastern side. Da Caltanisetta was easily able to visit each of them except *nkenge* from his residence at the *mbanza*, and everyone could have attended at least two of
them.[32] Indeed, it would seem that nearly every household did attend
the market. Da Caltanisetta's baptismal statistics provide us with an idea
of the attendance at them, which seems to have varied, but reached at
least 200.[33] Thus, if about 800 people attended the market each week,
there might have been one representative from every household of the
some 4,000 people in the area (800 households at five people each).[34] In
this rural region it is obvious that while markets were not central to the
economic organization, they were an important source for some items.
Indeed, da Caltanisetta was impressed by the variety of items sold at the
markets, both hard goods and soft goods, so that he remarked of one of
them, "At this market they get everything that they need."[35]

The importance and extensiveness of the market system can be judged by the extent to which money was developed as a means of universal exchange. In fact, Kongo had several different monies which could be exchanged against each other. The shell money, *nzimbu*, which circulated especially in the west of the country, could be exhanged against *lubongo*, a monetary cloth, which circulated in the east.[36] In addition, there continued to be barter, and some items, such as chickens or iron bars, were so widely exhanged that they almost took on monetary roles at times.[37] At any rate, it seems clear that the Kongo recognized the principle of money as a universal medium of exchange, and the fact that monetary taxes were charged reinforced this principle. Even bridewealth, which lay at the center of their social institutions, could be paid in money earned in the market. Indeed, there even existed a money market in which currencies were compared against each other, their values rising and falling according to the play of supply and demand.

Many authors have assumed that the Portuguese and Dutch, who introduced cowrie shells from India and other shells from Brazil into Kongo's money supply, destabilized the currencies and caused runaway inflation. This contention is supported by pointing to records of the *nzimbu's* falling value against European silver currencies. This logic does not prove anything about price levels in Kongo, however, for serial data on prices, outside of isolated quotations, do not exist. The devaluation of *nzimbu* was probably not the result of imports increasing the money supply, in any case, for the local production was sufficiently large to make the mass of money available in Kongo immune to flooding.[38] Instead, the fall in the value of *nzimbu* represented a fall in the value of Kongo's exports, and while limiting Kongo's purchasing power for imported goods, would not have affected general price levels within the country. While upper classes might feel the pinch of increased prices for luxury goods, the normal supply of goods to villages might undergo no change at all. Kongo's monetary system was too well established to be so easily destabilized.[39]

The busy and complex system of intervillage and interregion exchange was made necessary by the unevenness of the distribution of key resources and skills. Few households, or even villages, could obtain all their necessities from their own production. Salt and iron, for example, present two classic cases of uneven distribution which have given rise to trade and markets, not only in Africa, but throughout the world. Both items, so necessary to life in Kongo's villages, were found unevenly around the country. Salt was produced mostly along the coast, where the people of Mbamba and Nsoyo processed the salt from their coastal pans and traded it inalnd.[40] Iron, on the other hand, was found mostly in the east, in the mountains of Nsundi province, although there were also iron producing centers in Mbamba and a famous alluvial iron works in Kiova which

reputedly produced the best iron in the country. (Kiova's iron was especially valued, according to Luca da Caltanisetta, for making agricultural
implements. [41]) In addition to these two minerals, the important tree
crops were not evenly distributed, so that in Mbamba no one could obtain
palm wine, but had to drink a beer brewed from maize. [42] While most
palm wine was too perishable to transport, Dutch sources mention one
wine called *mboma,* possibly a sugarcane spirit, which was traded around
the kingdom from its original site of production along the Zaire River. [43]
Even more important than plam wine was palm cloth, which also could
be produced only in certain areas.

Because of the large market for such products, some regions specialized
in their production: the iron mines and salt works formed the centers of
groups of specialized villages whose inhabitants became quite prosper-
ous. Dutch "ten percent" traders who visited Nsoyo in 1700 mentioned a
large salt pan on the coast of the province, and when they visited the
place they found about one hundred women engaged in the work of
extracting salt. Salt, which was traded to markets inland, was said to
provide these women's chief livelihood. [44] These same merchants also
mention an extensive trade in fish along the Zaire River— at one point
along the river, "Jittar," the King of Kongo, had a customs post to tax the
fish trade. [45] Dionigio Carli also mentioned specialized villages working
iron and salt, and one where the entire male population was engaged in
palm cloth production. [46] Unfortunately, the meagerness of available information does not allow us to develop a complete understanding of this
regional trade and industrial specialization, except to note that it was
extensive and important.

While regional specialization and trade made the village sector largely
independent structurally from the towns, in that town workers did not
provide vital economic resources to the villages, it did create one important link between the two, that being the money generated by trade. As
we have seen, specialized producers paid dues to the towns in the form
of their products, but in addition to this special production, money taxes
were regularly extracted from the rural sectors of Kongo.

While the "republic" of lineages and households in every village did not
engender any inequality in the lives of the villagers, the two economic
structures outside of the household—the dominant classes and the work-
ings of the market—did foster inequalities in the village world. This is
obvious in the case of the *nkuluntu,* but less obvious in the case of
specialization and the market. In any case, the inequalities arising out of
participation in the market were not structural inequalities, such as the
class system introduced. The fact that a wide variety of products could be
sold on the market meant that some individuals who were either skillful

or lucky might, by accumulating money, be able to enjoy greater material abundance than otherwise possible in a village setting. The most obvious way in which this accumulation was revealed was in plural marriages. We have described the household in Kongo as if it were monogamous. Indeed, the evidence seems to suggest that monogamy was the normal marriage pattern, if for no other reason than that the generally high level of bridewealth prevented much plural marriage.[47] No doubt at older age brackets plural marriages became more prevalent, for widows in the village probably married into other households so as to keep together the two parts of the sexual division of labor. There were those, however, who had multiple wives even at a young age, as they could afford the cost of bridewealth in their youth. The *nkuluntu* was one such person, beyond a doubt,[48] to whom we might also add other specialists, such as artisans. Iron workers, according to seventeenth-century accounts, were always held to be fidalgos, "as they practice a noble art."[49] Their high status, and access to money as a part of the rewards of their art, could give them the opportunity to obtain more than one wife. These extra wives were not simply an expression, as some missionaries thought, of Kongo "sensuousness,"[50] nor were they obtained, as Antonio de Teruel maintained, because women "did the work," since their work provided only part of a household's needs.[51] Rather, the extra wives provided an element of prestige and show, and they permitted the man who had married them to live in a simple but elevated style. For example, of the three wives of one man who spoke with Luca da Caltanisetta, "one is necessary to cook for him and serve him his food, the second to cultivate his fields, and the third to receive strangers who come to pay him visit."[52] However, this was about as many wives as could be obtained, whether by the *nkuluntu* through his share of the surplus or by a specialized producer through his accumulation of money. In rural districts few if any men had more than six wives,[53] and for the most part those who did have multiple wives numbered among them the aged widows of kinsmen.

Despite its lively production and trade, the village sector of Kongo struck visitors from Europe as being poor—indeed the term "miserable poverty" peppers their reports of rural regions.[54] Even those who were rich by village standards, like the *nkuluntu* and his retinue, did not seem so terribly rich, being characterized by a few extra clothes, and perhaps a bit more food.[55] As for the average villagers, men wore only a simple cloth called a *tanga* around their waists which reached to their knees, while women wore the same, sometimes adding a second cloth which covered their upper bodies.[56] The villagers did not seem to have an abundance of material objects, and missionaries often had to forgo any charge for their services, as the people complained that they were too poor to pay, although they were often observed to be open-handed when they did obtain something.[57] To a certain extent, however, this appearance of poverty was an illusion. Their homes were made from palm leaves and a few poles and were furnished with only a simple bed and a few pots and household utensils. Yet they were sturdy and dry, and certainly provided adequate shelter.[58] By the same token, the villagers' diet was not poor. Kongo women grew a variety of grains—not only maize and cassava (American imports), but also many grew the three types of African millets and sorghums favored by the rich, as well as a host of garden vegetables, legumes, and fruits. Although the diet was relatively meat-poor, protein was provided by chickens (abundant even in dry and inhospitable Mbamba province) and fish, and the balance of legumes and grains.[59] This varied diet probably provided them with sufficient nutrition, and indeed their infant mortality rate and average life expectancy show them to have been at least as healthy as contemporary Europeans.[60]

What was lacking in the rural regions was a visible surplus, outside of the small amount that was rendered to the *nkuluntu* and the *kitomi*, or that went into the market network and generated some money which was often quickly consumed either by bridewealth or taxes. Production everywhere in the rural regions was for immediate use, and everything seemed to be consumed without regard for the future or for more extensive commercial activity.[61] This was true even of the surplus that did exist, for the *nkulutu* made no attempt to regulate production to increase the surplus, but was perfectly content with the share of the harvest that was essentially controlled by the households of the village. Thus, what was lacking in the rural regions was not so much an adequate productive base for the survival of its inhabitants as visible signs of a more luxurious life among its rulers. Kongo peasants were rational within the limits allowed by their technology and opportunities, as has been observed of peasants over the world when they control production.[62] It was, in short, the rural rulers who really lived in "miserable poverty."

There was, no doubt, the possibility of a potential surplus in rural Kongo far greater than the one produced for the village sector's rulers. Kongo peasants were far from being overworked. To prepare the fields for a crop they used a simple slash-and-burn technique. After burning the fields in September, and removing the roots from them, the women would simply "scratch up the soil with a little hoe to make small mounds in the field where they place the seed . . ."[63] This was probably combined with a system of a long fallow, so that the soil was not restored by human activity, but simply left after two or three crops to restore itself.[64] This light labor, which conserved work and used much land, was capable of producing harvests which by all accounts were "exceedingly abundant."[65] Even the need for extensive storage was reduced by the system of planting crops so that the harvests of different fields could be taken in at different times.[66] Although villagers occasionally suffered hardship during the dry season, and had to resort at times to wild foods,[67] this pattern was normally adequate to meet their needs. The Kongo were skilled agriculturalists. The women who planned and planted the fields were well aware of the potential yields of their crops when they set aside seed for the next year, and made good use of local patterns of drainage to obtain the maximum yield from the land they did use.[68]

It was Kongo's social structure, rather than irrationality or (as some missionaries thought) laziness, that kept the rural regions from producing a larger surplus. The dominant sector of Kongo's society, the town sector, was the center of a single economy in which the villages were expected to produce only a certain quantity of specific products. While these products were vital to the life-style of the towns, other economic activities of the villages were considered inessential. Thus those at the highest levels of Kongo's political and economic elite, as long as they obtained a certain portion of the village sector's production, remained essentially unconcerned with what happened in the villages. The persistence of rent in kind, and the permitting of direct control of the production process by the producers themselves, reflected this unconcern. Such a system did not require Kongo's rulers to organize or supervise production, to be concerned with the subsistence economy of the villagers, or to involve themselves in other aspects of social control in rural areas.

The end result was that the continued economic dominance of São Salvador fostered the economic independence of the villages, or rather their apparent independence and poverty. In was this feature of the political structure that made Kongo's economy appear to the Capuchin missionaries to perpetuate poverty. Thus one mid-century observer wrote that it was the "barbaric" policy of the king to keep the people in "miserable poverty," in order to "dominate them more easily." And were it not for this policy, he noted, the country would produce "not only necessary things, but surplus," which might be marketed or exported to offset the country's external dependence on the slave trade.[69] Indeed, other missionaries suggested a solution to what they saw as a problem of Kongo's rural production: the creation of more *mbanza* like São Salvador, in which the population could be concentrated and greater surplus realized.[70]

In fact, both these proposed solutions missed the main problem, even as they revealed it. The original population concentration in São Salvador had led directly to the two-sector economic organization, and the policy of the king was incapable of changing it. Only special circumstances, such as led to the growth of the town of Mbanza Nsoyo, could create another center of slave production like São Salvador. As it turned out, the rise of a second center to rival the first was the beginning of the end for Kongo.

4

Economy and Politics in the Towns

THE DIVISION of Kongo into two sectors, one centered in the towns and producing a large surplus, the other centered in rural villages and producing a smaller surplus, had profound implications for the political structure of the country. As we have seen, the relative poverty of the villages was a fundamental structural part of Kongo's economy. This poverty in rural regions highlighted São Salvador as a center of consumption and luxurious life, and thus perpetuated a centralized, royally controlled polity. Among the nobility who operated this political and economic system, the distribution of surplus, as well as the supervision of its production, fell to the household, as in the villages. But because the nobility faced entirely different circumstances in their vast and centralized economic system, noble households became the center of the political system and were in turn formed into great political-familial alliances which we will term "houses." Finally, the entire political system, having a single center, was a source both of considerable stability, as its center was overwhelmingly powerful, and of instability, as competition for the control of that single power source was intense. In the end, it was the more or less accidental rise of another town center that turned the small-scale instability of lineage competition into an instability capable of undoing the structure of the entire country.

In order to understand fully the implications of Kongo's economic divisions, it is first necessary to grasp the implications of the small surpluses available in rural regions for the life of the rural rulers. Although São Salvador was a densely settled region, containing more than 60,000 people, the rural *mbanza* were scarcely more than overgrown villages. In terms of population, the *mbanza* of the countryside rarely exceeded one or two thousand people.[1] Mbanza Mbata, seat of one of Kongo's most powerful dukes, was in fact little more than a small collection of buildings, scarcely distinguishable from the villages that surrounded it. Antonio de Teruel wrote of it in 1648:

> Even though the Duchy of Bata is very extensive and populous, and this duke is very important and recognizes the vassalage of several Gentile Kings, as they have told us, with all this the city or Banza of Bata is not very large, because only some of these lords and their servants live here, and a few fidalgos with their families. [2]

Only a few children could attend the school that de Teruel established, and when, in 1650, the king summoned the duke to court, his departure with his clients and servants left the city so depopulated that the missionaries decided to leave the town themselves, as their work there was practically fruitless. [3] In fact, the small population of Mbanza Mbata, as well as of other rural *mbanza*, was all that the taxes and dues of the surrounding countryside could support. Dapper noted that the wealth of the nobility consisted mainly of slaves, [4] but the slaves in the rural areas were primarily personal servants who moved about with their masters from one province to another.

There were obstacles which prevented the putting of slaves to work in agriculture in the provinces and the creation of population centers to compete with São Salvador. In the first place, the provincial nobility did not have a hereditary claim, with some exceptions such as Nsoyo and Mbata, to the districts they ruled, being moved frequently (in theory every three years) from one place to another. [5] All provincial concessions made by the king were still a part of the royal domain, the holder having rights to the income, and the property reverting back to the crown upon the holder's death or transfer. [6] This inheritance law was intended, we are told by witnesses of the time, to prevent the accumulation of wealth. [7] Although there may have been some hereditary succession to estates around the capital, even there there was the constant fear of sudden expropriation. [8] The imposed itineracy of the nobility would have prevented any permanent establishment of an agricultural base in any location, for no sooner would the groundwork have been laid than its founder would have to move and start anew elsewhere.

A second, possibly more important reason for the lack of investment in rural regions was the very attractiveness of the town of São Salvador itself, and the fact that a successful career would lead to it. The nobility could gain access to the wealth of São Salvador as a normal part of their careers, and did not need to engage in the risks and difficulties attendant upon setting up agricultural estates in their provinces. Their stake in the prov-

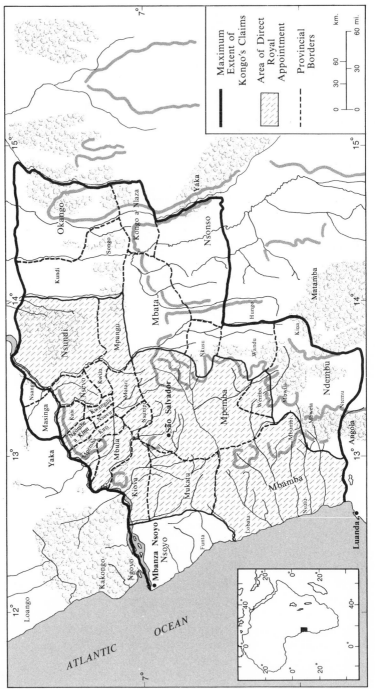

Kongo in 1641

Maximum
Extent of
Kongo's Claims

Area of Direct
Royal
Appointment

Provincial
Borders

km.
mi.
60
60
30
30
0
0

Okango

Kongo a' Nlaza

Yaka

Nsonso

Songo

Kundi

Matamba

Nsundi

Mpangu

Mbata

Hungu

Kina

Nsanga

Skusu

Wandu

Masinga

Nseto

Kwilu

Matari

Wembo

Mbwila

Ndembu

Yaka

Nsonga
a' Kimu

Kwangila

Nsongo

São Salvador

Nsuku

Mpemba

Wembo

Mbwela

Kasi

Nsongo

Kasi

Mbamba

Mbula

Khambi

Mpemba

Ndemu

Mbamba

Angola

Kiova

Mukatu

Ndibi

Kakongo

Ngoyo

Mbanza Nsoyo

Nsoyo

Funta

Lobata

Loango

Luanda

ATLANTIC

OCEAN

7°

15°

14°

13°

12°

7°

15°

14°

13°

7°

inces they might be given to govern was so low that in Nkusu missionaries noted the nobles were even reluctant to marry locally, for they all wished to make a match with a woman from São Salvador, as this would help them to make a career there.[9]

Given the structural importance of the rural sector of Kongo's economy, the rural posts were important ones for insuring that the revenue of the provinces flowed to the town. Even so, service in rural areas was something of an "ordeal," or a test of loyalty, since it involved a certain hardship for a class used to luxury. The task of collecting taxes and transmitting them to the capital was the most important standard by which nobles' careers were judged, and failure to perform it might hinder their return to São Salvador, or allow return only under reduced circumstances.[10] Often they took to this task with great zeal, as in the case of the Marquis of Mpemba in about 1652, when his enthusiasm for collecting taxes led to a widespread revolt among the villagers, which was suppressed at great cost.[11] Otherwise, the provincial nobility were not particularly well-supervised, and frequently chafed at the poverty of their lives in the provinces. Often they would casually despoil the province, for when they travelled they were accompanied by a fairly large band of servants and retainers—even missionaries who lived frugally would have bands as large as twenty or thirty—who would seize the goods of the rural villagers to provision themselves.[12] If this behavior met with resistance, as was often the case when the demands on a particular locality were excessive, villages were burned and people fled. Antonio de Teruel passed one such village which had been burned to the ground and abandoned because the villagers had not met all the demands of the Duke of Nsundi and his train.[13] Not surprisingly, sometimes people were captured and made into slaves; and the nobility, by selling them to townspeople or traders linked to the Atlantic trade, could thus relieve some of the poverty that life in the rural *mbanza* entailed.[14] This aspect of the town-village relationship was not without costs, however, as it was because of the frequent visits and arbitrary exactions of the nobility that rural inhabitants were said to "refuse to sow abundantly and to raise cattle," as they would "rather suffer penury than to work for someone else."[15] At the same time, the villagers built their habitations away from the main roads so as to avoid the casual plunder by their social superiors.[16]

If pressed too hard, the villagers might revolt, as they did when the Marquis of Mpemba became too demanding for taxes in 1652. At times the peasants would violently expel *mani mbembo* (tax collectors) from the country.[17] In a more peaceful vein, villagers might also take grievances against overbearing nobles to royal courts whose judges were situated in the countryside.[18] But while such courts might from time to time find in the villagers' favor, the judges' origins as nobles themselves normally made them subject to the nobility's point of view.[19] In general, the villagers' most effective recourse was simply passive resistance, as we have already mentioned—keeping their villages out of sight and refusing to produce more than absolutely necessary.

This peasant resistance and revolt must be clearly distinguished from the revolts of the nobility. While the villagers wanted nothing more than to be left alone to manage their household economy and pay their dues to the *nkuluntu*, the nobles were not concerned with local autonomy at all. The most important revolts of the nobility occurred at the death of the king as an integral part of the struggle to determine his successor, and were motivated by hopes that one or another potential candidate would support their careers better than would his opponent. Matheus Cordoso, the acute Jesuit observer of Kongo politics, noted in the context of a revolt in 1622 that the peasants revolted in order to steal (or more correctly in order to avoid exactions), while the nobles revolted to "avenge themselves on each other," or to "make a king who conforms to their pretensions."[20]

Thus the aim of nobles' revolts in most cases was not to secure the independence of their provinces. Independence of a province would have meant nothing more than permanent condemnation to a life of poverty in the province, and the permanent loss of the possibility of returning to the luxury of São Salvador. The very poverty of these provinces made revolts during the reign of a king who was well established in São Salvador impossible, at least if the rebel hoped to unseat the king or secure his own career. The poverty of rural areas meant that provincial nobility could not support large military forces on a permanent basis—fifty musketeers was an absolute maximum in most cases, and the king had easily ten times as many in São Salvador.[21] The low population density of rural areas made even the task of assembling an imposing number of irregular combatants difficult. Not only did the king have a standing army of some 5,000 troops (including about 500 musketeers), but he could draw irregulars from the mass of people, some 60,000, living within a few kilometers of his palace. Rural nobles would have had to pick their troops from a larger area—Mbamba's 60,000 people were scattered over some 17,000 square kilometers.[22]

The ease with which military action against São Salvador could be defeated was illustrated by the revolt of Daniel da Silva, Duke of Mbamba, against King Álvaro IV in 1633. Álvaro IV, an indolent adolescent, was not even popular in his own capital, which probably explains why da Silva decided to revolt in the first place. In fact, when the army of Mbamba approached the capital, the king promptly fled to Nsoyo. Despite this lack of resolution, however, the nobility of the capital decided to defend the king, and faced with the power of São Salvador, da Silva's forces were easily crushed.[23]

The power of attraction of São Salvador and the effect of its power on Kongo's politics is made all the more clear when one examines the behavior of nobles whose position was not the gift of the king. Kongo possessed two classes of nobility. One (probably the more important) was dependent on the king for their lands and income. The other held rights to land and the income of that land independently of the king, which they transmitted among themselves from generation to generation, although by the mid-seventeenth century the independent group's power was hedged by the king's ability to veto selections, influence elections of titleholders, and remove holders considered disloyal.[24] Into this latter class fell the rulers of Nsoyo, Mbata, and a host of smaller districts, mostly in the eastern mountains, such as Nkusu and Wandu.[25]

Although they possessed their own means of wealth, they sought the life of São Salvador rather insistently. Mbata's rulers, for example, jealously guarded their right to marry into the ruling family of Kongo, and by the 1650s they were closely tied by kinship to Kongo's ruling houses. Thus in 1648, the duke, Dom Manuel Afonso, had just celebrated his marriage to Garcia II's cousin, while his surname shows that he could trace his own descent back to King Afonso I.[26] As already noted, Antonio de Teruel complained that it was impossible to get the ruling nobles of Nkusu to marry locally, for they preferred a match with a woman from São Salvador who could advance their careers.[27] Such alliances would allow the descendents of the union to join the nobility dependent on the king and to obtain royal favor and possibly court titles and positions. The House of da Silva, hereditary rulers of Nsoyo, regularly held positions as nobility dependent on the king, and contributed to the ancestry of kings Álvaro III and Pedro II.[28]

Therefore, rather than attempt to secede from Kongo, or to become powerful "overmighty subjects" as such independent groups of nobles did in other societies, the independent group of nobles in Kongo sought to bind themselves as much as possible to the king and to the town. The Duke of Mbata, for example, proved to be very loyal, for Capuchins observed in 1648 that when the Duke was called upon to pay his tribute, he responded as promptly as did the most dependent of the nobility.[29] The surrender of local power was even more complete in Nkusu, where tax collection in the province was managed by an official dependent on the king and stationed in São Salvador. This official oversaw a great many other affairs as well, putting the ruler of the province in the position of a pensioned noble.[30] Given the relative poverty of Nkusu, the pension was not large. The only exception to this rule (to be discussed at length later) was the rebellious province of Nsoyo, which did assert its independence after 1636. But Nsoyo had its own town and its ruler possessed a large income, unlike even Mbata, the large eastern province whose capital was little more than an overgrown village.

It is instructive in this regard to consider those revolts which appeared to aim at provincial independence. In fact, they normally involved those who had lost out in the struggle for royal favor and office, and were left with no other choice. One quite successful revolt, for example, was that of Afonso Mvemba a Mpanzu, brother of King Álvaro III. In 1621 he was deprived of his office in Mpangu and recalled to the capital. Chafing at the poverty of an untitled position in the capital, and despairing of any further promotion, Afonso fled São Salvador and raised a revolt in rural areas of Mpangu, where he had shortly before been marquis. The revolt was successful, and he managed to seize parts of neighboring Nsundi province as well. Álvaro III was not very concerned about the revolt, and made only halfhearted attempts to expel Afonso. Ultimately the very success of the revolt was its own punishment, for the province was a poor one, bound in by mountains.[31] A similar revolt also occurred in Wandu in mid-century, under similar circumstances. Wandu was under an independent nobility with elected succession, but Garcia II intervened in an election around 1650 to have a brother of the locally elected count succeed. The overturned brother, however, refused to allow his sibling to rule, and forced him to withdraw into the mountains west of the capital. There the brother remained, confident of Garcia's support, until he was eventually able to oust the rebel brother. Garcia's support ultimately counted for more than the income of the province.[32] In 1665 another such disappointed candidate in Wandu, removed under similar circumstances by King António I, fled to Mbwila, a neighboring province, to raise a revolt which became dangerous to Kongo only because he also involved the Portuguese of Angola in it.[33] These revolts were the actions of desperate men, out of favor with the powers that dominated the country and in many cases fearing for their lives. Under such circumstances some form of independence was better than imprisonment or even greater poverty in Kongo. Such revolts were treated lightly by kings, for they were not an example readily to be followed by other nobles.

Therefore, the rulers of the capital could enforce their will on the country. They were too powerful to be overthrown solely by provincial revolt, for even by itself the town was more powerful than any province, and their way of life was also too rich and attractive to be scorned by those who might seek independence. These rulers were the king and a group of titled and dependent nobles who formed the royal council. Most sources give their number as twelve, and a list of their functions left in 1664 by Antonio de Teruel shows that they could be divided into several groups. There was a bureaucracy, headed by several royal secretaries and including tax collectors, military officials, or other functional divisions.[34] There were also judges, whose powers were wider than simply administering justice. They had branches in the countryside and insured loyalty and uniform enforcement of law.[35] Finally, there was a retinue of personal servants, who in fact influenced policy and administration. The Mani Lumbo (which sources in European languages rendered as *majordomo*) was one the most consistently powerful members of the royal council.[36] After the formation of the Kongo church in the sixteenth century, some selected members of the clergy might also exercise power that went beyond religion. The king's personal confessor, like his majordomo, could be powerful—Father Bras Correa rose to such a height in the 1620s as president of Álvaro III's royal council that he could almost dictate succession to the throne.[37]

So significant was the power of these urban titleholders that a king could rule with their loyalty alone. Álvaro III, faced during the early years of his reign (especially in the period 1614–20) with revolt and disloyalty from his jealous kinsmen, kept the country together by relying on the royal council. They met to decide strategy, made delegations to the rebels, and decided matters of policy, as Álvaro III's own descriptions of the events reveal.[38] Garcia II also relied heavily on his royal council during the early years of his reign. Capelle's description of 1642 has them as an important force which was a party to every major decision the king made.[39] He also relied on the clergy—a cannon of the cathedral was instrumental in arranging for his rise to power, and religious congregations organized by the regular clergy were the recruiting grounds from which he selected loyal officials.[40] Not surprisingly, the membership of the council was dependent on the king. An observer of the early seventeenth century chose the fall of a Mani Lumbo from power to illustrate how absolute the king's power was in his country.[41] Álvaro III, who relied so heavily on his royal council to remain in power, had replaced those who had sat on it under his predecessor and father with his own nominations shortly after his accession to power, as he felt that the earlier council would not be sufficiently loyal.[42] Often, only a handful even within the council would have the real power—Álvaro III relied on only six of the twelve members, while Antonio de Teruel makes it clear that Garcia II favored certain titleholders over others.[43]

A necessary corollary to the centralized power of the king and his council was control over the country's wealth. The wealth of the nobility was derived from the mass of income taken in by the various forms of rent of the country. The state machinery, from the king down to the lower ranks of the nobility, collected and distributed the rent, following closely the lines of power, all the more so since few Kongo possessed incomes independent of their grants from the state—such as might have been the case with commercial classes, or classes more actively involved in production.

Indeed, the basic unit of income in Kongo was called a "rent" (*renda* in the Portuguese of the documents).[44] A rent might be the income of a piece of land, raised by the titleholder from its taxes and dues, or it might be a direct money appropriation made by the king or another rich title-holder from his income. In rural areas, this income was derived from the collection of the royal tax. The holder would transmit some of the income to the king, and retain the rest for himself.[45] Some rents, such as those of the major provinces like Mbamba or Nsundi, gave the holder the right to grant smaller portions to his followers, thus giving the followers access to an income similar to the ones that the major provincial rulers had ob-tained from the king.[46] In the end, the kingdom was divided into many small, and quite stable, rental units, each of which included the revenue of a dozen or so villages which were ruled most frequently by a person holding the title of marquis. Some marquises were dependent directly on the king, even if their lands were fairly small, such as in the case of Matari or Nsumpi north of São Salvador.[47] Others might be dependent on an intermediate office, such as that of the Duke of Nsundi or the Duke of Mbamba; and in at least one case, a region of northern Mbamba traversed in 1625 by Matheus Cordoso, there was another intermediate level be-tween the Duke of Mbamba and the rulers of small income-bearing territories.[48]

The income available to these rural titleholders must have been consid-erable, if taken as a whole. If we assume that the annual head tax in Kongo was similar to that of late seventeenth-century Nsoyo, then each Kongo subject had to pay 7,000 *nzimbu* in taxes.[49] From a population of 500,000 the king would be due 175,000 *kofu* (3,500,000,000 *nzimbu*), yet in fact his income was only 14,000 *kofu*.[50] The remainder must have been divided among the many regional and local officials as their share in the state's income.

The same logic also applied, it seems, to the nobles in charge of the royal estates around the capital, even though the economic system of the estates was different. This is exactly the way in which Girolamo Merolla explained the pattern of estate holding around Mbanza Nsoyo in the late seventeenth century, and it seems to have been the pattern of the Kabata of the São Salvador region as well.[51] Other royal officials, however, were given cash incomes by the king. Perhaps other powerful nobles provided incomes for their followers and assistants from their own income, though the documents do not prove it. Pedro II, writing to the Pope in 1622, explained how the funds to support the clergy of the royal chapel were to be generated. A total of 440 *kofu* were to be paid annually: 140 from "my royal income in the Duchy of Bamba," 100 from "royal rights and revenues" in the marquisate of Mpemba, 100 in renderings from the kabata of the Mbala from the royal estates, and the last 100 from "bembo [mbembo or tax collector] of the chief justice of the kingdom, who is Dom Custodio Afonso today, and by those who succeed him in that charge."[52] The fact that the chief justice seems to have had an independent income and his own tax collector suggests that incomes of members of the royal council were derived from land grants. The rest shows clearly that some salaries were paid directly from the royal revenue, just as provincial revenues might be shared by the titleholder with his inferiors.

Another form of income granted to titleholders in the capital came from membership in Kongo's military order. In his letter to the Pope requesting authority to form the military order, modelled on Portugal's Order of Christ, king Álvaro II said that its stipends would be paid from royal income, and not from the income of the church.[53] Cavazzi noted that most of the minor officials of the capital were members of the Order; and there can be little doubt that they received incomes as a benefit.[54]

Structurally, then, the Kongo state was headed by the king and the powerful officials of the capital, who disbursed income to favored people and took it away from the disfavored. But its appearance of detached, bureaucratic impartiality was *only* an appearance, for in fact in was not an impersonal state apparatus that really governed appointments, titles, and wealth, but the family and household structure of the nobility. Positions were given more frequently for loyalty and family connection than for merit or some other impartial test, and as a result the struggle for control of Kongo's wealth was not that of individuals but of large agglomerations of households ("houses") that formed political factions and ruled the politics of the country.

If Kongo was ruled by households of the nobility, however, it was not a household organization like that of the peasants. While the peasant household united various branches of production through the union of male and female labor in the marriage, the noble household did not undertake any such productive activity. For the Kongo nobility, the sexual division of labor meant nothing. Perhaps the Kongo nobility of the seventeenth century had ideological throwbacks from its peasant past, but by Garcia II's time these were only a memory.

For example, the nobles of Kongo may have believed that political power should only be exercised by males—and for this reason always chose a male to rule the country. However, females were quite active politically. The retired queens of dead kings could not rule officially, but they exercised considerable authority as queen mothers. Matheus Cordoso, when he visited São Salvador in 1625, noted several "Queen Mothers" (wives of deceased kings) at the time of Garcia I's reign.[55] Some other women officially held high office. There were districts in Nsoyo where only women ruled, and travelling missionaries frequently encountered female rulers at the marquis level.[56] Cavazzi noted that provinces were often given to a woman to rule, and such women were even allowed to take a male as a consort.[57] Similarly, around 1650, four of the twelve members of Garcia II's royal council, who, next to the king, were responsible for the crucial decisions in São Salvador, were women.[58]

Because the royal household did not have to unite male and female labor by marriage, it could stand the loss of one of its members. Widows who survived their husbands often remarried.[59] Even when they did not, however, these women continued to exert influence in Kongo politics through their positions as heads of households, and in the case of queen mothers this influence was especially important, as they might head the household of which the king himself was a member. Later, during the civil war period, women acting as heads of households would behave just as if they ruled, even if they continued to allow male relatives to exercise legal power. Surely the most famous of such women was Dona Ana Afonso de Leão, whose activities played a central role in all the politics of the civil war era.[60]

In addition to their functional differences, noble households were much larger than the households of the villagers, even those of the *nkuluntu*. For one thing, nobles possessed many wives, even if one of these wives was clearly the main wife and exercised important political functions. In larger households, where as many as several hundred wives might live together, this principal wife would be assisted by a second wife who also had superintendent duties.[61] Not all the wives had equal status, and in fact many were slaves or the children of nobles of much lower status.[62] In addition to numerous wives, of course, noble households possessed servants, often in large numbers. These were integrated into the household of the nobles and often had a say in the disposition of property when their masters died.[63] The concentration of such a number of people in one settlement was a marked feature of noble residential structure. The palace of the king, which was also the residence of all his wives and servants, was so large that observers said it formed a "second city" within São Salvador.[64] Elsewhere in both town and country, the housing arrangement of the nobility was a complex set of buildings, rooms, patios, and passageways, all of which were surrounded by a hedge. In the towns these complexes were aligned next to each other to form streets.[65]

Even more important than the unique sexual division (or nondivision) of labor and large size of the noble households were the complexly structured relationships between noble households. In the village, several related households might be held together by marriage or lineage (membership in the same *dikanda*). Noble households also formed lineages, but their lineages were far-reaching, complex, and hierarchical, such that in many ways they resembled political factions more than simple kinship units like lineages. For this reason, it is better to use a different terminology for them than for the village lineages. The term "house" satisfies this criterion and has the advantage of having been used by at least one contemporary source, Matheus Cordoso, to describe noble descent–family units in Kongo, by analogy with the noble houses of Portugal.[66]

Houses were bound together by several types of relationship. Descent from common ancestors was a very important one; and following very closely in importance were relationships by marriage. In addition to these ties, which determined groupings also in villages, there were bonds formed by clientage and by slavery. Both clientage and slavery often involved marriage as well, and in any case the descendents of clients and slaves also were bound to the house. Thus a typical noble household contained a male head; several wives, who might be drawn from the nobility, from clients, or from slaves; clients who served the head of the household, and to whom he might have distributed an income or rent, or who might have married one of his sisters or daughters; slaves; and, possibly, a mother or aunt of the head, even if she had retired from active political life.

Status within this extended household was conferred by position in the Kongo state structure, and with it a corresponding portion of the state's income. Since few of the important positions in the country were inherited, status could and did change often, depending on the favor that the household enjoyed with the king. A good illustration of this is the household of the ruling king, Garcia II, in the mid-1650s. Garcia's eldest son was made prince and heir apparent and given several rents, while his second son António was the Marquis of Mpangu.[67] Miguel de Castro, who was either a son of Garcia or a nephew (through his brother, formerly King Álvaro VI), was the dean of the cathedral (the bishop's position being vacant) and had an annual income of fifty *kofu*.[68] Garcia married his cousin to the Duke of Mbata,[69] and his daughter was given to one Sebastião, who was given the Duchy of Mbamba as "dowry."[70] Since Sebastião was from a lesser house in Kongo, he was a client to the royal household, as was Pedro Valle das Lagrimas, who held Nsundi.[71] Pedro Valle das Lagrimas was recruited for his post through his membership in a lay congregation of São Salvador organized by the Capuchin priests.[72]

Most of the people whom Garcia had favored with rents and positions were themselves heads of households, and they gave out whatever largess their position allowed them to extend to their relatives and clients. Garcia's Marquis of Mpangu, for example, gave out all the dependent offices in this extensive province to his relatives.[73] Those who had less power, often called "fidalgos of the royal household" or simply "criados" (*servants* in Portuguese), might not exercise any patronage beyond a group of personal servants (often slaves) and immediate relatives. This less powerful group might receive a knighthood in the Kongolese military order, with a corresponding income, or a position in the staffs of royal council members, or perhaps an ambassadorship.[74]

Garcia II's house, known to later generations as the House of Kinlaza, included not only all these people, but in fact most officeholders in Kongo by the end of his long reign. At the start of his reign, however, there were two other houses in Kongo—the House of Kimpanzu and the House of Kinkanga a Mvika[75] and much of Garcia's reign was spent in gradually removing them from power and replacing them with members of his own house. They had obtained their positions as members of the households of previous kings, those of the House of Kinkanga a Mvika from Pedro II and Garcia I (who ruled 1622–24 and 1624–26) and those of the House of Kimpanzu from Kings Álvaro III, Alvaro IV, and Álvaro V (who ruled 1614–22, 1633–36, and 1636), and had retained them by making temporary alliances with the ruling household when their own head was out of power.

The situation was made possible by the flexibility of the house as a form of social organizations. For example, although it was a kinship unit, kinship was widely defined indeed. Kinship was determined by matrilineal descent in the villages—indeed the vocabulary of kinship in the seventeenth century confirms it[76]—but the nobles reckoned descent from both the male and female lines. Moreover, the status of one's ancestors was of little importance in a country where most status was conferred by appointment rather than by hereditary succession. Several seventeenth-century kings were born to enslaved women, for example.[77] Anne Hilton has suggested that this flexible reckoning developed rather late in Kongo history,[78] but in fact, it is clearly found in a letter written by King Diogo I in about 1550 in favor of his son. He urges his followers not to support members of his rival's house, neither "son nor daughter nor male nor female relative, nor even slaves."[79] It is clear, at any rate, that many kings favored relatively obscure clients over close relatives when their loyalty and past service recommended them. Álvaro III, for example, built his reign around a council hand-picked for proven faithfulness which was largely composed of outsiders to his family, including a foreign priest, and gradually edged his own brothers out of their rents.[80]

The flexibility of the house allowed the head to extend it to include many, or narrow it to include only a selected handful, and the fissioning of one house, or the rise of new ones to political power, resulted from political eventualities, and not simply from dynamics of descent. Kings with long reigns, like Afonso I (1506–43), Diogo I (1545–61), Álvaro I (1568–87), Álvaro II (1587–1614), or Garcia II (1641–61), could expect to place their houses firmly in control by the end of their reigns. There were almost always succession disputes at the ends of these reigns, normally between adult brothers, over who would head the house in the next reign. This happened at the end of Diogo I's reign;[81] and Álvaro II's succession was decided (according to a Jesuit witness) by single combat between the brothers.[82] Similarly, most of Álvaro III's reign was spent in a struggle against his brothers.[83] When António I took over after the death of Garcia II in 1661 there was a bloodbath, as he eliminated potential claimants from his generation, which bcame legendary.[84]

However, in none of these cases did a new house develop from the struggle. Only after the death of Afonso I after a reign of thirty-seven years did generational conflict lead to the formation of a new house, and that matched his grandson against his son.[85] Instead, the rise of new houses to power normally occurred by promotion of one house within these struggles. For example, in a situation where brothers fought each other, they could not rely on kinsmen for support, and so they turned to clients. Álvaro III, for example, obtained considerable assistance from the House of da Silva, hereditary rulers of Nsoyo, as well as from the House of Jordão; and eventually, when he found the da Silvas proving difficult, he promoted the House of Kinkanga a Mvika.[86] Indeed, his royal council even had the House of Kinkanga a Mvika promoted to the kingship when they elected Pedro II to rule after Álvaro III's death in 1622.[87] However, when Pedro II's son Garcia I tried to force his formerly client house into full power, the residual supporters of the House of Kimpanzu (Álvaro III's house), led by the leader of the House of Jordão, Manuel Jordão, ousted him.[88]

Garcia's own house, the House of Kinlaza, came to power in a similar way, also working on behalf of the Kimpanzu. The young king, Álvaro IV, faced by an overambitious client house, the da Silvas, called on Garcia to save him from attack. Garcia and his elder brother Álvaro agreed, and their action saved the day.[89] As a reward, they were made Duke of Mbamba and Marquis of Kiova, and Álvaro used that base to eventually become king.[90] In fact, the situation that Garcia faced when he became king in

1641 was very unusual in Kongo history. Because of the complicated political crisis that followed the death of Álvaro II, in which the Kimpanzu retained power only by promoting other houses and then playing them off against each other, while the clients even captured the kingship from time to time, Garcia faced two potential rival houses. Garcia did finally manage to obtain complete power for the Kinlaza, but only after many years of struggle.

Garcia's early days as king are not well documented, but apparently he relied heavily on the royal council and the church. As already remarked, it was a canon of the cathedral that warned him of the death of his brother and allowed him to be elected. Witnesses of the time often commented on the power of the royal council in Garcia II's early days.[91] Both he and his brother had been connected to the Kimpanzu through lay congregations organized by the Jesuits, and both were very close to the Jesuits, who had considerable power early in Garcia's reign.[92] Church ties were reinforced when the bishop of Kongo ordained four clergymen, one (Manuel Robrerdo) a Kimpanzu and the other three (Miguel de Castro, Simão de Medeiros, and Estevão Castanho) Kinlaza.[93] These connections, forged in 1636 and 1637, allowed the Kinlaza to retain power after Álvaro VI's death in 1641, and kept Garcia in power after that.

Garcia's first moves were made to consolidate control of his own house. When Capuchin clergy arrived in 1645, several of Álvaro VI's children and his wife were refugees in Nsoyo, probably having fled there as Garcia eliminated his brother's kin from office.[94] He also removed Dom Pedro from Nsundi in 1650, who was another of Álvaro VI's relatives.[95]

Next he turned to the Kimpanzu, his erstwhile patrons, who had held offices for him as he consolidated power. He had one of their senior members, Dona Leonor, a member of the royal council, exiled and secretly killed, while he tried to remove and then to descredit Manuel Robrerdo, the Kimpanzu member of the cathedral staff.[96] The latter saved himself by joining the regular clergy as a Capuchin in 1652 (thus legally severing his kinship) and by being conspicuously loyal to Garcia. He eventually became royal confessor and died alongside Garcia's son António in the battle of Mbwila in 1665.[97]

Finally, Garcia moved against the Kinkanga a Mvika, the house with the closest kinship ties to him.[98] While he was maneuvering against his other opponents he had sought close ties with the three brothers, sons of King Pedro II, who led the house, offering his daughter in marriage to two of them.[99] They rejected his overtures, however, as they felt they might have sufficient power to overcome him, but after he had defeated his other enemies, it was clear that they were next. In 1656, Garcia announced his intentions more or less openly by designating his son,

Afonso, as prince and heir apparent. This set off a plot involving the Kinkanga a Mvika, who were still powerful and controlled posts in São Salvador as well as the Marquisate of Mpemba.[100] Garcia discovered the plot in time and crushed it, killing some of the plotters and forcing others to flee to Nsoyo. There they continued agitation, involving the Portuguese in their plans, but an attempt to move against Garcia in 1657 failed and the Kinkanga a Mvika were, in the words of an eighteenth-century writer on Kongo history, "put totally to the ground."[101] Sixteen years after his succession to the throne, Garcia's house, the House of Kinlaza, were masters of Kongo.

During the course of his struggle, Garcia had used all the avenues open to a house to build its membership and increase its loyalty. He had cultivated relations with the church, both the cathedral and the regular orders (the Jesuits and Capuchins). He had played off the major opposing houses against each other, and had made use of minor houses as loyal allies. Dom Sebastião, Garcia's choice as Duke of Mbamba, for example, was so pleased with his marriage to Garcia's daughter that he chose to ignore her blatant infidelity, and was a leading force in putting down the 1657 plot.[102] Nor had Garcia forgotten to make use of his natural allies, junior kinsmen. In the end, it was his sons who got major positions, like control of the Duchy of Mpangu. But his house, like those that preceded it, was not simply a kinship unit, nor were the struggles that rent Kongo from time to time primarily ones involving kin. The lack of hereditary succession to title and office reduced the primacy of kin relations and opened options both for alliance and for opposition.

Ultimately, all the struggles over control of the center of affairs in Kongo, whether they were within a house over who should control it, or between houses, were resolved by the inherently centralized political structure of the country. As long as São Salvador remained the magnet that it did, as long as discontented members of the nobility found secession to be less attractive than loyalty, the struggles would never damage Kongo's basic solidity. The crucial issues of a struggle were often decided quickly, within a year or two of the death of a king. Warfare was normally briefly and decisive. If the capital was attacked, as it was from time to time, the attacker would only succeed if he had allies there to help him. No matter how weak the king might otherwise be, if the capital supported him, he remained in office, as Álvaro IV demonstrated in 1634 when attacked by the Duke of Mbamba. Manuel Jordão's attack on São Salvador of 1626 that overthrew Garcia I was successful because of the extensive plotting going on in the capital, as were Garcia II's attack in 1641 and Álvaro VI's in 1636.[103]

It was, in the end, the gradual erosion of the centrality of this capital that led to a change in Kongo's politics, even if the apparent manifestation of the change was a seemingly uncontrollable struggle between competing houses. The erosion of São Salvador's place at the center of Kongo came about, not through São Salvador's decline, but through the rise, almost accidentally, of a new town center at Mbanza Nsoyo on the Atlantic coast.

Nsoyo had long been the home of an independent nobility. The House of da Silva were well-established rulers of the county, their control dating probably from the fifteenth century. Since they did not shift locations as frequently as the dependent nobility did, they were more prone to develop local infrastructures. However, in itself, independence was not enough, for Mbata, Wandu, and Nkusu were also under independent nobles. Nsoyo, in addition, was the main port of exit for slaves shipped out of Kongo for the transatlantic trade. The need to handle large numbers of extra mouths, and the availability of servile labor, would have predisposed Nsoyo to develop a rather large, surplus-producing agriculture. The royal estates documented for the late seventeenth century probably had their origins feeding slaves awaiting embarkation.

Other towns also trans-shipped slaves, but Nsoyo, being the end of the line, and main catchment for all slaves arriving from different directions, naturally had to handle many more. Moreover, from the mid-sixteenth century, shipping from Nsoyo was sometimes delayed, as a pained protest of merchants living in Kongo to the Portuguese King João II in 1548 demonstrates.[104] The building of Luanda in the 1570s may have drawn slaves away from Nsoyo, but the revival of a northern slave trade after the Dutch began trading there in 1597 brought Nsoyo to new heights.[105] By 1645, in any case, the combined population of Mbanza Nsoyo and Mpinda, its port, had reached approximately 15,000.[106] This was easily the second largest town in Kongo, behind São Salvador (with about 60,000) but well ahead of the one or two thousand inhabitants that lived in other towns in Kongo.

The House of Da Silva, rulers of Nsoyo, were also deeply involved in Kongo politics, which made the fact of their independence and the building of a rival town there all the more significant. Since the early seventeenth century the da Silvas had participated in Kongo politics as a minor house, generally in the service of the Kimpanzu. They had helped Álvaro III to the throne, but because of their special ties and independence, they were tricky allies. Álvaro III moved against them in 1620, and Álvaro IV also had to deal with them in 1634.[107] Their involvement in Kongo politics may have been due to the struggle of houses in Nsoyo itself, which had a political structure internally much the same as Kongo's, complete with central towns, appointive local officials, and clientage and descent.[108] During the early years of the seventeenth century, while the da Silvas were involved in the affairs of Kongo, Nsoyo was ruled by a house with the name of de Sousa.[109] That they were hostile to the da Silvas is suggested by the fact that when Álvaro IV faced attack by the da Silvas in 1634, he fled temporarily to Nsoyo, which provided him asylum.[110]

In any case, in 1636, the da Silvas returned to the thone in Nsoyo, and promptly refused to permit Álvaro VI to meddle in their affairs. He tried to remove Daniel da Silva, the new count, from office, and when Dom Daniel refused to obey his call to the capital, Álvaro sent troops. It was the first in a long series of confrontations between Kongo and Nsoyo, in which Nsoyo successfully defended its de facto independence. Contemporary witnesses attributed its success to the wild, untamed border with Kongo that swallowed Kongo's armies, and munitions obtained through successful trade with the Dutch.[111] The possession of a major town, with a population eligible for call-up to military service, was no doubt equally important.

Ties with the Kongo ruling houses did not cease when Nsoyo broke away from Kongo's orbit. Two houses had close ties to the da Silvas—the Kimpanzu (King Álvaro III's wife was a da Silva) and the Kinkanga and Mvika (Pedro II's mother was also a da Silva).[112] Nsoyo rulers were quick to offer asylum to their kinsmen from Kongo, as they did to Kimpanzu and Kinkanga and Mvika who lost out in Garcia II's consolidation of power.[113] They even supported Álvaro VI's kinsmen, perhaps to spite Garcia II.[114]

This political involvement, combined with the rise of Mbanza Nsoyo as a rival town, had a strongly destabilizing effect on Kongo's politics. It provided an alternate route for the losers in Kongo's succession struggles to take. It would contribute to the prolonging of those struggles, and during the succession struggle after the battle of Mbwila in 1665, it would decisively alter the whole nature of Kongo's politics.

5

The Mental World of Kongo

THE MENTAL world of Kongo had as profound an impact on its development in the seventeenth century as did other factors such as environment, relations of production, or social structure. Of course, the mental world of Kongo was not independent of these other factors—on the contrary, they conditioned it in important ways; but their complex effects would be difficult if not impossible to trace. Changes in environment, social structure, or relations of production could quickly deform the world view of the Kongo people, but they might not change it completely. The set of attitudes and beliefs held by Kongo people in the mid-seventeenth century was the result of a long historical process in which rapidly evolving attitudes in some areas were placed side-by-side with older, traditional beliefs that showed much greater continuity through time. Although these beliefs might be attacked or reshaped by outside forces, those who held them did not yield unresistingly, but preserved as many of their traditional beliefs as possible, accepting change only as necessary and only within the limitations of the already existing system.[1]

The beliefs of the Kongo offered explanation and justification and set down courses of action for a great variety of activities and eventualities, from paying rent or performing labor to establishing a household, raising children, being sick (or staying well), and dying. But at the same time, Kongo beliefs were not uniform throughout the society. There were profound differences in outlook between the residents of the towns and the residents of the villages—this division, so central to economy and society in the country, had its effect on world view as well. Perhaps at some time in Kongo's past, well before the formative years of the society that Garcia II ruled, a more or less common belief system prevailed throughout the country. But by the seventeenth century, although echoes of this system

remained, indeed played a substantial part in the integrating of society to
the degree that it was integrated, on the whole Kongo's two sectors had
divided. Each sector had evolved in its own way, the towns tending
towards one set of beliefs, the villages towards another, each guided by
the logic of its own development and the logic of the system as a whole.

At the center of these separate developments were notions of economic
integration and political sovereignty. In the villages, as we have already
seen, the sexual division of labor, and the complementary contributions
to the household made by men and women, were fundamental principles.
Those who lived off the surplus of the village economy justified this
privilege by their talents and services—the *kitomi's* special prerogatives
were justified by his ability to mediate the unseen natural forces of the
spirit world, and while the *nkuluntu's* claims are less clear, he too provided leadership in some aspects of community life.[2] It was not so with
the town sector, however. Even if the king might provide some spiritual
direction to the town sector, and find his position justified within that
sector, in his relations with the country as a whole his rule was justified
simply by the right of conquest. The myths of Kongo's origin related how
an adventurer, whose father had made his name as a raider, conquered
the kingdom and divided it among his companions.[3] No further justification for the taking of taxes and rent seemed necessary, even in the seventeenth century, for the myth was spoken aloud in the coronation
ceremonies of the time as a charter for the kingdom.[4] Even beyond the
right to seize goods deriving from conquest was another concept—that of
slavery. The slaves who labored to produce the town sector's wealth and
luxury were themselves "conquered" in a fashion, so that their condition
was derived more or less directly from the right of conquest.[5] Yet, while
in their relations with the villagers and slaves who provided their needs
the nobility of the town emphasized their power as a right, among themselves they were still profoundly governed by the ethics that applied in
the villages. Household and lineage, even though they no longer played
a role in production, continued to govern consumption. The spoils of
conquest were divided up by households—Kongo politics, after all, was
largely a story of the struggle for power of various houses. Christian
priests exhorted young Kongo nobles to honor and obey "our priests and
those who lead the *dikanda* (lineage)."[6]

If the nobles of the towns considered the right of conquest a sufficient
justification for their systematic exploitation of slaves and villagers, there
is substantial evidence that the later did not. The villagers revolted against
taxes from time to time,[7] and engaged in more subtle passive resistance
by moving their villages away from roads or reducing their production.[8]
But at the same time there was a certain grim acceptance of the ideology

of conquest, acted out in the ceremony of installation of provincial rulers. This ceremony, which was described in 1652 in detail by Girolamo da Montesarchio, reveals clearly the way in which political and economic beliefs coalesced at the level both of the town sector and of the village sector, for it was here that the two came most closely into contact. Before taking control of the Duchy of Nsundi in 1652, the Capuchin witness relates, Dom Rafael Valle das Lagrimas had first to go to the village of Ngimbo a Mburi, where the *kitomi* of the district lived. There his following and the *kitomi* staged a mock battle, fighting with arrows made of reeds. The duke and his retainers won the "battle," and in the aftermath the *kitomi* ceded rights to land and water. If the duke did not engage in this ceremony, da Montesarchio noted, "he would not be able to exercise any power whatsoever, and no one would have given any obedience or tribute . . ."[9] Besides emphasizing the nature of the justification of town rule in the country, the ceremony showed older themes as well. In the battle, the men fought with the men, and the women fought with the women (the duke's wife with the female companion of the *kitomi*),[10] emphasizing that for town and country alike the division between the sexes was still important, even central, to any systematic exposition of beliefs.

If town and country, with their differing economic structures, had contrasting beliefs about the justification of Kongo's structure, and found themselves in conflict, symbolically if not in actual fact, there was still some consensus on ethics and the supernatural. Despite the differences imposed by history on their particular ways of life, both town and country, slave and freeman, noble and peasant, responded to an older and deeply entrenched set of ideas about the proper role of humanity in the greater world of nature. Most Kongo beliefs, both social and political, had reference to higher powers, natural forces that governed humanity and established what was right and just. These natural forces and human society were deeply intertwined and each affected the other, so that the actions of a society might just as easily affect nature as the actions of nature might affect society.

The study of Kongo's religious life in the seventeenth century is difficult, especially because the only sources available are foreign missionaries. They provide a wealth of descriptive data on rites, but very little in a systematic way on cosmology or the belief system that underlay the rites. Anne Hilton has written extensively on these beliefs, using the missionaries descriptions informed by knowledge of modern Kongo cosmology. Her version is as convincing as possible given the sources available for this most difficult task of historical reconstruction.[11] My object, however, which is to examine the social manifestations of this cosmology, is somewhat easier and less hazardous, since it need involve only a minimum of the biased judgements of outsiders.

One can start by looking at the roles of religious actors in the mental world of Kongo. These roles can be separated into actions for the public (or social) sphere and actions for the private sphere, although the borders between them were not clearly defined.[12] Ideally, in the seventeenth century a *kitomi* was strictly a public figure, while the *nganga* was a private one.[13] *Itomi* (plural of *kitomi*) stayed fairly closely within their public role, at least as far as the rather sketchy record shows, but the same records reveal that the *nganga* regularly performed public roles as well. In addition to helping private persons overcome hardship or obtain luck, *nganga* regularly sought to bring rain, cure epidemics, and engage in other functions on behalf of society at large. Cavazzi, for example, was careful to delineate the differences in ceremonial usage between an *nganga a ngombo*'s activities for private persons and those for the public.[14] Thus all religious actors engaged in both private and public functions—despite theoretical differentiation, it was difficult to separate the individual from society.

The public role of mediating between society and nature belonged typically to the *kitomi*, and examining his actions reveals something of the attitudes, at least ideal attitudes, of Kongo religion. Missionaries likened the *itomi* to "bishops and patriarchs," and one describes their role as like that of a "god of the earth." They were seen as central to agriculture— fertility and rainfall were said to be dependent upon them. At harvest time they received the first fruits, and it was held that eating the first fruits without giving them to the *kitomi* would kill the consumer.[15] So delicate was the balance between the *itomi* and the forces of nature that it was considered unwise to let them die a natural death, as this might upset nature. As a result, moribund *itomi* were ritually strangled by their successors.[16] Not only were *itomi* guardians of the relations between humans and nature, but they also protected and continued the most cherished social institutions. Although *itomi* did not set up a household of marry (having instead, female companions to provide them with agri- cultural products), it was a crime punishable by death to be faithless in marriage if the charge were brought to the *kitomi*.[17] Likewise, the *itomi* legitimized the political order, whether with apparent reluctance as in the case of the installation of the provincial rulers, or willingly as when they acted as oracles on behalf of the political rulers.[18]

The *kitomi*'s role indicates how closely the balance of nature depended on the balance of society; each was intimately related to the other through the actions of the *kitomi*. The role of the *nganga*, although ideally a private one, shows this precarious balance even better. Frequently, even normally, an *nganga* would do some sort of service on behalf of a particular client in exchange for payment in kind or in money, such as predicting the future, curing an illness, providing charms for luck in hunting or agriculture, or preventing accidents and similar misfortunes. Some *nganga* specialized in a very narrow range of services.[19] The individualism implied in this private role with clients contained an inherent danger for a society like Kongo's. Personal ambition represented a threat to the cooperation and solidarity that were essential to village life. Moreover, in a close-knit society tensions and jealousies might also enter into this private role, and it was easy for the *nganga* to step across and become *ndoki*, witches, people who helped their clients by hurting others.

The tension and ambiguity of the *nganga*'s role is well illustrated in the detailed observations of Luca da Caltanisetta made in late seventeenth-century Nsundi. At Mpangala, on 28 January 1698, he witnessed one man throw a curse on another after a fight, and at Lemfu a month later he encountered an *nganga a ngombo* who was in a ritual psychic combat with another who was trying to poison him. Similarly, at Damma in March, 1699, people explained that during the night someone had left his body and was ruining the crops, and they were chanting to make him flee.[20] *Nganga* could obviously work on both sides of what Kongo society considered ethical, and the very fact that they worked on behalf of private clients made much of what they did suspect. Therefore, the Catholic priests, who were widely regarded as simply another type of *nganga*, were at times accused of dealing in evil. Luca da Caltanisetta and Marcellino da Atri, travelling in Nsundi, regularly had to submit to baggage inspection, which was a precaution village authorities took to insure that travellers were not working evil by means of various devices. Indeed the accusation that priests worked for private and antisocial ends was not uncommon.[21] No amount of denial could help; and when, conversely, the priests rounded up "fetishers" whom they claimed (using the witchcraft terminology of seventeenth-century Europe) were working for the Devil, their actions were both acceptable and understandable to the Kongo who hosted them. Locating witches and subjecting them to various punishments was legitimate and frequent activity of any *nganga*.[22]

Just how closely related social and natural forces were assumed to be in seventeenth-century Kongo is illustrated by aspects of the public role of *nganga* as well as of their private roles. Public as well as private misfortune was often blamed on witchcraft, and in both instances the practice of witchcraft was ascribed to resentment, jealousy, or other social tension. A public ritual, the *mbumba kidongo*, which Luca da Caltanisetta observed in 1697, instances how closely the balance of nature was held to be dependent on social solidarity. "When in a libata there is a lot of sickness or death, they call one of the principal fetishers . . . to ask the devil the cause of the sickness or deaths."[23] This *nganga* then consults the forces of the spirit world, and "the devil tells him the cause of the sickness or the general mortality, and he also reveals that someone wishes it because of a wrong done to him or because of an argument between this person and that one. . . ."[24] Charges of witchcraft were not always brought against specific individuals; in this case, for example, the *nganga* recommended that all the people recognize and repent their faults, and the community as a whole raised and altar (the *mbumba kidongo*), which they dedicated with objects such as cinders, pieces of wood, and so on that belonged to both the living and the dead members of the community.[25]

The *kimpasi*, a well-documented Kongo initiation cult, also demonstrates how important social unity was conceived to be in a properly ordered natural system. *Impasi* (plural of *kimpasi*) were normally not established in every location; one that Bernardo da Gallo observed in the early eighteenth century was to "cure the sick,"[26] and a regional increase in mortality might have been a cause for their establishment. They were probably regional rather than simply local, for the *nganga a ngombo* who was called in to establish one would travel over the district assembling potential initiates who would then go to a secret meeting place away from all settlements, which was taboo to all who were not a part of it.[27] From the seventeenth-century accounts, it appears that the *kimpasi* symbolically destroyed and rebuilt society, perhaps in order to rid it of all jealousies and tensions. Initiates were symbolically "killed" upon entering the *kimpasi* and were then resurrected from the dead by way of possession by a spirit, *nkita*.[28] Among the most prominent activities of *impasi* was the rearrangement of sexual and marriage relationships along the initiates, including, apparently, members of the same family and household.[29] In the end, new households would be established, so that people might have husbands or wives of the *kimpasi* as well as their own husbands or wives.[30] After this, people would return to their communities, although in some cases a *kimpasi* might last a long time; for example, in 1664 Girolamo da Montesarchio disbanded one that was held to be "an old and respected one."[31]

These cases show that the Kongo valued actors playing the public role ahead of those in the private role, if for no other reason than that the private role always was threatening to the community. They also valued the *kitomi's* role ahead of the *nganga's* because *itomi* communicated with the natural forces directly.

While the *kitomi's* physical person was valued, he carried with him nothing save a staff of office, "six palms (120 cm) high and moderately thick, with a carved end";[32] whereas the *nganga* often operated with the aid of numerous charms, *nkisi* or *iteke*. These came in a wide variety of sizes and shapes, and were worn on the body or placed in houses.[33] The *nganga* claimed to charge them with power, and they were sold for a price that depended upon their power and efficacy.[34] An *nganga's* livelihood depended upon the sale of *nkisi* or fees for the services rendered to clients. Thus an unsuccessful *nganga* might go hungry,[35] while successful ones might be like the one in the Ntanda Kongo region of Nsundi who was so well known that people came from miles around to see him, or the old man known to missionaries in 1652 who claimed to be the patriarch of all the *nganga za ngombo* (plural of *nganga a ngombo*) of Kongo.[36] Such a life-style was foreign to the *itomi;* rather than charging for services they obtained subsistence from the first fruits of the harvest or were paid by the local nobility out of their revenue.[37] Once again, however, the roles were not as distinct as this ideal description makes them sound—*nganga*, too, might perform a public role, and without use of material objects. For instance, the *nganga a ngombo* was said to be able to predict the future solely by means of an inborn power called *kutamanga*.[38]

Catholic priests, who were placed in the same class with *nganga*, were subject to the same expectations and rules as applied to the latter. When Capuchins refused to collect a charge for baptisms or other services, they were honored as would be a *kitomi* or another *nganga* who did service in the public good.[39] However, the secular clergy, who regularly charged for the sacraments they administered, were not abused as greedy, nor was any objection made by the Kongo if Christian priests made use of what seemed to be *nkisi*. Indeed, the priests even called the Bible *mukanda nkisi* (holy book) and the church *nzo a nkisi*, (holy house) clearly suggesting by the names, as well as by the apparent reverence with which these material objects were regarded, that they had charged these "charms" with energy.[40] Like their Kongo counterparts, the Christian *nganga* were more honored when they performed their functions without mediation of physical objects and in the public interest. Their own penchant for destroying *nkisi*, which so many historians have cited as evidence of their cultural chauvinism, was no hindrance to their effectiveness in Kongo.[41]

Thus the religious and ethical systems of Kongo, and their beliefs about the relationship between humanity and nature, were conditioned by human society itself. Not only was social equilibrium considered important as an end in itself, but the entire natural order dependent upon it. Therefore, in religious rituals, social actors were preferred over private actors, direct contact preferred over indirect contact. The overall tendency of this belief system was to favor social equality: individual advancement would be seen as occurring at the expense of the community at large. But in seventeenth-century Kongo there were large, systematic inequalities. Village rulers stood in unequal relation to the villagers, and the entire town sector was likewise set above the villages. Within the town as well there were inequalities between the slaves and the nobles. These inequalities were justified by the right of conquest and by the *itomi's* sacralizing of the rulers. We have already seen how local *itomi* installed rulers from the towns in the country districts. The king himself was also installed by a *kitomi*, the Mani Vunda, who was said to be descended from the *kitomi* of the São Salvador region at the time of the foundation of the kingdom.[42]

Despite the right of conquest, which implied violence and destruction of social solidarity in the positions of rulers and kings, these figures did perform religious roles as well as purely secular ones. Perhaps the roles were inherited from earlier periods in which rulers performed less exploitative political roles, or perhaps they stemmed from the rulers' position among their own particular class. Olifert Dapper noted in the 1640s that rain was said to depend upon the king.[43] More important still, the Prince of Nsoyo in the 1670s and 1680s was not only held responsible for the rain, but also engaged in a number of ceremonies opening the agricultural season, fishing season, and hunting activities.[44]

An important aspect of this religious role played by the nobility was the opportunity for its extension and control offered by the Christian religion. The Christian religion has often been seen as an ephemeral part of Kongo's religious structure, and indeed, viewed from some perspectives, it was. It is clear from the research of Wyatt MacGaffey and Anne Hilton that Christianity was thoroughly Africanized, in that there was a more or less direct translation of Kongo cosmology and religious categories onto Christianity.[45] This process was greatly helped by the adoption by the priests, in their religious texts, of key Kikongo religious terms—such as *nganga* for "priest" and *nkisi* for "holy," or *Nzambi Mpungu* for "God." These terms effectively turned a declaration of Christian faith, such as the Credo, into a declaration fully comprehensible to any Mukongo. To say that one believed in Nzambi Mpungu, that the priest was an *nganga*, and that his religious paraphernalia (cross, church, images, etc.) were all *nkisi* (which missionaries translated as simply "holy") was not to change one's religion much.

On the other hand, most scholars who have seen Kongo Christianity in this way have assumed that such a declaration did not constitute true conversion, or that the missionaries were deluded in their notions about their parishioners' beliefs. Such an analysis has normally been predicated on the modern missionary definition of Christianity, formed in the twentieth century and applied in a colonial situation. By the terms of this modern definition, Christianity makes stringent demands on converts, requiring them to change their lives radically. If such modern missionary standards are applied retrospectively, it appears clear that the Kongo did not qualify as true converts. But the context of the sixteenth and seventeenth centuries was quite different, for there was then never any real doubt that Christianity was the official religion in Kongo, and the Popes accepted it as such. Most missionaries themselves accepted the Kongo as Christians, even though they often denounced them as superstitious. The Propaganda Fide in Rome was convinced that conversion required only minimal cultural alteration, and ruled that only practices strictly forbidden by the Councils could be suppressed.[46] Moreover, in many mission fields of the world in the sixteenth and seventeenth centuries, some truly remarkable combinations of Christianity and local religions were considered to be orthodox, at least for a time, as in China and some parts of India.[47] It was only in colonial areas such as Mexico that a strict definition of conversion, such as was widely in use in twentieth-century missionary work, was applied.[48]

It is in this context that we ought to view the missionaries' activities in seventeenth-century Kongo. If we take as a starting point two of the Kikongo words from the religious vocabulary of the Christian religion in Kongo, we can see more clearly the direction of missionary practice. These two words are *nganga* and *nkisi*. Essentially, the goal of the missionaries was to replace all *nganga* in the country with Christian *nganga* (priests) and to replace all *nkisi* in the country with Christian *nkisi* (the cross, religious medals, etc.). Thus a Catholic priest would perform the same principal rites as his non-Christian counterparts, utilizing the Christian equivalents of his rival's charms (*nkisi*). Girolamo Merolla's account of his activities in Nsoyo in the 1680s clearly and directly shows this active substitution, which indeed went on everywhere.[49] Kongo would have been as completely Christian as any missionary would have wished if only the entire practice of the *nganga* were in the hands of ordained priests. To the ordinary people, however, this transformation would have had no religious significance, for Kongo religion as a system would have survived the transformation intact, save for its renaming as Christianity—a condition that was more or less satisfied in any case, since even Kongo peasants who had little contact with the Church were happy enough to call themselves Christian.[50]

The primary tool by which the priests intended to work this transformation was the concept of witchcraft, which in the seventeenth century was widely shared in both Europe and Africa, although its precise cosmological definition was different in the two areas.[51] In Europe, the sixteenth and seventeenth centuries witnessed an increasingly harsh def-

inition of witchcraft whereby many healers or other odd types were identified as active agents of the devil and consigned to the flames.[52] This
definition was likewise applied by Europeans in Africa, where the local
nganga were seen as diabolic agents, and those who utilized their services
as practicing "diabolic superstitions."[53] On the other side of the coin, the
Africans clearly understood what was meant in this sort of attack on
nganga, for they recognized that anyone with powers to deal with the
supernatural might use that power for personal, private, and harmful ends
and thus be labelled as practicing witchcraft. Not surprisingly, the *nganga's* answer to this attack was to accuse their accusers of doing the same.[54]

The "war" which raged across Kongo's rural areas in the mid-seventeenth
century and pitched the priests against the local *nganga* can be properly
seen only in this way. Far froim being a fundamental attack on Kongo's
religious self-determination, it was fully supported by Kongo's ruling class
and nobility, and it was understood by all the participants, Kongo and
European. The burning of "fetishes"[55] and the imprisoning of *nganga*,
and (on the other side) the poisoning of priests, did not represent a
struggle between rival religions—it was a struggle between rival religious
actors for control of the same religion, the ancient religion on the Kingdom of Kongo, renamed Christianity by offical decree in 1491.

The support for the Christian religion by the upper classes from that
early date can best be understood by seeing the consequences of a completely Christian religious establishment. Under Kongo's traditional religious organization the role of *nganga* was quite open—in any case the
nganga were not officially commissioned or ordained by some other *nganga*,
but won their respect through general acclaim. Some failed to achieve
that acclaim and lived in poverty, while others were widely recognized.
Under a Christian system, however, all the *nganga* of the country would
be strictly controlled in a hierarchical system, from the humble parish
priest to the bishop in São Salvador. By controlling this elaborate clerical
organization, the kings of Kongo and the noble classes could guarantee
control over the formerly democratic and somewhat untamed religious
sector of the country. They could move loyal clients into clerical positions,
bolster their own legitimacy, and suppress rival religious claimants under
the rubric of witchcraft. It is hardly surprising that the Kongo priests
ordained in 1637 were all of noble origin, nor that the many catechists
and students of the schools were also drawn from the upper classes.[56]

The failure of the nobility to Christianize the entire religious establishment in Kongo was not due to their lack of desire or good will, but to
their struggle with the Portuguese over control of the bishop—the center
of the whole scheme. When Kongo was made an episcopal see in 1596,
the Portuguese Crown, invoking the right of "Padroado" (patronage), in-

sisted that the King of Portugal had the right to choose the bishop. His tendency to choose high-ranking Portuguese, who in turn used their position against the kings of Kongo, led to permanent conflict which culminated in the abandonment of São Salvador by the bishop and a part of the cathedral staff in 1624 to join their countrymen in Luanda.[57] Pedro II, who was ruling Kongo at the time, reorganized the remaining clerics around his chapel of Saint James and effectively gained control of the church in Kongo—but at the price of losing the bishop.[58] The ultimate result was a hesitancy on the part of the bishop to ordain Kongo to the priesthood—although some were ordained in 1637—so that by mid-century the number of clerical personnel in the country had sunk dangerously low.[59]

To make up for this loss of the secular clergy, the kings of Kongo turned to the regular orders—first the Jesuits, who reestablished their mission in São Salvador in 1619, and then the Capuchins who arrived in 1645 and whose mission provided the vast majority of ordained priests in Kongo for the rest of the seventeenth century and all of the eighteenth century.[60] While the Jesuits confined themselves largely to education, and the seculars (of whom there were eight in Kongo at the time the Capuchins arrived)[61] took on the lucrative posts in São Salvador and the largest of the *mbanza*, the Capuchins were sent into the countryside, barred from performing the sacraments within five leagues (twenty-five kilometers) of an *mbanza* where there was a secular priest.[62] This proved a satisfactory arrangement to all involved, after a period of some inter-order struggle, and was to last for over 150 years.

To make up for the lack of genuinely clerical positions open to Kongo, the foreign regular clergy were surrounded by noble Kongo who acted as interpreters and school teachers (masters). As they were largely responsible for instruction and organization of the rural chapels and churches, they became the unofficial clergy of the country, while the Capuchins were placed in the role of travelling dispensers of the sacraments—the one clerical role denied the noble laymen. Capuchin priests often did little more than baptize children, travelling on long journeys from their hospices accompanied by their interpreters and mission slaves (*nleke*) and baptizing thousands every year.[63]

Although this arrangement allowed for the survival of the Christian religion in Kongo, it did not create the Christian Kongo that the kings hoped for, in which they controlled the religious establishment simply and directly. Garcia clearly hoped that he could change things to his advantage, and one of the principal tasks of his ambassadors to Rome in 1645–48 was to arrange for a bishop in Kongo to be free from Portuguese rights;[64] he settled for the haphazard arrangement of travelling Capuchins and noble lay assistants only after that endeavor failed. The Capuchins did provide some functions, however. They assisted the Kongo kings in diplomacy, and by organizing several lay congregations they provided a focus for Garcia's consolidation of power.[65] Rivalry with the seculars kept them from assuming an overtly political role—in the 1650s seculars convinced Garcia that the Capuchins were plotting against him and were carrying munitions into the country to arm his enemies[66]—but in the end the Capuchins' reputation for political neutrality, acquired in part because they were foreigners and short-term residents (the normal tour of duty for a Capuchin in Kongo was seven years), gained them some advantages. Indeed, it was through membership in the Capuchin order that one secular—Manuel Roberdo, ordained as Francisco de São Salvador—managed to break his problematic ties with the Kimpanzu and eventually rise to a position of trust as Antonio I's personal confessor.[67] While they could not create a Kongo clergy in Kongo and naturalize the church, the Capuchins played their limited role consistently and well.

In the countryside, the Capuchins, while aware of their own acceptability as *nganga*, also recognized the fundamental political and social realities of Kongo that limited their influence. While their schools in the rural districts provided education outside the normal schooling available in São Salvador, this schooling was very noble-oriented. As late as 1722, when Capuchin schools in Mbamba had been functioning for nearly three-quarters of a century, literacy was still restricted to the nobility. Of the witnesses in a legal case that year which involved ordinary servants of the hospice (freed slaves), the only one who could read and write was a "fidalgo of Mbamba."[68] In exchange for this preferential education, the nobility backed the Capuchins with force, if necessary. When one Capuchin, Joris van Gheel, was killed by initiates of a *kimpasi* he was attempting to disrupt, Garcia II seized all the inhabitants of the village and sold them into slavery.[69] Similarly, Garcia backed a plan by Girolamo da Montesarchio to suppress the *itomi* of the provinces in which he worked. His vigorous activities in the small marquisates west of Nsundi in 1650 succeeded in getting a number of *itomi* to convert, but also apparently provoked a revolt against both the campaign of suppression and the ruler of Nsevo, Dom Gregorio.[70] It would have been in Garcia's and the nobility's interests to suppress the *itomi*, who always represented, in part, rivals for the claim of legitimate authority, and replace it with the much more loyal and easily controlled priests. The campaign continued into 1652, when da Montesarchio succeeded in getting Rafael Valle das Lagrimas to bypass the *kitomi* of Nsundi in taking up his office as duke.[71] In the end, however, this particular effort failed, perhaps because of peasant resistance.

The mental world of the Kongo therefore remained quite constant throughout the early part of the seventeenth century. The tendency of Christianity to expand, and at the same time to do so without altering fundamental belief structures of Kongo, continued from the sixteenth century. If there was a general direction to these movements, it was for an increasing legitimacy of the noble rule in Kongo through their alliance with the Christian church. The arrival of the Capuchins not only continued this development within the nobility, but also helped to propagate the new source of legitimacy in the countryside. However, in no case did any of these movements represent a radical break with Kongo's religious or ideological past; rather, they simply emphasized already active tendencies in the world view of the Kongo.

6

The Civil Wars Begin

OF THE many adjustments necessary for complete stabilization of the socioeconomic system of Kongo that had been established around 1650, adjustments in attitude and belief were the latest to develop. By the mid-seventeenth century, there still was not a completely accepted ideological justification for the rule of the countryside by the towns. This laggard development, however, was not the primary threat to the system; for there were other circumstances, some of them outside the country, which were menacing the destruction of Garcia's Kongo even before it was consolidated. The rise of Nsoyo by mid-century and its alliance with the Kimpanzu against Garcia posed a significant threat. Kongo faced another threat from still another town sector, that which the Portuguese had established in Angola, just beyond Kongo's southern borders. But despite the tendency of historians in recent years to see the Angolan threat as paramount to Kongo, and a principal contribution to the end of Kongo's power,[1] in fact, the role of Angola in Kongo's fall was less important than that of Nsoyo.

There are a number of reasons why Angola was a less important threat, but the most important in the end is that Angola was foreign, established in a marginal area and ruled by non-Kongo people. Nsoyo, on the other hand, with its close connections to the Kongo throne and its intimate relations with Kongo's ruling houses, was an internal threat much more serious than the essentially external and military power of Angola. Kongo could deal with such an external threat directly, since it had obtained through trade or diplomacy most of the military technology which the Portuguese could use.[2] Portuguese military might could never equal the potential political power that the ruler of Nsoyo possessed, which can be gauged by the fact that Nsoyo had once been entitled to participate in the election of the ruler of Kongo.[3]

In fact, moreover, Kongo had little reason to be hostile to Angola by Garcia's time. It is true that relations between the two countries had not been good since the late sixteenth century, and in the early seventeenth century Portuguese troops with their allies, the dreaded cannibal Imbangala, had attacked Kongo's southern provinces, culminating in the wars of 1621–24 when they seized several southern districts of the country and annexed them to Angola.[4] The Portuguese had also shown a keen interest in Kongo's internal politics, actively supporting disgruntled claimants to positions in Kongo and flirting with invasions during Kongo's many succession disputes. But much of this overt hostility had calmed by the 1630s or '40s. The Portuguese were increasingly drawn into affairs east of Angola, in Ndongo and Matamba, so that by the middle of the seventeenth century the majority of Angola's slaves came from there and not from Kongo.[5]

Moreover, Portuguese residents of Angola had turned the rivers that marked the southern border of Kongo into great plantation areas whose products had gone to feed Luanda. By 1635, according to an account of Pero Tavares, a well-travelled Jesuit priest, there was a great chain of *arimos* (slave-worked farms and plantations) along the Bengo and Dande Rivers, in which not only Portuguese, but local African rulers had an interest.[6] Slaves for this region were overwhelmingly recruited from eastern parts of Angola, and as a result the language along these rivers changed during the first part of the seventeenth century from Kikongo to Kimbundu.[7] What military expeditions the Portuguese of this area were able to mount against Kongo were normally only to retrieve runaway slaves, and not major raids or wars.

Thus, from the point of view of São Salvador, Angola was a relatively minor threat. Incursions from Angola, as long as they did not threaten São Salvador, would be handled by local governors as best they could. This was in accordance with Kongo practice concerning other occasionally hostile neighbors. Thus the raids of the Yaka of the Niari, which were constant in the region along the south bank of the Zaire, and quite disruptive locally, were met by local rulers.[8] Similarly, the Marquis of Nkusu's battle with invading forces of Nsonso on the east was without help from São Salvador, as was the resistance put up by Wandu when invaded in 1648 by forces from Matamba.[9] This policy regarding invaders reflected the general unconcern exhibited by the town sector towards events in the village sector (which of course included all the border areas). Kongo nobles themselves might despoil their own provinces from the *mbanza* just as easily as did the outsiders.

The Portuguese of Angola did pose a threat in one respect, however. While the rulers of São Salvador might care little about small-scale raids and border wars, they were concerned about the seizing of valuable resources in Kongo which either were rare or might provide the town with extra luxury or foreign exchange. We have already seen that the function of the rural areas, from the point of view of the economic rulers, was to provide just such resources, and a threat to this function must have been perceived as a direct threat to Kongo's larger economic interests. The Portuguese of Angola did pose such a threat at times, first in their occasional demand to be allowed to work mines (for various metals) in Kongo and second in their desire to have a monopoly of all external trade on the Kongo coast. Most of Angola's designs in both these regards were drawn up on paper and never got much beyond the planning stage, or wound up as consistently opposed clauses in various Kongo-Portuguese treaties.[10] Throughout the seventeenth century the Kongo had been adamant in not allowing either plan to be realized.[11]

An especially sticky point of contention was Portuguese insistence that she had the right to exclude Dutch merchants, who had frequented the Kongo coast since the early seventeenth century, and by 1640 had a string of posts along the coast.[12] As the Dutch offered better merchandise at lower prices, the Portuguese resented their competition and constantly drew up plans and importuned Kongo rulers for a fort at Mpinda in Nsoyo province.[13] As a result of both Dutch commercial contacts and mutual hostility to the Portuguese intentions, Kongo-Dutch relations were good, and would get better when the Dtuch seized Luanda in 1641. The Portuguese insistence on mining rights caused fewer problems, since no one was even quite sure what mines existed, or what metals they might contain.

In addition to these direct (even if mainly paper) threats posed by the Portuguese, they also posed a significant indirect threat. This was their contention, legalized through the right of Patronage granted the King of Portugal by the Pope in the fifteenth century, to control the church establishment in Kongo.[14] We have already seen that the church played an important role in Kongo internal politics, both ideologically and in the struggles between houses. It had caused some concern to Kongo, then, when the pro-Portuguese members of the See of São Salvador withdrew to Luanda in 1624.[15] While Pedro II reorganized the loyal members of the See during his reign, and probably strengthened it, a real hope of various Kongo kings during the rest of the century was to obtain complete control of the Kongo church, and to have this control accepted in Rome. This struggle over the right of Patronage was Kongo's most ambitious in its foreign relations, for unlike the struggle over freedom of trade and mining rights, it was waged in Europe, Portugal's home ground.

Thus these complex contests with Portugal, involving the Dutch and indirectly the Catholic church leaders in Rome, provided the background for a significant Portuguese threat to Kongo. If it still represented less of a threat on structural grounds than that posed by Nsoyo, it could never-theless not be overlooked by those concerned with Kongo's politics. In the end, this secondary threat led to events which forced Kongo off-balance and allowed the primary threat posed by Nsoyo to operate fully. The currents of the Kongo-Portuguese struggle reached a climax in a series of events that began with the Dutch seizure of Luanda in 1641 and ended with the battle of Mbwila in 1665.[16]

In retrospect, the Dutch occupation of Luanda can be seen to be the beginning of the final crisis for Kongo, but at the time it could only have appeared as a fortunate stroke for Garcia, for it gave him a decisive edge in his struggle with the Portuguese. Holland's action had been preceded by an abortive attempt in the 1620s and Luanda had been subject to frequent alarms. Nevertheless, the attempt of 1641 took Luanda com-pletely by surprise. At the first news of the event, Garcia II, newly established on Kongo's throne, promptly contacted the Dutch in Angola and began negotiations for a treaty that he hoped would establish better commercial outlets for his products and drive the Portuguese perma-nently out of west central Africa.[17] Garcia's negotiations did secure him an important new trade outlet through southern Kongo, connecting Ma-tamba with a port at the mouth of the Mbrize River, which avoided both Luanda and Mpinda, whose rulers might be hostile to him.[18] Nsoyo, whose hostility to Garcia was matched by its friendship with the Dutch, also sent embassies to the Dutch conquerors in both Luanda and Brazil (and eventually even to the Low Countries themselves) to make treaties and to protest Dutch military aid to Garcia, who, they claimed, was using weapons intended for fighting the Portuguese to carry on his struggle with Nsoyo.[19] Nsoyo's ambassadors were not wrong in this contention, either, for in 1645 Garcia's emissaries asked Dutch cooperation in a land-sea attack on Nsoyo to free his son Afonso, who had been captured leading Kongo's most recent attack on the province.[20] The Dutch, for their part, tried to stay as neutral as possible in order to secure the maximum trade from both areas, while still enlisting their aid in the ongoing struggle they were waging against the Portuguese who had fled inland from Luanda and were holding out in strongholds in eastern Angola.[21]

The defeat of Portuguese arms in Luanda had provided Garcia with another weapon to use against them, and to regain control of the church in Kongo. Garcia began to press hard in Rome to get a new bishop to replace Francisco do Soveral, who had been firmly pro-Portuguese and had recently died while with the Portuguese armies in eastern Angola.[22] In 1645, the first Capuchins came to Nsoyo in answer to a request for the missionaries made over a quarter-century earlier by Álvaro III.[23] Despite the hostility between Nsoyo and Kongo, the Capuchins managed to secure missions in both areas; to Garcia's advantage, they proved to be good diplomats in Kongo's service. The arrival of the Capuchins had been one episode in the struggle waged by Roman authorities to regain control over the overseas missions, which had been lost in the granting of the right of Patronage to the Crowns of Spain and Portugal.[24] As such, it corresponded nicely with Garcia's similar attempt to reduce the right of the Portuguese to control the functioning of Kongo's church. Thus, Kongo diplomats and Roman officials were in general accord as to what should be done, and Rome was responsive to Garcia's proposal for an extensive reorganization of Kongo's church, including an archbishop for São Salvador and bishops in the major provinces, all free from Portuguese control.[25] Indeed the Roman officials did appoint a non-Portuguese temporary bishop for Kongo, the Neapolitan Francisco Staibano.[26] The fact that this concession was won in Europe against the vehement protests of the Portuguese ambassador to Rome shows how successfully Kongo diplomats could maneuver in Europe by 1648.[27]

If 1648 then represented the high point of Garcia's military and diplomatic career, it also represented a turning point. Just as his ambassadors in Rome were beginning to break through on the issues of ecclesiastical organization, the troops of Salvador de Sá stormed Luanda, and in a few days had totally neutralized the Dutch presence in Angola.[28] Suddenly, Kongo and the other central African powers were on the defensive. Salvador de Sá's troops were as well equipped and numerous as Portuguese finances would allow, and they came to Angola to restore Portuguese rule and punish those who had aided the Dutch. The period that followed the Portuguese restoration, from 1648 to 1671, was one of the most militarily aggressive periods of Portuguese rule in Angola. Salvador de Sá and his successors in office ran Angola in the interests of Brazil, paid themselves by acquiring slaves in their wars, and eventually so alienated even the Portuguese residents in Angola with their constant warfare and destructiveness that on occasion governors were expelled from the colony.[29]

Portuguese troops waged war on all of Angola's enemies—Libolo in the south, Ndongo and Matamba in the east, the Ndembu region to the north—and, in 1649, Kongo. Garcia, anxious to avoid all-out war against the Portuguese, sent an embassy to Luanda when the Portuguese invaded southern Kongo, securing their withdrawal and beginning negotiations for peace.[30] The initial versions of the treaty, one from São Salvador, the other from Luanda, were each rejected by the other party, although Portuguese in Angola maintained for years afterwards that Garcia had agreed to a harsh and exacting treaty proposed by Salvador de Sá.[31] At any rate, Garcia was studiously friendly to the Portuguese, even when their troops violated his borders, and the Portuguese, tied up with other enemies to the south and east of Angola, did not seriously threaten Kongo over the following few years. It may be that the Portuguese were themselves a bit frightened by Kongo's strength, as their incursion of 1657 shows.

This was their most serious campaign in Kongo territory, and was planned to link up with the last revolts of the leaders of the Kinkanga a Mvika lineage against Garcia. Such a combination of antagonists might have been dangerous to Kongo, but the internal revolts were crushed swiftly in 1656, and Garcia was ready for the Portuguese when they came in 1657. Kongo troops easily smashed hostile factions of the last renegade members of the Kinkanga a Mvika who had fled to Nsoyo to join the Portuguese army, and when the Angolan forces reached the Loze River, the troops refused to proceed, saying that any white man who went farther into Kongo would never return.[32] Garcia, nevertheless, placated the Portuguese by returning some runaway slaves, and both sides retired, each a bit too nervous about the other's capabilities to risk full-scale war.[33]

In the spring of 1661, Garcia died and was succeeded by his son Antó-nio I, who was duly elected by the Kinlaza of Kongo, and quickly elimi-nated his rivals, both real and imagined, with great cruelty.[34] This new king, young and impetuous, was faced with an equal implacable new governor of Angola, André Vidal de Negreiros. With most of Angola's rivals to the east and south beaten or cowed, Vidal de Negreiros turned to Kongo and began, with the Crown's blessings, to renew the old Portu-guese plans for a fort at Mpinda and prospecting for mines in southern Kongo.[35] His principal legal weapon against Kongo was the unratified treaty of 1649, in which mining rights and free commercial passage had been demanded, and he did not wait long to repeat these demands to António.[36]

Vidal de Negreiros' insistence was based on the rather desperate eco-nomic situation of Angola as a result of the Dutch occupation and the warfare that had followed the restoration. Trade routes to Kongo were closed off, and the cloth currency normally obtained from areas north of Angola was scarce, its price rising.[37] In addition, exports were being routed around Angola, through Kongo either by the route in southern Mbamba, or more commonly through Loango. In 1656, Portuguese com-plained that the Vili, "vassals of the King of Kongo," were frequenting eastern markets in greater numbers and stealing the Portuguese trade.[38] With slaves becoming harder to obtain, Vidal de Negreiros hoped to diversify exports by exploiting the minerals of the colony (or its neighbors) and even minting its own currency to supplement or supplant the cloth *mabongo* which were only available from hostile neighbors.[39] Suddenly, mines, even if only copper mines, were much more important than they had been, and the need to secure better passage through Kongo was rising in importance.

Therefore, Vidal de Negreiros began to meddle in the affairs of the Ndembu rulers of southern Kongo, with an eye towards discovering mineral wealth. António, worried that the Portuguese might begin to exploit these rights to his disadvantage, began to reiterate the ancient claim that Kongo ruled the Ndembu region (which for years had had *de facto* independence) and did some meddling of his own. The Angolans launched wars in the region in 1664, and António's ambassadors began to attempt making an anti-Portuguese alliance in the Ndembu area, promising that Kongo would be obtaining aid from the Spanish.[40] Although their geographical position made them difficult to subdue militarily, the Ndembu region's internal politics, with various mutually hostile contenders for many offices, made it easy for outsiders to interfere in disputes, especially over succession. In 1664–65 such a succession dispute broke out in Mbwila, one of the most important Ndembu areas and strategically located near a supposed mining region. Both António and the Angolans quickly became involved on opposite sides. Taking advantage of the recent appeal by a rebel count of Wandu to Angola for help, along with the struggle over Mbwila, Vidal de Negreiros mobilized an army. António, fearing the intentions of the Portuguese and aware of their stated desire to obtain mining rights from Kongo, issued a general call to arms, in the interests of Kongo's defense.[41]

The two armies met in Mbwila, in the valley of the Ulanga River, on 29 October 1665, in the most significant confrontation between Portugal and Kongo in the two countries' history. Unlike the raids of earlier hostilities, the full military capacity of each was displayed at Mbwila, and the confrontation shows how equal the two sides really were. Both armies were organized in the same way, with a core of regular musketeers surrounded by a much larger assemblage of irregulars. In most respects, however, the Portuguese had a slight edge. First of all, they had more musketeers—Luís Lopes de Sequeira, the Portuguese field commander, could muster 450, while Kongo's Afro-Portuguese captain, Pedro Dias de Cabra, commanded 380.[42] In addition the Portuguese were able to trundle two light field pieces into the mountains.[43] Finally, the Portuguese irregular forces were superior. Although Portuguese reports claimed that António headed an army of 100,000 (and despite the obvious exaggeration of this figure, he probably did have numerical superiority in irregulars), the Portuguese had a significant advantage in quality.[44] The Portuguese *guerra preta* ("black army") was drawn from areas that had participated in the many campaigns waged since 1648. Their forces also included a detachment of Imbangala, fierce fighters who were trained for war from birth and probably the best troops on either side.[45] António's irregulars, on the other hand, were little more than a mass of peasants with no military experience to speak of.

The battle itself was a set-piece affair typical of the Angolan wars of the seventeenth century. The Portuguese formed a square with their musketeers and artillery, surrounded by irregulars, while António launched attacks against this formation. The irregulars were quickly swept away, and the final struggle was a direct attack, led by António himself, against the Portuguese square. The attack failed, António was killed by a musket shot, and his army broke. At that moment the Imbangala launched a counterattack on the disorganized Kongo army, and defeat turned into rout. Thousands of Kongo were killed, including ninety-eight titled nobles and some 400 lesser fidalgos. Also dead on the field were Francisco de São Salvador, António's chaplain and the only Kongo ever to become a member of the regular clergy, as well as another secular cleric. A third priest was captured, as were some other important members of António's personal retinue.[46] The Portuguese left the field in glory, carrying António's severed head with them along with his crown and scepter. The celebration in Luanda lasted several days, and António's head was buried with great pomp, while his royal regalia were sent to Lisbon as trophies.[47]

The battle of Mbwila is rightly considered one of the great decisive battles of central African history, but its decisiveness had little to do with the fact that the Portuguese had triumphed over one of their capital enemies. The Portuguese followed up their victory by making treaties of submission with several Ndembu rulers and Wandu, as well as extracting ore samples from the region, which continued to supply Portugal until 1668.[48] However, Kongo's sovereignty was not seriously threatened and the Portuguese were not in any better position to dictate terms to the losers after the battle. In the end, even the treaties of submission made by Ndembu rulers proved to have only paper force, as were all treaties made by Portugal with the inhabitants of that rugged country until well into the twentieth century.[49]

What made the battle of Mbwila decisive was the effect it had in the conflict between Kongo and Nsoyo, a struggle between town sectors whose relations were far more intimate than those between Kongo and Angola. Throughout the reigns of António and Garcia, Nsoyo had been on the defensive, but with the death of António at Mbwila, Nsoyo moved to the offense. Nsoyo's count, Paulo da Silva, took advantage of two weaknesses in Kongo to make good his attack. In the first place, the disastrous defeat at Mbwila had deprived Kongo of considerable military strength, especially in musketeers, whose casualties had been heavy. Secondly, Paulo da Silva's alliance with the Kimpanzu house allowed him great leeway to intervene in the succession crisis that followed António's death. It was the second of these two weaknesses that was to prove decisive in the long run.

Of course, succession disputes had been common enough in Kongo history, but in the case of the dispute following António's death, it was made worse by the fact that his heir apparent and some other possible contenders had died in the battle.[50] Thus, there was no clear choice for the succession, and several Kinlaza attempted to succeed. Three candidates emerged. A certain Dom Álvaro, the Marquis of Matari, who announced his desire to kill all Europeans in Kongo as well as make himself king, was among the first. Then there was Afonso, husband of Garcia's sister Ana Afonso de Leão; and finally, Álvaro Mpanzu a Mabondo, simply "a relative of the dead king," who eventually came out the victor.[51] This King Álvaro VII killed the upstart Álvaro of Matari and his confederates and backers, the Duke of Nsundi and the Mani Vunda.[52] Afonso, for his part, fled São Salvador with his wife Ana and took refuge in the Nkanda mountains of the east, in a place called Kingi.[53] By Christmas of 1665 the new king felt secure enough to dispatch a trusted Capuchin priest, Girolamo da Montesarchio, to Luanda to make peace with the Portuguese. But da Montesarchio, held up by a rebellion in Mbamba, could not complete his mission, and when he returned to the capital in June, 1666, he found Álvaro VII dead and a new king, Álvaro VIII, on the throne.[54] Nsoyo had intervened in Kongo, and a new era of Kongo's history had begun.

As soon as the rains had broken in 1666, Paulo da Silva and his Kimpanzu allies, including the man who would become Álvaro VIII, marched on São Salvador. The attack fell at a time when the city had not yet solidified its support for Álvaro VII, and when its military capacity had in any case been reduced. Paulo da Silva's troops not only sacked the city, but they installed Álvaro as king, ousting the House of Kinlaza temporarily from the throne.[55]

While Nsoyo was able to place the Kimpanzu on the throne, its eighteen-year-old candidate ruled uneasily in a country where the Kinlaza still controlled many offices and bore him considerable hostility. One of his first actions, in fact, was to attempt to reduce the number of his enemies by placating the Portuguese. He sent his ambassador, Dom Anastacio, to Luanda in 1667, where he negotiated a peace treaty with the Portuguese that conceded mining rights in Kongo to them.[56] If the Portuguese were satisfied with this treaty, the Kinlaza were not, and so Álvaro went personally to Mpemba to try to get the marquis, Dom Pedro, to come to an understanding with him over the future of the Kimpanzu in Kongo.[57] But in the end, Álvaro failed to obtain harmonious relations, and was not secure enough even in São Salvador to continue to rule for long. In an attempt to force a settlement, Álvaro decided to take control of the southern provinces of Mbamba and Mpemba, oust the Kinlaza governors, and place his own kinsmen in command. Dom Teodósio, Duke of Mbamba, began to comply with Álvaro's recall, but Pedro, the Duke of Mpemba, refused. Pedro raised a small army, attacked Mbamba, and killed Duke Teodósio, then successfully resisted an attack by the king, led by two loyal Kimpanzu from the court. Strengthened by his two victories, Pedro marched on São Salvador, and with Álvaro still not fully in control of the city, was able to throw the young king out and place himself on the throne as King Pedro III. The Kinlaza canon, Estevão Castanho, crowned his new lord in January, 1669, and the Kinlaza once again ruled in Kongo.[58]

The reign of Álvaro VIII proved that despite Nsoyo's military aid, it was impossible to rule in Kongo without completing control of the principal offices in the town and countryside. On the other hand, events were soon to prove that the Kinlaza could not rule Kongo in peace without the compliance of Nsoyo. Unless a king in São Salvador could obtain complete control of the town sector, he would not be able to withstand the military strength of Nsoyo. Thus the period between 1666 and 1678 was marked by the rapid, and eventually devastating fluctuation between these two forces, neither one of which was able to control Kongo completely.

Pedro III was crowned king in January, 1669, and by June the army of Nsoyo, led by the new Count Paulo II da Silva, was at the approaches of São Salvador, bringing a new Kimpanzu contender again named Álvaro, with them. Paulo II da Silva's troops mercilessly sacked the city, demolishing buildings and carrying off booty before they established their latest Kimpanzu ally as Álvaro IX.[59] Pedro III managed to escape the city, and led a band of followers to the wooded hills of Mbula some distance to the north of São Salvador on the banks of the Zaire River. In addition, Pedro III's newly appointed Marquis of Mpemba, Rafael, fled with another group to Mbumbi, and, possibly thinking that his king had been killed, attempted to obtain Portuguese aid to restore the Kinlaza to the throne of Kongo.[60]

Between the sack by Nsoyo's army and the flight of the various Kinlaza authorities, São Salvador was being ruined. The slaves of the estates were no doubt disappearing as well, some carried off as booty or following their masters into exile, others perhaps simply taking advantage of the confusion to melt into the population of villagers in the lands around São

Salvador. Whatever the reasons, the town was becoming rapidly depopulated. From a mid-century population of 60,000, São Salvador had shrunk
to 5,000 by 1670, and witnesses in Rome in 1672 put its population at
only 3,000.[61] Not only were none of the contending factions able to control the town, but the town itself was rapidly losing the power to influence
affairs of Kongo as it had throughout the earlier part of the seventeenth
century.

Rafael, who had fled from São Salvador to Mbumbi in the wake of Paulo
II da Silva's attack, sought new allies to counteract the military strength
of Nsoyo and to assist him in the restoration of his house. He turned to
the only likely ally to appear, the Portuguese of Angola, who were quite
willing to hear what he had to offer in the hopes of realizing some of their
commercial and economic plans for the country to their north. Rafael
approached the Portuguese governor, Francisco da Távora, with a tempt-
ing offer—payment of an indemnity of 20,000 cruzados, cession of mining
rights, and granting of permission to build a fort at Mpinda, in exchange
for military aid to restore his line to power.[62] It was all the Portuguese
could ask for, and they willingly granted him all the assistance they could
give.

The Portuguese raised their most powerful army, with 400 musketeers,
a detachment of cavalry, four light cannon, and the usual irregulars—
including an Imbangala detachment under the dreaded Kabuko Kan-
dongo. To this was added a quickly raised, but mostly irregular, Kongo
army under Rafael and a naval detachment of six ships which would attack
from the sea in coordination with the land forces. Their target was Nsoyo,
and their aim to destroy it and allow Rafael to restore himself in São
Salvador. These powerful forces left Luanda on 15 March 1670, and plunged
into the land to their north. Paulo II da Silva also raised a powerful army
which included four light cannon of his own to meet this Portuguese
force. This second Portuguese attack to the north in five years took place
when the two armies met in southern Nsoyo in June, 1670. Paulo II da
Silva's army was badly beaten, and he himself was carried, mortally
wounded, back to Mbanza Nsoyo. His army was smashed, his cannon
were lost, and the Portuguese had little to block a triumphant march on
Mbanza Nsoyo.

Confident now of victory, the Portuguese were content to take their
time in the march to the north. Rafael was detached to march on São
Salvador, where he was duly proclaimed King Rafael I of Kongo, after
easily deposing the Kimpanzu puppet, Álvaro IX. The main army pro-
ceeded slowly northwards, looting the countryside and terrorizing the
inhabitants even as they gradually began to lose their discipline.

The Portuguese advance was so slow, in fact, that it gave Nsoyo time to rebuild its forces. Estevão I da Silva, Paulo II da Silva's brother and successor, girded the Nsoyo people for a desperate struggle. His determination was assisted by the fortunate arrival of a Dutch ship, loaded with military supplies. The Dutch were not going to sit idly by and watch the Portuguese squeeze off their lucrative trade along the Zaire and inland. On 18 October 1670, a reconstituted Nsoyo army fell upon the Portuguese force marching north and annihilated it at Kitombo, not far from Mbanza Nsoyo. The Portuguese were taken totally by surprise, and were unable to deploy their artillery. The Imbangala fled, the artillery was all lost, and hundreds died trying to swim the Mbrize River in the retreat. When the Portuguese fleet showed up a few days later, the troops of Nsoyo sent them the dismembered parts of Portuguese soldiers killed in the battle, and according to legend recorded a decade later, the Nsoyo offered Portuguese as slaves to the Dutch.[63] It was one of the worst defeats suffered by Portuguese arms in Africa, and their last campaign into Kongo territory for over a century.

Kings of Kongo, 1661–1718

Lobata	São Salvador	Mbula	Kimbangu
	António I (Kinlaza) (1661–65)		
	Álvaro VII (Kinlaza) (1665–66)		Afonso (Kinlaza) (1665–70)
	Álvaro VIII (Kimpanzu) (1666–68)		
	Pedro III (Kinlaza) (1668–70)		
	Álvaro IX (Kimpanzu) (1670)	Pedro III (Kinlaza) (1670–83)	Garcia III (Agua Rosada) (1670–89)
	Rafael I (Kinlaza) (1670–72)		
	abandoned 1672–73		
	Afonso II (Kimpanzu) (1673?)		
	Afonso III (Kimpanzu) (1674)		

Kings of Kongo, 1661–1718 (*continued*)

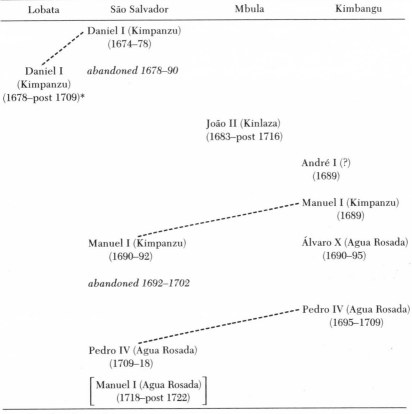

Lobata	São Salvador	Mbula	Kimbangu
	Daniel I (Kimpanzu) (1674–78)		
Daniel I (Kimpanzu) (1678–post 1709)*	*abandoned 1678–90*		
		João II (Kinlaza) (1683–post 1716)	
			André I (?) (1689)
			Manuel I (Kimpanzu) (1689)
	Manuel I (Kimpanzu) (1690–92)		Álvaro X (Agua Rosada) (1690–95)
	abandoned 1692–1702		
			Pedro IV (Agua Rosada) (1695–1709)
	Pedro IV (Agua Rosada) (1709–18)		
	[Manuel I (Agua Rosada) (1718–post 1722)]		

---- transfer of capital.
*Also called Daniel I de Gusmão and Daniel I de Nóbrega.

Because of the struggle with the Portuguese, Nsoyo was temporarily exhausted and thus unable to intervene in the affairs of Kongo. As a result, Rafael I was left to sit unmolested in his largely depopulated capital. But if he was now free from the threat of the Kimpanzu in Nsoyo, he had a new threat to face from the other Kinlaza still in Kongo.

One such group in the east of the country had elected one of their number as King Garcia III (who was descended on one side from the Kinlaza and on the other from the Kimpanzu) upon the death of their first leader, Afonso. Afonso had been one of the contenders for the throne after the death of António I and had been driven out for São Salvador after Álvaro VII declared himself king in 1666. Afonso died sometime around

1670 in his mountain fortress of Kimbangu, where he had for long been forgotten and neglected as the life and death struggle of São Salvador was played out between various Kinlaza kings and the counts of Nsoyo. When Garcia III was elected, however, his choice was not unanimous, for Afonso's wife, sister of King Garcia II, Dona Ana Afonso de Leão, refused to recognize him and withdrew with a group of discontented Kinlaza to Nkondo on the upper reaches of the Mbrize River.[64]

To the north, however, was Rafael I's greatest threat. The Kinlaza there were not happy with his choice of allies, or his attempt to regain control of São Salvador for himself. They were the followers of King Pedro III, Rafael's one-time sovereign, who still felt he had a valid claim to Kongo's throne. It finally came to war, in 1672, and Pedro III was the victor, dethroning Rafael and renouncing his treaty with the Portuguese at the same time. In any case, the Portuguese were scarcely in a position to enforce the treaty after their disaster in Nsoyo.[65]

Pedro III, once he had dethroned his Kinlaza rival, chose not to remain in São Salvador, which was not only mostly depopulated, but vulnerable as well. His army therefore withdrew to the relative safety of Mbula once he had made good his victory over Rafael. São Salvador was thus left temporarily without a king.

By 1672 or 1673, Nsoyo had recovered enough from its fight with the Portuguese to resume its meddling in Kongo affairs, and placed still another Kimpanzu, Afonso II, on Kongo's throne. Afonso II died shortly after his coronation, but was succeeded by his son, Afonso III. In 1674, Pedro III attacked this latest product of the Kimpanzu-Nsoyo alliance, but although he was able to kill Afonso III, the king's nephew, Daniel I, managed to hold off Pedro III and have himself crowned as king to succeed his uncle.[66] But Daniel I was not content to leave well enough alone. Without the constant help of his allies in Nsoyo, he was unable to do much more than simply rule over São Salvador. Accordingly, in 1678 he decided to take the initiative and attack Pedro III in Mbula. His attack failed totally, and Pedro III, along with his new allies, the Yaka of the Niari Valley, carried the war back to São Salvador. Pedro III, at the head of the Yaka, stormed the city and destroyed it totally. Those who could not flee to Lobata (in southern Nsoyo) with the remains of Daniel I's following were killed by the Yaka or sold as slaves. The crops, which were just ripening as Pedro III's army entered the town, were left to rot in the fields, and Michele da Torre di Camerino, the Capuchin then resident in São Salvador, reported when he left the abandoned city a short time later that elephants had invaded it, trampling the nearby villages and eating the bananas from the town's many trees.[67]

Kongo lay in ruins, its capital destroyed, its ruling group dispersed, and its politics now dictated more by Nsoyo than by internal forces. Kongo's great centralized power, which had been at its height just a quarter-century before, was no more. The rivalry between Nsoyo and Kongo, combined with the instabilities of the lineage struggle and the losses to Portugal at Mbwila, had blown it apart. With its reconstruction by King Pedro IV some thirty years later, it was to be built upon entirely different principles and with an entirely different structure.

7

Kongo in the Civil Wars

ALTHOUGH PEDRO III did not realize it, when his troops left the smoldering ruins of São Salvador in 1678, they had put an end to a whole era of Kongo's history. The final destruction of São Salvador had deprived Kongo of its most important, vital town. Recognition of this fact was slow in coming, as is all such change, for people born in the Kongo of Garcia II always would tend to conceive of the country as it was in their youth, even when changes had altered it quite fundamentally. The destruction of São Salvador, the great centralizing town which all the nobility outside of Nsoyo took to be their home, put an end to the real distinction between town and village in Kongo. Despite this reality, however, the nobility who had grown up before 1678 still saw the distinction between town and country as the basis for Kongo's society. No doubt this is why Bernardo da Gallo was still able to cite traditions, given him by older nobles, relating the foundation of the kingdom to the foundation of São Salvador, and making the ethnic-social distinction between town and country, as late as 1710.[1] But by 1710 this distinction had vanished in fact, and lived on only in the minds of older generations of the nobility. In the early eighteenth century a new attitude was beginning to grow among the nobles, one that accepted the new structure of the country. Already in 1701, Francesco da Pavia, prefect of the Capuchin mission to Kongo and Angola, noted a new oral tradition of Kongo's origin among youthful members of Pedro IV's court that had replaced the conquering army of Nimi a Lukeni with a "very skillful blacksmith" who had founded the country by uniting warring factions.[2] In 1710, the same year that da Gallo was writing down traditions and attempting to recreate the old São Salvador through the efforts of Pedro IV, his superior in Luanda, Columbano da Bologna, was announcing to Rome that the old Kongo was dead, the forces of unity were gone forever, and the church would do well to recognize those facts.[3]

Pedro III's attack of 1678 was of course only the final touch to the destruction of São Salvador, which had been going on since the aftermath of the battle of Mbwila, certainly since the sack of the town in 1669. The forces that would be unleashed by the abandonment of the capital in 1678 were already fully in play by then, even if it would take a quarter of a century for the full implications of the event to be felt in both daily life and thought.

Under Garcia II, as we have already seen, everything depended upon São Salvador, the great town, with its large population, huge surpluses, abundant luxury goods, armies, and servants. In the new Kongo, young men would no longer troop out of the city to the provinces hoping to make a name for themselves and their houses as they had for Garcia II, nor would old men retire there to enjoy its prestige. The loss of São Salvador had ended the forces that prevented the building of independent rural *mbanza* based on slave labor, but it had not replaced them with a sudden growth of new São Salvadors in new locations, save of course for Mbanza Nsoyo, which had existed before the sack of Kongo's capital. Between 1666 and 1678 the entire nobility of Kongo with their servants and slaves struck out from São Salvador and settled in the provinces, leaving one town but not replacing it with another. The same wars that had gnawed away at São Salvador once it had lost military supremacy would prevent the rise of another such town, and the residences of the new ruling nobility of Kongo would be hidden away in the mountains, safe from enemies but unable to recreate the slave-based economy that had characterized São Salvador.

The exodus from São Salvador had not freed the slaves, of course; slaves continued to be bought and sold, employed in agriculture, and put to personal service.[4] But the great slave estates that characterized São Salvador, and the large, concentrated group of leisured aristocrats that the estates made possible, were no more. None of the most important regional capitals, except Mbanza Nsoyo, were large or occupied an extensive area of dense settlement. Kimbangu, in the eastern mountains, capital of the line of kings after Garcia III, was in an area where the average population density was not much above four per square kilometer.[5] Mbula, the small provincial town which Pedro III made his capital, although situated on more favorable terrain south of the Zaire River, did not have a significantly different hinterland—it, too, was only a slightly oversized village, and was in a region of scattered *mabata* whose population density was no greater than that of the area around Kimbangu.[6] Luca da Caltanisetta provided ample witness to its relative poverty in his account of a visit in 1696. The Capuchin was incensed to discover that the chapel of Mbula had been converted into a barn for the king's cattle; this makeshift barn, which held all the king's wealth in cattle, housed only eight head.[7] Similarly, when Luca da Caltanisetta decided to build a fitting chapel in Kimbangu, the work went extremely slowly (in contrast to the speed with which a much larger structure was built a half century earlier in São Salvador), and the finished edifice was far from impressive.[8]

These hints suggest that no town in Kongo apart from Nsoyo could produce a large surplus or an impressive show of wealth, nor did any contain a population density sufficient to make it a military center. As a result, none of these impoverished capitals could act as the magnet that São Salvador had in the time of Garcia II, when the nobles had been forced to either accept the king's will or be permanently banished from the city. No town of Kongo after 1678 could offer a young noble much more than any other; and for that matter, the towns had scarcely more to offer than the larger villages. Consequently, nobles were more content to settle in rather remote parts of the country, less willing to accept the orders of a superior who had neither the military strength to force obedience nor the luxurious life to elicit it. The end result was that kings, dukes, and other regional lords found their most loyal supporters from among their close personal entourage—granting nobles rule over remote provinces was likely to produce breakaway rivals, not loyal servants. Succession passed along among a closely knit group that surrounded the ruler, and not from district or provincial officers from more remote regions. All the rulers of Kimbangu in the late seventeenth century resided near its *mbanza*,[9] and the Duke of Nsundi reigning in 1697 had served in the court of his predecessor as majordomo.[10]

Initially, of course, before all the implications of the loss of São Salvador were evident or accepted, power was transferred out in the old way. The kings who ruled in 1668–78 continued to appoint members of their household, their house, or allied houses to provincial offices, and these appointees in their turn appointed district rulers from among their close allies and dependents. But as the power of the kings declined and São Salvador ceased to act as a magnet to the ambitious, provincial nobles found it less advantageous to bow to royal will. Furthermore, the rapid alternation of Kimpanzu and Kinlaza rulers at São Salvador in the period meant that rulers appointed one year might be removed by a hostile successor in the next. The result was inevitable—provincial rulers refused to recognize the right of kings to recall them, and refused to return to São Salvador, instead setting up as independent rulers of their provinces.

These same provincial rulers, however, faced an even worse situation with regard to their dependents than did the king. Just as they no longer found it worthwhile to return to São Salvador, so their dependents found no advantage in linking their careers with the provincial rulers, who could offer them neither a luxurious life in São Salvador nor any material advantage in the provincial capital. As soon as a provincial ruler declared himself an independent duke or marquis, he lost control over the more remote districts of his realm. The district rulers would make no career in the ducal capital, it being as small and wretched as the district capitals, and the lure of São Salvador was gone.

At the upper levels of the nobility, this process was underway by 1680 at the very latest. When Cadornega listed the enemies of King Garcia III in 1681, he mentioned not only his rival King João II of Mbula (who had succeeded Pedro III), but also the provincial rulers of Mpemba, Nsundi, and Mbamba, all of whom were independent of royal control.[11] The same process was probably going on at a local level as well, although we must make use of the detailed reports of Capuchin travellers of the 1690s to see the local pattern in full development.

This diffusion of political sovereignty was matched, naturally, by a diffusion of the ties of the houses that had formed the glue holding the older Kongo political system in place. Since a career no longer depended on loyally following the ruling house or allying with it at any cost, the tendency for households to form a vast pyramid capped by the household of the king was reduced. It was replaced by a plethora of households, each holding the political office it had originally obtained through the working of household politics in Kongo years or decades earlier. These households were localized by the 1680s or 1690s, each of the rulers being surrounded by a staff drawn from members of his household or its immediate allies, consisting of a secretariat, a council, and several offices of personal service, such as captain general or majordomo. Not only did kings possess this small group of officers; even relatively unimportant rulers, such as the Marquis of Nkusu, possessed one.[12] They were recruited from the ruler's household, which is why Pedro Constantinho da Silva, when he revolted from Pedro IV in 1702, was able to build a similar group around him as soon as he had made his break with the king.[13]

To these bureaucratic offices were added local territorial offices in the immediate vicinity, so that Pedro IV's half brother Rafael ruled the fortress of Ntari a Nzundu near Kimbangu, while another brother ruled Nzolo a few kilometers to the north, and a female relative ruled a village on the border of Nkusu.[14] This group was extended by clerical personnel, usually of the ruling household, but staffing offices in the church. Thus Capuchin catechists often were well represented in royal councils. For example, Manuel Deliciado, a catechist, was on the royal council of Mbula, and another catechist, Miguel Fernandes da Paiva, was secretary to the

Duke of Nsundi and performed diplomatic functions.[15] It was from this group of bureaucrats, personal servants, and rulers of nearby villages that the successors were chosen, and the household continued to operate as integrating function. Whatever original ties of blood and marriage may have united the heads of these local households to other households nearby played no necessary part in the making of their careers or politics. Even then the ties of blood and marriage were significant, as in the end they often were, their significance was radically different from that of the same ties in Garcia's Kongo.

While the lineages and households of Garcia's Kongo were thrown together by common interests in the great pyramids that culminated in Garcia's household and the House of Kinlaza, the houses and households of Kongo in 1680 were only occasionally operating in accord. They did form alliances at times, though, and these great alliances of households, which often preserved some of the appearances of the pyramidal lineages of Garcia's Kongo, were an important force in the history of the civil wars in Kongo. This was especially true in the southern part of the country, where battles raged between allied households nominally headed by Dona Ana Afonso de Leão and King Manuel I in the late 1680s and 1690s.

Dona Ana Afonso de Leão was a sister of Garcia II, and was married to Afonso, who tried unsuccessfully to succeed António I in the confused struggle that followed the battle of Mbwila in 1665. Ana followed Afonso to Kimbangu, where she played a role in its politics until his death in about 1680. Ana and her group lost in the subsequent succession struggle to a house bearing the surname Agua Rosada, headed by King Garcia III, and she retired to Nkondu, a small marquisate on the Mbrize River. By 1680 Ana was perhaps the senior member of the House of Kinlaza and a queen mother, and as such the natural head of the house. As a result, many of the Kinlaza who had been appointed to territorial office in the years following Mbwila looked up to her as an important senior figure. These relatives not only controlled the Marquisate of Nkondu, Ana's new home, but also the Marquisate of Mpemba and the Duchy of Mbamba, as well as occupying lesser posts in the southern part of the country.[16] Dona Ana made no pretense of ruling the area, nor did she in any way attempt to remove or replace her relatives in various ducal posts, but the alliance of blood and respect for the old queen mother allowed them all to operate in concord. Indeed, they had few real differences with each other precisely because no career was to be made beyond their posts, and each was content to let the others rule in peace.

Throughout the 1690s Ana and her group were resolutely, and sometimes successfully, opposed by a Kimpanzu group headed by Manuel I and backed by the military might of Nsoyo, traditional allies of the Kimpanzu. When Manuel I marched out from Nsoyo at the head of a large army (supplied by the Prince of Nsoyo) and took over São Salvador in 1690, his cousins Pedro Constantinho da Silva and Alexio led forces to the south to attack Ana Afonso de Leão's group. The Kimpanzu forces quickly conquered most of the territory, and for six years ruled the same area in the same loose style as had Ana's group before.[17]

Taking control of a regional center during this confused time did not mean that all the small outlying districts would fall also, as they might have under a more centralized system. Although Dona Ana and her nephews drove Manuel's group out of Mpemba and Mbamba in 1696, they had failed even by 1707 to reconquer Wandu or southern Mbamba, where members of the households of Pedro Constantinho da Silva and Alexio still ruled.[18] Likewise, it should be clear that the cohesion that came from simple blood alliance and mutual respect for a central figure was much less than the cohesion of more complete commonality of interests. In a particularly cynical episode, Pedro Constantinho da Silva and Alexio delivered their cousin (and nominal leader) Manuel I to his rival, King Álvaro X Agua Rosada of Kimbangu, to be beheaded, just for the sake of a temporary alliance with the Agua Rosada of the mountain capital.[19]

In the end, the local households held the real power in Kongo, and they bargained with their neighbors and relatives as their interests dictated. Alliances formed by marriage were as strong as blood ties. Thus Pedro IV tried to tie his line to that of Pedro Constantinho da Silva by taking Pedro Constantinho's sister Hipolita as his wife.[20] Similarly, João II of Mbula tried to unite his household to that of his eastern neighbors, the Dukes of Nsundi, by a judicious exchange of wives, although his overtures of 1696 were unsuccessful.[21] What went on between kings and dukes was also true at the level of the less mighty, some of whom in fact were scarcely less powerful than the various pretender kings. Luca da Caltanisetta found that many of the district rulers of Nkusu were allied by marriage with district rulers of neighboring Nsonso, so that all along the border there were intermixed families.[22]

As the seventeenth century wore on, descent counted much less than more immediate alliances of marriage in making cooperative units. Dona Ana could hold a large area together through relatives who were all descended from her, but she was in her eighties by the turn of the century.[23] The great houses that had fought in Garcia's Kongo, the Kinlaza and the Kimpanzu, thus held less significance by the end of the century, although all nobles in Kongo could describe descent from one or the other. The importance of these great houses for binding households together was considerably reduced by the dispersion of households to rural areas. The fact that João II of Mbula and Ana Afonso de Leão were both Kinlaza did not make any sort of alliance between them easier, as Luca da Caltanisetta found in 1696.[24] Nor did the fact that the Duke of Nsundi was a Kimpanzu and João II a Kinlaza prevent them from seriously discussing alliances, intermarriages, and Nsundi's recognition of João II as King of Kongo the same year.[25] Pedro IV and his brothers of the Agua Rosada line were Kimpanzu on one side and Kinlaza on the other,[26] but considerations other than descent dominated their relations with other leaders. Local power, local careers, and local politics had come to govern before anything else, even among those who claimed to be kings and dukes, whereas before nothing was done without reference to the king, and above all, to São Salvador.

The dispersal of authority and the fissioning of houses had come about directly as a result of the loss of São Salvador, which had held all the centralizing institutions in place. There were still some town-centered careers, but their focus had shifted from São Salvador to other towns— notably Mbanza Nsoyo and Luanda. The best examples are the careers of the priests. Those seculars who surrounded Garcia II had won their positions by their family ties and by going from parish positions to the cathedral staff in São Salvador, thus making careers that paralleled those of the territorial rulers. After the final sack of São Salvador they dispersed to the provinces, just as the nobles did. It was in this way that Miguel de Castro, a son of Garcia II, left São Salvador and ended his career in the service of Ana Afonso de Leão in 1685, serving the Kinlaza faithfully to the end.[27] But a new group of clerics emerged in the generation following the sack of São Salvador who felt they could make no successful career unless it led to Luanda.

The career of Francisco Fernandes de Sousa illustrates the change well. De Sousa had been trained by the Capuchins in Nsoyo, and was related to one of the most important Nsoyo houses, but was ordained through the chapter of São Salvador. In 1673 he returned to Mbanza Nsoyo to begin a career, perhaps with the hope of settling there. The Capuchins, however, controlled the capital's chapel, and de Sousa found himself making many rural tours.[28] He therefore continued his career in Luanda, where he secured a position on the cathedral staff and served out his days outside his native land.[29] The careers of all the secular clergy became centered on Luanda, and the whole country of Kongo formed, from their point of view, a rural province where one could make a name, especially if one spoke Kikongo. From these rural areas, priests who had been ordained in Luanda returned after making a fortune, perhaps in the slave trade, to retire to a sinecure in the Luanda Cathedral.

Another good illustration of such Luanda-centered clerical careers, of which there were many in Kongo in the late seventeenth century,[30] is that of Luis de Mendonça. Mendonça, a mulatto, left Luanda for Kongo in 1687, "because" (in his words) "of my poverty." He spent many years in Kongo, travelling to Nsundi and Kimbangu and eventually attaching himself to the service of Pedro IV, whom he crowned in 1696.[31] This career must have eventually ended his poverty, for he later returned to Luanda, where he was serving on the cathedral staff when he wrote his life history in 1727.[32]

Not only clerics sought wealth and fame in Luanda after the fall of São Salvador. Lay people also sometimes followed a career pattern that led to Luanda. Such seems to have been the case with Lourenço da Silva e Mendonça, who proclaimed himself to be of "the race of the Kings of Kongo and Angola" and was Procuror-General of the Congregation of the Rosary in Luanda in 1684.[33] Equally interesting is the career of Agostinho Rodrigues de Sá, a cousin of the Duke of Mbamba, who made a career in the Portuguese army in Angola, and served not only in campaigns against Matamba but even against his own uncle, Álvaro, then Duke of Mbamba. By the 1690s he had risen in rank and was leading a successful career in Portuguese service.[34]

If Luanda proved attractive to some people, the most significant remnant of town-center glory was still in Nsoyo, where Mbanza Nsoyo operated in much the same way that São Salvador had earlier. Its presence not only preserved a structure similar to Kongo's in Nsoyo province, but it also spawned hope among some Kongo nobles, especially of the House of Kimpanzu, that the old system could be restored in Kongo.

Mbanza Nsoyo's population doubled between 1645 and 1700 to over 30,000, due in part, it seems, to the acquisition of slaves taken from São Salvador when they city was sacked.[35] Mbanza Nsoyo was surrounded by slave-worked plantations, and while it never reached the size that São Salvador had attained at mid-century and its churches and palaces never rivalled those of São Salvador, it was clearly an important town center, sufficiently populated to provide for a large leisured class, many personal servants, and substantial military forces.[36] Because of its position, Mbanza Nsoyo played São Salvador's role, even if over a smaller area of the Atlantic coast.

The Prince of Nsoyo (whose title, upgraded from count, first appeared some time in the 1640s) was elected by a conclave of several territorial nobles, mostly from districts immediately surrounding the capital, but with one or two electors from more remote districts.[37] These outside districts, which were annexations and conquests added to the "Marquisate of the State" (Mbanza Nsoyo and its immediate environs, apparently the original nucleus of the County of Nsoyo), were ruled by members of the prince's household, and the office of prince was attained through a career that could come either by holding territorial office or by membership in the bureaucracy of the Mbanza. When Paulo II da Silva was killed in the battle of Kitombo in 1670, his brother Amadoro was ruling the far western province of Kiova, while his other brother Estevão was holding the title of captain general in the Mbanza. Estevão was elected to succeed the fallen prince.[38]

As in Kongo, alliances of households made up the units in which power was exercised. The struggle that developed in the 1680s during the rule of António I Baretto da Silva illustrates just how closely offices were held within one household, and how the tensions between households could flare up into open conflict. António had appointed his brother's son as captain general and had also given him the post of Mbamba a Nsoyo in the south of the country, while António's own two eldest sons held important posts in the Capuchin hospice (which at this time was very like what a post in the cathedral staff had been in São Salvador). The captain general had a conflict which developed into armed struggle with three cousins (sons of one of António's sisters) who held the title of secretary general and two territorial posts in the Mbanza region.[39] For all the struggle and violence that accompanied such household struggles, however, they did not significantly disrupt the structure of Nsoyo. Thus, although it occupied a smaller territory and was less complex, Nsoyo reproduced the essentials of the structure of Kongo, complete with lineage and household politics.

The struggles between houses paralleled the struggle between households. Since the fifteenth century the counts of Nsoyo were descended from the first count to be baptized, Miguel da Silva, and da Silva had been the family name of all counts, just as Afonso was the family name of the kings of Kongo. In the 1620s there was a struggle between the da Silva house and the House of de Sousa. In the 1680s there were again two houses in conflict, the da Silva e Castros and the Baretto da Silvas. There was a long series of struggles between these lines, the throne passing from one line to the other, sometimes with violence, as when António III Baretto da Silva killed his rival, "a certain Francisco de Castro, whose line had ruled before," on election day in 1697.[40]

There were also some differences between Kongo in mid-century and Nsoyo at the end of the century. The church made deeper penetration in Nsoyo, possibly because Nsoyo had more or less cut itself off from the secular organization based in Luanda, and obtained its priests from Italy and the Capuchin order. Church careers were thus made in the service of the Capuchins, and such careers, being lay, could lead to the highest offices. In 1702 most of the important territorial offices in Nsoyo were held by people who were also "masters" of the church there for the Capuchins.[41] António III Baretto da Silva, who became prince in 1697, began his career as a cook and porter in the Capuchin mission, later rising to the position of sacristan, then "aiudante" (lay assistant), and finally "master" of the church in Mbanza Nsoyo.[42] This close relation between the Prince of Nsoyo and the Capuchin hospice staff became so central to Nsoyo's political organization that traditions of Nsoyo set down in the nineteenth century represented the chief of the hospice staff as playing a part in the foundation of the state.[43] The role of the church was therefore quite different from the position of the church in Kongo at its height, since church careers there, though important, had not been in line for succession to the throne.

Still, however different in details, Nsoyo represented a continuation of the tradition of Kongo. Although rocked by succession disputes and near–civil war, the basic social and economic structure of the principality remained intact throughout the seventeenth century and well into the eighteenth.[44] And, while Nsoyo had by degrees become almost a separate realm, it continued to play a significant role in the future of its one-time overlord, the Kingdom of Kongo. This role was Nsoyo's support of one or another branch of the House of Kimpanzu in the Kongo civil wars. We have already noted that the Kimpanzu were extensively intermarried with Nsoyo families, and though none of them ever became prince, some did hope to become King of Kongo with Nsoyo's aid.

In the 1690s Nsoyo harbored two such groups of Kimpanzu. One was headed by Dona Suzana de Nóbrega, whose line had once provided Kongo with Kings Afonso II, Afonso III, and Daniel I. Driven from São Salvador by Pedro III in 1678, they were settled by 1690 in Lobata, a small marquisate in southern Nsoyo.[45] The second Kimpanzu group was nominally headed by Manuel I, whom Nsoyo installed in São Salvador in 1690. Neither of the two groups had any real chance of restoring Kongo to its former glory, even if both might claim its kingship, but because they thought they could, and could count on some help from Nsoyo, many nobles were slow to acknowledge that fundamental changes had occurred in Kongo. Nsoyo's interference kept the struggle between the Kimpanzu and Kinlaza alive even after the economic base to sustain such a struggle had been destroyed. Nsoyo's interest in Kongo was sufficient to keep it meddling, but insufficient for it to attempt a genuine reconstruction. In the end, it was the House of Agua Rosada, half Kimpanzu and half Kinlaza, ruling in the remote eastern mountains, that would recognize the nature of the new Kongo first and restore the country, if only partially.

The old order in Kongo, except for a few vestiges, was gone. And not least among the many changes that took place in the decades after the battle of Mbwila were changes in the attitudes and outlook of the people. The dispersion of the great estates meant that the nobility of Kongo were now living in much closer contact with the villagers, who now, rather than slaves, were providing them with their livelihood. Of course, the nobility had often lived in rural areas, subsisting on rural surpluses in keeping with the earlier economic patterns of Kongo. But in former times such a life was seen as a temporary inconvenience, and the rural population was ignored or even despoiled. Now people who had once been fed by slaves were fed, permanently, by peasants. During his travels at century's end, Luca da Caltanisetta met a son of a former king of Kongo ruling a few *mabata* in Ndidi, a district of Nsundi.[46] This noble, like a great many others of similar status who peppered the eastern regions of Kongo, had to face the fact that he would live out his days ruling a collection of *mabata*, with little or no hope for a career leading anywhere else.

As a result of this fact, new ideological forms were emerging among the nobility of Kongo. Changes in oral tradition first noted by Francesco da Pavia provide some evidence for the new attitude of nobles towards their rule. Nobles, now forced to live permanently in rural areas, sought new justification for their right to live and rule there. According to the new tradition, the country's founder had succeeded in unifying diverse and mutually hostile people, not simply in conquering.[47] This newly conceived founder was thus a much more integrative figure than Nimi a Lukeni had been; and the nobility, whether they deliberately originated this new figure or simply did not challenge it, were tacitly declaring that they had a stake in the rural districts. In time the traditions would become still more integrative, until the whole of the Kongo people were seen as one stock who had migrated from São Salvador to settle in virgin territory, their social division into noble and commoner being based on a supposed order of arrival in the villages, with first arrivals being nobles and later arrivals being commoners.[48] To this was added a third status, that of freed slave, whose conditions were not much different from those of commoners.[49] These changes in belief, and the deeper changes in attitude that underlay them, would not fully mature, however, until those who still remembered and hoped to restore the old Kongo had passed from the scene.

The new changes in thought that were occurring throughout Kongo were matched by changes in, and confusion about, religious and ideological roles. With the disappearance of São Salvador, many of the confirmation rituals involved in the coronation of the king had to alter, and the local *itomi* were given new powers. Thus, in 1701 the *kitomi* of Kimbangu emerged as an important force in the politics of the royal fortress. Pedro IV had to have his blessing before he could build anything, and the two met one day a week.[50] At the same time, the missionaries were making their own claims to a role in the legitimizing process, in conflict with the *kitomi*. In about 1700 one such conflict involved Luca da Caltanisetta: he wanted to smash a spherical ball said to have important powers in rain and fertility, and the *kitomi* forbade it. In the end, the stone was smashed, but the man who had revealed its location to da Caltanisetta was punished.[51] A new, working relationship between all who claimed legitimizing powers was yet to be worked out.

The fact that the nobility was accommodating itself ideologically to life in the village sector did not mean that noble and peasant lived in harmony. It is impossible to say if there was any attempt to place new burdens on the producers to accommodate a class that was used to luxury. Genuinely heavy burdens would have had to involve reorganization of production, and this did not occur. However, one additional burden was imposed on the countryside, and that was an increase in warfare caused by the rivalries between various lineages and households. This warfare was disruptive, for fields were burned, harvests seized, and people enslaved in the affected areas. Although the scale of warfare was not great, it had become endless, and took a social toll far above its cost in battlefield casualties. Severe skirmishing on the Nsundi-Ngobila border in 1697 so disrupted fishing that the market price of fish skyrocketed.[52] Constant hostility in Mbamba province among partisans of Manuel I's group, Ana Afonso de Leão's followers, and the faction of Suzana de Nóbrega led to serious confrontations in 1682, 1696, 1702, and 1714.[53] So great was the cumulative devastation that when Lorenzo da Lucca crossed the province in 1714 he and his party were forced to sleep in open fields, as the villages were all burned and abandoned, famine had struck, and the people had fled.[54]

Another ill effect of the warfare was the frequent seizure of people as slaves. In addition to their assignment to the limited entourages of the nobles, many of these slaves were sold to Luanda or to the Vili for overseas shipment to bring in European goods. Luca da Caltanisetta recorded one relatively minor incident that he observed while living in Kimbangu in 1701:

The night of 10 February, . . . the Mani Lumbu returned with 58 slaves captured by order of the king; he had destroyed a libata of one of his vassals, accused of treason for having entered into relations with the Duke of Bata, enemy of the king; among these slaves were many free people, some inhabitants of the libata of the vassal judged traitor and others who were just there on business; all of these were captured by the Mani Lumbu, majordomo of the king.[55]

The sum of dozens of such incidents, and the example they set to those who were even indirectly touched, greatly increased the fear and insecurity of the common inhabitants of Kongo's villages. While the actual human cost was probably not so great as to cause widespread depopulation,[56] as the areas most severely ravaged were limited, it nevertheless had far-reaching consequences for those whose lives were affected. King Pedro IV, urged by his council to make war on one of his rebel vassals, expressed his concern about the situation when he said

> . . . that in no way would he make war, as it was the continual warfare which had already destroyed the kingdom, and also the Faith. Nor did the Congolese want any more troubles. They were already tired of being like beasts in the fields and wastelands: outraged, murdered, robbed and sold, and their relatives, wives and children killed on all sides.[57]

The warfare and insecurity had a lasting effect on the pattern of settlement in Kongo. People increasingly sought out strategically inaccessible mountains in the wilderness areas to relocate their villages. Lorenzo da Lucca found that all the villages in the south of Nkusu were in inaccessible locations in the mountains.[58] Luca da Caltanisetta made much the same observation with regard to roads, which often were built with safety in mind more than convenience.[59] Nor was it simply commoners who fled to the hills. Not only were kings building their towns in the safety of the mountains such as those in Mbula or Kimbangu, but the increase in warfare in Mbamba forced the duke to remove his residence in 1702 from the flat coastal plains to the rugged mountains that Lorenzo da Lucca dubbed the "Alps of Mbamba."[60] This general flight from disturbed areas often led to extensive localized depopulation, such as on the road between Nkusu and Nkondu along the upper Mbrize River, where Lorenzo da Lucca found not a single person, and only one deserted village, in an entire day's journey.[61]

The forces that would transform Kongo from the two-sector economy of the mid-seventeenth century into a more socially integrated but politically disunited country were already beginning to operate at the end of the century. But they were still operating inconsistently, often in contradiction to the thinking of the actors. In the last years of the seventeenth and the first years of the eighteenth centuries, nobles and commoners would finally come to grips with the new Kongo, and each would attempt in their own way to build a new order. For the nobles it would be a matter of compromising as to who would rule, and how the rule would be conducted; to the commoners it would be an attempt to unite the country under a Kongo saint who would proclaim a new order.

8

The Restoration

IF THE near-constant state of civil war that engulfed Kongo from 1665–90 had proved anything, it was that the kingdom was not likely to be reunited by force, and if it were reunited at all, it would have a very different structure from the Kongo whose armies António I had led into battle in 1665. Sovereignty was totally splintered, and even if powerful people could keep some factions united by blood and marriage, the natural tendency in Kongo was for the limits of effective political control to contract to the area easily controlled by one household—perhaps an area with a radius of thirty to fifty kilometers. This was the largest area in which the system of rent in kind was feasible;[1] beyond it, real power would have to decline. No military power, although it might draw on a population somewhat beyond the frontier of such an economic unit, was likely to dominate a large region, and no one ruler—save the rulers of Nsoyo, of course—was likely to have any more than a temporary military advantage over any other. Nsoyo's rulers, however, were unwilling to make any more than sporadic attempts to unite the country, and then usually only by backing a pretender.

As the seventeenth century drew to a close, hopeful visions of a restored Kongo began to emerge, spurred by growing recognition of the nation's fundamental disunity and the disastrous effects of the continuing civil wars. If real centralized control was impossible, then perhaps some sort of generalized truce could be arranged, whereby one or another king was universally recognized as ruler, while local sovereignty was respected and warfare thus reduced.

Missionaries had been especially active in attempting to promote such a ruler, since it was in their interest to have a peaceful Kongo for safe travel and effective proselytization. As early as 1679, Filippo da Gallese, one of the Capuchins in Kongo, tried to get universal recognition for King Garcia III, and even won the support of Nsoyo, but in the end, nothing came of it.[2] Capuchin politicking behind one or another ruler who was said to have some special claim to the throne was a regular feature of the time.

Such a solution met with several problems. First, and most important, recognition that the old Kongo was irrecoverable was not yet universal. The old mentality died hard, and there were always one or two pretenders who felt that with the right circumstances they could reunite the country around their own power. As a result, peace negotiations tended to be laden with treachery and double-dealing. A second problem was simply in finding a suitable candidate for king—someone who was willing to accept the restrained place required in political affairs, and who was at the same time acceptable to the other major powers in the country. Finally, it would be difficult to establish a constitution for this person's rule—how would the new king be selected, how would he be succeeded, where would he rule, and in what matters would he have authority?

Despite the obstacles, however, time had greatly increased the possibility of a restored Kongo. Year after year of civil war had the effect of demonstrating the reality of Kongo's demise. What is more, as the century wore on, the major powers increasingly accepted the natural regional limits on their dominion. It became less important to rule the whole country directly, and at the same time, certain lines became so deeply entrenched in specific areas that it was clearly impossible to dislodge them. As the regional groups emerged, the character of warfare changed from major contests aimed at winning the throne or overthrowing a major rival to border skirmishes between regional leaders, often fought not by the leaders but by local powers along their borders. Both the emergence of regional powers and the increasingly local character of warfare are apparent in a political survey of Kongo around 1690.

All the heads of major factions in 1690 had to take similar measures to maintain their rule and their way of life. First, they had to have enough military power to enforce their rule, or, barring that, they needed enough defensive strength to protect the heartlands of their realms. Secondly, they needed access to trade—for despite the much more local character of their rule, and the considerable limits imposed by the lack of slave estates and surpluses, these rulers still maintained a life style that required at least some luxury goods. These goods generally were only obtainable from people with access to Europe on the one hand, and the slave trade on the other. Even though the estates were gone, slaves provided valuable personal services. Since slaves were trans-shipped across

Kongo from other points, even the simple charging of dues on the trade might bring some luxuries to the noble rulers of the country.[3]

In the north of the country the Kinlaza line of kings ruled the forested hills of Mbula. Originally founded by Pedro III when he fled São Salvador, by 1690 the area was ruled by his brother João II. João had two implacable enemies, the Kimpanzu rulers of Lobata who had treacherously killed Pedro III in 1683[4] and the princes of Nsoyo. Nsoyo and the de Nóbregas had together plotted the death of his brother, and he would brook no adherent of either group. João made up in part for his military disability vis-à-vis Nsoyo by an alliance with the Yaka of the Niari Valley, nomadic warriors who had harassed Kongo since at least the 1620s.[5] The alliance was an old one, for the Yaka had joined Pedro III in sacking São Salvador in 1678, and by 1696 some of the Yaka had even settled in the country and mixed with the inhabitants.[6] Although such an alliance might have been dangerous, the Yaka aided João II against Nsoyo; with their help, he had successfully attacked and annexed Kiova kia Nza from Nsoyo's eastern border.[7] In the east João's military presence was also felt, for the entire south bank of the Zaire River, up to the bluffs along the Lukunga River which bordered on lands controlled by the Duke of Nsundi, were under his control.[8]

Foreign forces helped João II in trade as well. Not only did he control the port of Mboma on the Zaire River, which later would become more important as an outlet for Europeans,[9] but he also had a close alliance with the Vili of Loango, who found hospitality in his capital on their expeditions to the south and southeast of Kongo.[10] They not only brought back slaves from Matamba and the lands to the east of them, but also provided him with European goods traded at Loango from English, French, and Dutch merchants.[11]

To the east of João II's lands were the lands of the dukes of Nsundi, who in the 1690s were Kimpanzu, perhaps originally appointed during the reign of the Kimpanzu king Álvaro VIII (1667–69), but long independent by 1690.[12] Nsundi was not a military power of much consequence, and as a result carried little weight in the struggles over the kingdom. While the bluffs of the Lukunga River protected her border with Mbula, the southern and eastern borders of Nsundi were frequently disputed by her neighbors—and indeed the duke exercised little authority over even his own appointees in many border districts. In 1697 the duke's appointee to Magoa on his eastern border had to fight to take up his office, while on the south his appointee to Mpangu faced a serious rival.[13]

The Duke of Nsundi was more fortunate with regard to trade, for a major trade route connecting Angola on the south, Nsoyo on the west, and the slave market of Mpumbu crossed his territory. *Pombeiros* (merchants from Angola) as well as secular clergy anxious to make some of their fortune frequented Mbanza Nsundi, and Luca da Caltanisetta often encountered them there in the 1690s.[14]

South of Nsundi, and sharing the same trade route, was the mountain fortress of Kimbangu. This stronghold had been ruled since the 1670s by the House of Agua Rosada of mixed Kimpanzu and Kinlaza descent who had produced Kings Garcia III, Álvaro X, and Pedro IV. They did not have much offensive military capability, but they did occasionally score victories against their rivals in the open field, such as that gained by Álvaro X against João II in 1692 or 1693.[15] More important, though, was the fact that Kimbangu was an impregnable fortress, which more or less granted the Agua Rosada hegemony over the area. This very invulnerability may have led to complacency, however, for they were hesitant to attempt exercising their power over a wider area.

The southeast portions of Kongo were less well fixed in the control of regional powers. The Marquisates of Nkondu and Mpemba, the County of Wandu, the Duchy of Mbamba, and the Marquisate of Wembo were all somewhat linked together by the mutual respect their rulers had for the queen mother Ana Afonso de Leão, leader of the House of Kinlaza.[16] This alliance was little more than an agreement to peace among relatives under the nominal leadership of the proud old queen, and it lacked much military power. Because of its relative military weakness, the major contests of the 1690s were waged in the area between Ana Afonso de Leão's faction and the group led by Manuel I with Nsoyo's support. Wars were fought in one or another part of the region in 1691–92 and 1696, and after that point the fighting was joined by the de Nóbrega group from Lobata and Mbamba. In the seesaw battles, neither group was able to score a decisive victory; yet it proved remarkably easy for one suddenly to oust its rivals.

Ana Afonso de Leão's faction controlled the southern end (in Kongo) of the great trade route that linked Loango with Matamba and also the route linking Mpumbu with Luanda. Both the Vili of Loango and the Ndembu rulers of the southern mountains were anxious to keep these routes open and avoid Portuguese attempts to close off the trade and concentrate everything in Luanda.[17] As a result, Ana and the local rulers of the area often allied against the Portuguese, so much so that the Portuguese governor was relieved to see her overthrown in 1691, although in the end Portugal benefitted little if any from the politics of her successors.[18]

The southwest of the country, in so far as it was not in control of Dona Ana's faction (who ruled most of Mbamba), was more or less under the influence of Nsoyo. Nsoyo actively supported Suzana de Nóbrega's Kimpanzu line and let them govern the province of Nseto in Nsoyo and Lobata in Mbamba.[19]

It was in Nsoyo, too, that another Kimpanzu line, that of Manuel I, sought asylum and obtained aid. Manuel had briefly held the kingship around 1688, following the death of Garcia III Agua Rosada; but, probably because he was not himself an Agua Rosada, he was eventually driven from Kimpangu, Álvaro X being installed in his place in 1690.[20] It was then that he fled to Nsoyo and recruited help for his campaign to establish himself in São Salvador and to set up his cousins Alexio and Pedro Constantinho da Silva in southern Kongo.

In the east, the emergence of stable regional powers altered the pattern of warfare that had marked the civil wars in earlier years. The great contests of rival kings, often fought for or around São Salvador, had given way to smaller-scale contests fought on the ill-defined borders of the regional leaders' spheres of influence. Typically they would involve clashes of households for the control of a small area, the head of each of the contesting households giving nominal loyalty or being related to the household of the regional ruler. Several such clashes occurred in the late seventeenth century. In Mpangu, for example, there were two rival marquises, one appointed by the Duke of Nsundi and holding one part of the province, the other supported by the kings of Kimbangu.[21] Likewise in Mbata there were two rival dukes, one basing his claim for the post on his descent from the ancient (once independent) ducal lineage, the other claiming descent from another branch of the same lineage, but also backed heavily by the rulers of Kimbangu.[22]

Rival claimants to the same province, each appointed by a different regional power, were not limited to the east, however, for Mbamba was contested throughout the early years of the eighteenth century by two dukes—Pedro Valle das Lagrimas under the aegis of Ana Afonso de Leão, and Manuel de Nóbrega of the Lobata-based House of de Nóbrega.[23] Likewise, in 1707, Lorenzo da Lucca found two dukes of Wandu, one appointed by Ana Afonso de Leão, the other by Manuel I's faction.[24] Even when major wars between groups ceased, these minor wars continued to take a steady toll of lives and resources.

But even while this new pattern was emerging in the east, the older pattern of extensive warfare continued, especially in the west and south, largely because of the presence of Nsoyo, whose political interests followed a different logic, and whose military strength permitted her to interfere in Kongo's affairs with impunity. Nsoyo's support of various Kimpanzu pretenders and local powers kept the hope for a reunited Kongo alive, even though a united Kongo actually would have been counter to Nsoyo's best interests. Thus for a time the two types of conflict coexisted:

large-scale war based on attempts to restore Kongo to one or another house by force, and small-scale conflicts growing up around the borders of the regional groups.

It is not possible to understand the events in Kongo at the end of the seventeenth century without understanding Nsoyo's interests in Kongo. Nsoyo had emerged after Kitombo as one of the leading military powers in central Africa, and her military interests were matched by extensive commercial interests. Nsoyo had obtained, by trade and warfare, some fifty pieces of artillery by century's end, and her army was strong enough to defeat not only any single Kongo power, but even her neighbors who counted European support. Around 1685 Nsoyo's army defeated the King of Ngoyo (her northern neighbor) and in so doing routed a detachment of English marines who had landed to support him, taking the Englishmen's colors and artillery as spoils.[25] These victories allowed Nsoyo to bargain from a position of strength when she finally made peace with Portugal in 1690, thus ending the technical state of war that had existed since the Portuguese attack of 1670.[26] The peace treaty restored Portuguese trade, but the trade with England and the Low Countries counted for more, as they were willing to supply munitions.[27]

Nsoyo's interest in this trade was so important that in 1673 she had gone as far as obtaining Flemish Recollets to replace the Italian Capuchins who had been serving in Nsoyo. Although the mission failed, it forced the Italian Capuchins to recognize the importance of Nsoyo trade with the Low Countries, whom they considered heretics.[28] Considerations of trade also influenced Nsoyo's policy with her northern neighbors, who also traded heavily (and more successfully) with the English and Dutch. Thus Nsoyo's attacks on Ngoyo were aimed at gaining a greater share of the northern trade, and were successful in so far as slaves obtained by Nsoyo were exported through Ngoyo's port of Cabinda as well as through the port of Malemba even farther to the north.[29] Marriage strengthened ties that had been made by force: and the families of Nsoyo intermarried with those of Ngoyo, all in the interest of strengthening Nsoyo's control of the trade on the north coast.[30]

It was the pursuit of military power and commercial domination that made Nsoyo anxious to intervene in Kongo. Since Kongo was active in the trans-shipment of slaves from further south, control of the country meant control of this lucrative trade. Thus Nsoyo hoped to restore Kongo under a puppet ruler who would be mindful of Nsoyo's interests above all else. However, the implementation of any such plan was dangerous. Nsoyo did not want the development of another powerful Kongo like that of Garcia, which had waged war on Nsoyo every two or three years, and the possibility of such a development could not be ignored if Kongo were reunited, however loosely. The central problem, which neither Nsoyo nor the pretenders she supported could resolve, was how a puppet kingdom could be supported without making it strong enough to threaten Nsoyo. The resulting policy was one of supporting pretenders enough to establish them, but not supporting them enough to maintain them. Nsoyo thus nurtured hopes among the Kimpanzu that Kongo could be restored, but killed these hopes with its hesitant policy.

Nsoyo's support of the candidacy of Manuel I in 1690 is illustrative of this contradiction. It was with an Nsoyo army that Manuel I marched out of São Salvador, and it was with Nsoyo support that his cousins, Alexio and Pedro Constantinho, conquered lands to the south. In spite of this, and the continued military support by Nsoyo, who sent him an army every year, he was unable to make his claim good. Lacking his own followers, and sufficient, continuous support from Nsoyo, he abandoned São Salvador for Nkondu, for the capital was still not defensible.[31] In the end, this hapless Manuel, who would have been a puppet of Nsoyo in any case, was executed by his own supporters as a part of a plan to create an alliance with the Agua Rosada.[32]

The gradual turning to small-scale wars, and the constant demonstration that even Nsoyo, with considerable military power, could not restore Kongo by force, had made it clear by the end of the seventeenth century that a Kongo conceived along earlier lines would not be possible. The best possibility was a compromise that recognized the realities of Kongo and bore some hope of ending the civil wars. To achieve this, diplomacy and moderated ambitions were required rather than force. It was left to Pedro IV Agua Rosada, who had become king in Kimbangu after the death of his brother Álvaro X in 1695, to attempt such a reconstruction.

There is no doubt that Pedro IV wanted to be king of all Kongo, for he had himself crowned at São Salvador on 2 August 1696. He marched out to the abandoned city with a small military detachment and the secular priest Luis de Mendonça for his coronation as King of Kongo. But it was a strictly symbolic gesture, for, fearing an attack by João II, Pedro left the ruined city the next day and returned to the safety of Kimbangu.[33]

Perhaps it was this very weakness that made Pedro IV champion of an essentially diplomatic restoration. The kings of Kimbangu were perhaps the weakest of all the pretenders. Their founder, Afonso, had been largely forgotten in the struggles immediately after Mbwila, and the territory they directly controlled was small and mountainous. Unlike others, who felt that they had good chances militarily, the rulers of Kimbangu had no such illusions. Secondly, and quite important, the Agua Rosada were descended from both Kimpanzu and Kinlaza. As such, they had ties of blood with most of the other pretenders. Both these factors made the House of Agua Rosada ideal for leadership of a new Kongo.

In his diplomatic campaign of 1699–1700, Pedro made clear what sort of political structure he favored for the new Kongo. He asked for no more than simple recognition of himself as king and a general truce. Perhaps it is not surprising, then, that it was in Pedro's camp that the new foundation tradition of Kongo was first recorded, and was reported to Rome linked with enthusiastic Capuchin support for his candidacy.[34]

First Pedro made peace with Pedro Constantinho da Silva, who had taken over leadership of Manuel's faction of the Kimpanzu upon the latter's death in 1693. Pedro Constantinho was in no position to assert many claims, as he had recently been driven out of his territory by the forces of Ana Afonso de Leão. Pedro cemented his bond to Pedro Constantinho da Silva by taking Pedro Constantinho's niece as his wife in a solemn ceremony at Kimbangu on 13 July 1699, followed by the appointment of Pedro Constantinho as his captain general.[35]

The next year, Pedro IV persuaded Ana Afonso de Leão to join the truce. Despite her conflicts with his new captain general, she and her principal kin signed a treaty of recognition of Pedro IV and a general truce among all the parties.[36] Pedro IV was not able to obtain similar satisfaction from João II of Mbula, however. Although there was some support in his court for accepting Pedro IV as king, especially since João II was sick and had lost the power of speech, in the end his sister refused to accept the overtures of Pedro IV's envoy, the Capuchin prefect Francesco da Pavia.[37] The Capuchins did back Pedro IV, even though, just three years earlier, Luca da Caltanisetta had been active in a campaign to obtain recognition for João II.[38] By 1700, the clerical establishment was firmly behind the new king, whose candidacy was championed by the prefect of the mission.[39] Rome accepted their reports, and the priests promised a papal blessing and crown to seal the Pope's approval.[40]

All that lacked in 1700 was a suitable capital. Kimbangu, while safe, was neither accessible nor neutral enough to satisfy all parties. At the urging of Francesco da Pavia, Pedro IV decided to reoccupy São Salvador permanently. Not only was that site the traditional seat of all of Kongo's kings, but it was in territory that no faction controlled. Pedro's reoccupation of it would thus show both his respect for tradition and his sincere commitment to neutrality.

As a first step in re-establishing his rule in São Salvador, Pedro IV decided to repopulate the site. Accordingly, in 1701 he dispatched his captain general Pedro Constantinho da Silva with a group of colonists to the capital to plant a crop and thus be ready to receive the king, who

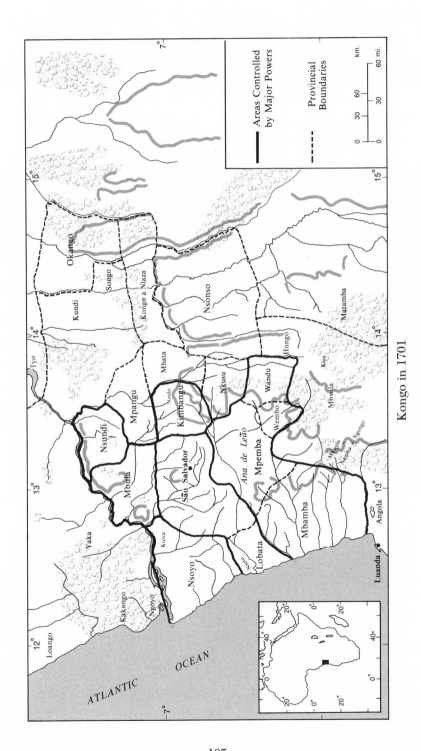

Kongo in 1701

105

would follow the next year. But Pedro Constantinho da Silva proved to be true to his opportunist nature, and began acting very independently once he was out of Pedro IV's reach. Sensing some sort of treachery, Pedro IV decided not to follow in 1702 to reoccupy the city personally.[41]

Pedro Constantinho's change of heart was one more example of the type of double-dealing that had crippled attempts to reunite Kongo, whether by force or diplomacy. Although Pedro IV had drawn closer than his immediate predecessors to establishing a realistically constituted Kongo, he still faced the ambition and defiance of those who themselves hoped to rule. Thus, despite Pedro's own belief that warfare in Kongo must stop, he was soon committed to still another war.[42]

To the villagers and peasants of Kongo, the complexities of diplomacy and the restoration of Kongo meant very little. All they had experienced since Mbwila was constant war, which affected them more than any other sector of the society. By 1700 nearly a whole generation of Kongo peasants had grown up under the threat of constant war, which meant not only the disruption of their daily lives, but great physical danger, either in the deadly cross fire of the opposed armies or the threat of transatlantic transportation. It is hardly surprising that when in 1702–3 a great leader rose up, proclaiming herself to be Saint Anthony and announcing that Kongo would be reunited in peace, not by mortal hands, but by the work of God, they eagerly followed.

The Antonian movement, born out of the desire of Kongo peasants for peace, resulted in the establishment of a powerful new religious ideology. The religious ideology itself was a result of Kongo's traditional religion in combination with the Kongoized message of the Christian priests. The Antonian movement represented an attempt of the Kongo to adjust their ideological perceptions to their new, changed circumstances. Just as Kongo's history was being reinterpreted in oral traditions at the beginning of the eighteenth century, so new sources of political legitimacy seemed necessary, given the warfare and strife engendered by the old. If the new oral traditions recorded in 1700 reflected the nobility's version of the ideological basis for Kongo's future, the peasants' version can be discerned in the Antonian movement.

Although Dona Beatrice Kimpa Vita, the "false Saint Anthony," had been born into the "highest nobility," she had spent some of her youth as an *nganga marinda* (a traditional religious actor.)[43] In 1686, the year of her birth,[44] membership in the nobility counted for little in the now ruralized Kongo, and her life as an *nganga* had no doubt brought her somewhat outside the circle of both noble and peasant. This background permitted her, like the young King Pedro IV (born about 1671),[45] to see

Kongo as it had become after the destruction of São Salvador, and thus to attempt to reconstruct it in accord with the economic and social realities of their time. She grasped ideologically what Pedro IV grasped politically.

Wyatt MacGaffey has examined, at some length, the various events surrounding the start of the movement: the announcement made by a child (who later proved to be an adult) that God would punish Kongo, the stone shaped like the head of Christ found by Beatrice's associate Appolonia Mafuta, Beatrice's claim that she was visited by two white children in her childhood dreams, and her possession, after a long illness, by Saint Anthony's spirit. All of these events, MacGaffey concludes, are evidence of her association with the cult of the *isimbi*. This cult involved tutelary spirits of particular localities who would be invoked both by the *itomi* and the *impasi* cults described earlier.[46]

Dona Beatrice's activities touched both the political and the religious life of Kongo. In the religious sphere, she claimed direct, unaided communication with the other world. Bernardo da Gallo recorded her changes in the Christian prayer "Salve Regina" which converted it to "Salve Antonio." In this prayer Beatrice emphasized that the normal Christian sacraments of marriage, confession, and baptism served no purpose, since God would know the intention of the believer.[47] Her burning of various objects used by both Christian and traditional *nganga*, like the cross, also reflected her belief in simple, direct spiritual communication.[48] Her defense of the burning of the cross, when da Gallo questioned it, fits this logic, for she argued that it was encumbered with "fetishes."[49] She claimed to die each Friday, visit heaven, and return to earth on Mondays to tell the Kongo what to do, so important was her personal mediation.[50] All this activity was perfectly understandable within the public service roles of *nganga* and *itomi*, who always insisted that direct mediation was superior to mediation by means of *nkisi* or other material objects.

Beatrice's operation of the *isimbi* cult had important political implications, and in the end it was these which both gave her her notoriety and led to the end of her career. Since the *kitomi* claimed to communicate with the territorial *isimbi* spirits, it was the *kitomi* who sacralized political officeholders, and as such the mani Vunda, *kitomi* for the kingdom, had long held the power to enthrone the king, a power he had come to share with the Capuchins or other clergy as the kingdom became Christianized. Now, however, Beatrice was claiming that power. She commanded that the nobility of Kongo reunite at São Salvador, recognize her (as their *kitomi*, no doubt), and allow her to choose one as King of Kongo. In any case, she insisted, they must stop their jealousies and fighting, as this was destroying the kingdom.[51] We have already pointed out how important in Kongo ideology the concept of harmony was, and likewise how many sorts of misfortune were attributed to jealousies which might manifest themselves in witchcraft. The misfortunes that befell Kongo's peasants as a result of the continual warfare of the late seventeenth century were certainly evidence for the effects that jealousies and evil-doing might have.

If Beatrice claimed the right to enthrone a king, and hence to resolve the political disputes of the kingdom, however, she could not exercise this power without alienating all others with a claim to royal office. The "little Anthonies," her ambassadors, who claimed, like her, to be resurrected saints, even went so far as to suggest that no one would be chosen king from among the present rulers, as all had contributed to the destruction of the country.[52] But despite her doctrine, and the potential in it, Beatrice was not fundamentally attacking Kongo's political ideology. Although she burned Christian objects, and was said to denounce the Pope, she claimed when interviewed by da Gallo that she respected the papal office, and even da Gallo himself as an *nganga*.[53] Although her followers were at times hostile to the priests, the movement was not hostile, in principle, to the European *nganga*—indeed Saint Anthony appeared to Beatrice dressed in the habit of a Capuchin priest.[54]

The Antonian movement was no more deeply hostile to Kongo's political ideology than it was to the country's particular type of Christianity (though it was opposed to the practices of some Kongo Christians). To be sure, the Antonians, like their secular counterparts of Pedro IV's party, no longer held to the tradition of Nimi a Lukeni as the conquering founder of Kongo. But Beatrice's explanation of Kongo's origins formed a natural counterpart to the new oral traditions that were circulating in political sphere by the beginning of the eighteenth century.

By her account, events traditionally associated with the founding of Christianity (the story of the birth of Jesus) took place in Kongo. This was not entirely original with her: other similar accounts of the beginning of Christianity in Kongo were circulating among Kongo Christians by the late seventeenth century. Andrea da Pavia recorded the story of King Afonso I's reign as it had been changed to suit a new Kongo in Nsoyo about 1688. In this story, Christianity had been started in São Salvador, but it was during Afonso's reign as governor of Nsundi that it eventually grew to be important, later becoming the dominant religion after Afonso defeated his brother to become king.[55] Beatrice's story of the baby Jesus being born in São Salvador and baptized in Nsundi preserved the essentials of that earlier account. Similarly, her contention that Saint Francis (patron saint of the Capuchins) was born "of the stock of the Marquis of Vunda" shows her acknowledgement of both the Capuchins and the Marquis of Vunda (*kitomi* for Kongo) as *isimbi* spirits who played a necessary role in the political and religious structure of Kongo.[56]

Thus, while Beatrice deeply threatened the political leaders of Kongo as individuals by threatening their ideological legitimacy, she did not threaten the fundamental ideological structure of the kingdom. While superficially anti-clerical, Antonianism was not fundamentally anti-Christian, at least not against the Christian faith as it was interpreted in Kongo and integrated into the social and political structure of the kingdom. Similarly, while it was radical with respect to individual kings and dukes, on the whole the movement upheld the evolving status quo of ruling groups.[57]

Whatever Beatrice believed the movement to be about, and whatever basis it had in Kongo ideology, its actual acceptance was conditioned by a wide variety of political, ideological, and social circumstances. Beatrice's message made an immediate impact on Kongo's peasants, who had suffered for such a long time under the ceaseless wars of the nobility. That she addressed herself to the issue of these wars, and proposed that a new Kongo be built on familiar but revitalized ideological grounds and that contests for control of the country end, was enough for them. It was the poor people, the peasants, who flocked to her when she called for Kongo to be reunited at São Salvador. They came, in Bernardo da Gallo's words, "from the forests and the wilds, ruder than rudeness itself, more ignorant that ignorance itself."[58] They quickly repopulated São Salvador after Beatrice moved there permanently in 1705. Even the Christian priests found it "an admirable thing to see the ease with which the blacks, young and old, men and women" took to her teaching, and went singing her prayers "on the roads, in the fields, everywhere."[59]

Their motives may have varied; some perhaps had their doubts about the validity of what Beatrice thought, and we may gather from da Gallo's description of the reunion that it had something of a carnival atmosphere:

> Therefore it happened that there were those who went to worship the supposed Saint, to see their homeland reborn, to see their friends: some to recover their health miraculously, and others to be first to reoccupy the place; São Salvador was rapidly repopulated. In this way the false saint became the restorer, ruler and lord of Congo, and was acclaimed adored and esteemed as such by everyone.[60]

Along with the peasants and their hope and celebration came the nobility, as da Gallo noted, "to be the first to reoccupy the place" or "out of greed in order to reign." Sensing the popularity of the movement, and its potential to count militarily in the struggles for power, some of the nobility joined Saint Anthony and her peasant following. Most important of these nobles was Pedro Constantinho da Silva, who was already in São Salvador when Beatrice arrived, leading Pedro IV's resettlement column. In exchange for his conversion to Antonianism, Beatrice proclaimed him King of Kongo.

In proclaiming Pedro Constantinho to be king, Beatrice achieved recognition of her movement and gained a force to defend it. She also guaranteed the enmity of all other aspiring groups of Kongo nobility, and in so doing set off a war that lined up herself and some of the Kimpanzu groups (though not all) against Pedro IV and all of the Kinlaza. For her opponents, the attack on São Salvador to overthrow her was more than just one more military and political maneuver in a series of such maneuvers: it was a holy war.

Beatrice consolidated the Kimpanzu hold on São Salvador—Pedro Constantinho's relatives, who treated her with great respect, deeming it an honor to eat from her hands, were granted important positions in her church.[61] Other Kimpanzu groups honored the movement as well, especially the de Nóbrega group of southern Nsoyo. In 1706, Lorenzo da Lucca found the Antonians firmly entrenched in the lands under the de Nóbregas. In the same year there was a revolt in Mbamba in favor of the Kimpanzu, which in turn embraced the Antonian movement.[62] Suzanna de Nóbrega's son Manuel, who entertained an ambition for the throne, joined Pedro Constantinho, and Manuel's son and brother Daniel also came to São Salvador.[63]

The movement was less unambiguously successful elsewhere in Kongo, even in lands controlled by the Kimpanzu, possibly because its strong popular and millenarian content made it dangerous and unwieldy. Thus the Antonians preached with some freedom in Nsoyo initially, but in 1708, actually after the death of Saint Anthony herself, a popular movement that was pro-Kimpanzu but against the ruling prince, António III Baretto da Silva, succeeded in overthrowing him and electing another prince, Amador da Silva. However, the movement overstepped its bounds, for Amador da Silva was not so anti-Christian as to acquiesce to the demands of the rebels that they be given the head of the Capuchin superior.[64] At any rate, he was killed by poison the next day, and his successor, Paulo IV da Silva, protected the missionaries and turned his support to Pedro IV as King of Kongo rather than Pedro Constantinho da Silva.[65] In Nsundi likewise, the movement had uneven success. At first the Antonians were tolerated, but later the "little Anthonies" were driven out of the province by the duke, a move with which Bernardo da Gallo agreed.[66] Although the dukes of Nsundi were Kimpanzu, they were quite an independent branch, and more friendly than any other lineage to the Kinlaza, being long-time supporters of João II.

If the Antonian movement had only partial support among the Kimpanzu and their allies, it is not hard to guess that it was firmly and resolutely opposed by the Kinlaza, and it was they who finally brought Beatrice to trial. In 1705 Beatrice travelled to Mbula to obtain from João II both his adherence to the cause and a papal document known in Kongo as "Santissimo Sacramento."[67] João II promptly drove her out of Mbula. She nevertheless claimed to have the papal bull when she returned to São Salvador (permitting no one to see it, as, she claimed, it was protected by her guardian angels, and seeing it would cause instant death).[68] The opposition from the Kinlaza rulers of Mbula was of course predictable, as was the even stronger reaction by the faction of Ana Afonso de Leão in southern Kongo. In 1706, Pedro Valle das Lagrimas, Ana's nephew and ruler of Mbamba, decided to undertake a major campaign to extirpate the heresy from his lands, as it had already caused a serious revolt on the west in the territory bordering the pro-Antonian Kimpanzu group of Suzana de Nóbrega. "The Duke of Mbamba," wrote Lorenzo da Lucca,

> advised that his State was in danger of loss or contagion by this heresy, showed holy zeal, took up a great Cross, and went with this throughout his Duchy, passing through the Marquisate of Pemba and then on to Mucondo where he joined the Queen Dona Ana, and with Father Gio. Maria da Barletta they worked, liberating those regions of the heresy, rounding up all the demons-incarnate there.[69]

It was ultimately as an offshoot of this anti-Antonian campaign that Beatrice was captured and brought to the royal court.

Ana Afonso de Leão sent her ambassadors to Kimbangu to seek Pedro IV's aid in driving out the heresy. On their way to Kimbangu the ambassadors encountered none other than Saint Anthony, Beatrice herself. She had become pregnant and had left São Salvador to go into the bush to have her child, accompanied by her principal "Angel Guardian" (named Barros but who had taken the name of Saint John when he became an Antonian).[70] The ambassadors seized the pair and the infant, carrying them up to Kimbangu to deliver them to the king. Pedro IV, while he was opposed to the Antonian movement both politically and religiously, nevertheless vacillated from April until June of 1706 before he and his council sentenced her as a heretic to death by burning.[71] On the night of 1 July 1706, Beatrice, Barros, and Appolonia Mafuta, the original prophet of the movement, gave their last confessions to Bernardo da Gallo and Lorenzo da Lucca. All three confessed to grave sins, and recanted—

Appolonia Mafuta was judged to be insane, and pardoned; Beatrice and Barros were condemned to die. Huge crowds attended the public execution in the square at the palace of Kimbangu, and they were so unruly that the two Capuchins failed to obtain Beatrice's public recantation of the movement, although they did manage to save her infant son, who was originally scheduled to die with his mother by Pedro IV and his council, against the wishes of the Capuchins.[72]

So that her remains would not be saved by her followers, the ashes were carefully reburned. Although the movement, notwithstanding, did not die with its leader, and continued under the nominal leadership of Pedro Constantinho in São Salvador,[73] it could not long survive the death of Saint Anthony, especially when its new head was a crass political opportunist. Indeed, the unifying character of the movement began to dissipate quickly after the death of Beatrice, and when Lorenzo da Lucca and his Capuchin companion Giovanni Paolo da Tivoli visited São Salvador in July 1706, they were able to reconvert a number of Antonian nobles back to Catholicism. Even Pedro Constantinho himself seemed to be wavering in the face of a movement that he had no hope of really controlling, for when da Lucca spoke with him, and an Antonian celebration suddenly broke out on a nearby plaza, he became visibly upset, so that "his usually black face became blanched."[74] Bernardo da Gallo, visiting the city in 1707, made still more converts; and the ideological movement that had bound politics and religion, rich and poor, villager and townsman, was apparently beginning to weaken.[75]

With the Antonian movement flickering out, normal politics resumed, and it was military affairs that began to count once more. In 1708 a series of battles raged over Kongo. Although Pedro Constantinho and his allies in Lobata under the de Nóbregas took the initiative, they were defeated, and Pedro IV meanwhile scored an important victory against the forces of Mbula.[76] In February, 1709, Pedro IV launched a successful attack against São Salvador, and amidst the cries and prayers of the Antonians, put an end to both Antonianism and the rebellion of Pedro Constantinho da Silva.[77] Pedro Constantinho remained opportunist to the last, and died by gunshot while trying to change sides and receive the king's pardon.[78]

The remnants of Pedro Constantinho's forces fled in all directions, many being rounded up immediately by allied rulers of Pedro IV, others taking refuge in Lobata, where the Kimpanzu of Manuel de Nóbrega continued to struggle against Pedro IV.[79] Many more took advantage of Pedro IV's offer of a pardon, and Pedro himself tried to heal the wounds of the struggle by allowing Manuel Makassa, the son of Pedro Constantinho, to marry his daughter.[80]

Nsoyo, now under the leadership of Paulo IV da Silva, offered to pay a nominal tribute to Pedro IV and to recognize him, as well as refusing aid to Pedro Constantinho's followers who sought asylum there.[81] Some years later, in 1715, João II also recognized the sovereignty of Pedro IV,[82] and in the same year the long struggle against the de Nóbrega lineage in Mbamba and Lobata culminated in the capture and beheading of Manuel by Pedro Valle das Lagrimas.[83]

Thus, with the death of Manuel de Nóbrega, Kongo was at last nominally reunited under one sovereign, Pedro IV. Pedro spent the last years of his life attempting to remarry, for his first wife, Hipolita, had proven unfaithful and run away to São Salvador to become an Antonian, eventually taking refuge in Nsoyo. The secular visitor, Estevão Botelho, agreed to allow Pedro IV to marry a second time, despite the denunciations of the Capuchins. When Pedro died in 1718, he was satisfied that he had accomplished his most important task, the reunification of Kongo.[84]

Epilogue

WHAT SORT of kingdom had Pedro IV reunited before his death? Certainly not the kingdom of Garcia II and António I. The fact is, Pedro IV remained, as did his royal successors, the ruler of São Salvador and Kimbangu only; his power beyond that region was constituted only in the tenuous ties of marriage, treaty, and alliance with equally powerful other rulers. While the state of the kingdom from about 1720 to 1767 is much less visible to historians than in the previous era,[1] the image of Kongo that emerges in mid-century shows how it was governed after the restoration of Pedro IV. Cherubino da Savonna, a Capuchin missionary who worked in Kongo from 1760–67, described the kingdom as it existed during the time of his apostolate. In its political structure the Kongo of 1760 was very similar to that of 1700, with the same groupings of regional powers, each being merely the center of a group of independent potentates, and all being tied together by a system of alliances and marriages. These then constituted a rather ephemeral Kingdom of Kongo, "better called an Empire," in Cherubino da Savonna's words.[2]

Cherubino da Savonna chose to call the subdivisions of this "empire" kingdoms, and a survey of them shows that they corresponded fairly well to the groupings that had allied with or fought against Pedro IV in his various campaigns to reunite Kongo from 1699 to 1718. In the south there was Nkondu, "ruled always by a woman" just as this same region had been ruled by a woman, Ana Afonso de Leão, in 1700.[3] The ruler of 1760 was not a member of the House of de Leão, but she was, according to da Savonna, Kinlaza.[4] Under her sovereignty were several subunits which included Mbamba Lobata, Mbamba Kongo, Mpemba, and Wandu, all tied together very loosely by intermarriages. Several rulers bore the surname Romano Leite or Agua Rosada Romano Leite (showing that they had intermarried with Pedro IV's lineage, the Agua Rosada).[5] The de Leãos had not disappeared, however; a ruler of Mbemba in 1781 was named Afonso de Leão.[6] Just as in the beginning of the century, this group of related rulers, who still valued their interconnections through the Kinlaza household of a century before, had intermarried with each other. Cherubino da Savonna continued this tradition during his stay in Kongo by blessing the marriage of Dona Christina, daughter of the Duke of Mpemba, to the Duke of Mbamba Kongo.[7]

In the north of the country, the kingdoms were smaller and had fewer interconnections of blood and alliance, just as in 1700. At Mbula there was a kingdom ruled by José de Vasconcelos e Menezes which controlled a large area south of the Zaire River, and appears to have been the direct descendent of the Kingdom of Mbula established by the pretender King Pedro III in 1668 and ruled in Pedro IV's time by the former king's brother João II.[8] Because of his access to European goods through posts along the Zaire River, José de Vasconcelos e Menezes was fairly rich and possessed three iron cannon, bought from European merchants.[9] Bordering Mbula on the north was the Duchy of Nsundi, ruled in 1760 by António Brandão and independent, as in 1700, from the rulers of Kongo.[10]

On the seacoast, and dominant as ever, was the Principality of Nsoyo, ruled in 1760 by Prince Miguel de Castro da Silva, who "held his court with more magnificence than the king himself."[11] Prince Miguel based his power, as had his predecessors, in Mbanza Nsoyo, whose population had not declined from its level earlier in the century.[12] By the mid-eighteenth century Nsoyo had abandoned its earlier policy of interference in Kongo affairs, and had shifted its emphasis to a vigorous policy of domination of the countries to the north of it.[13]

Finally, in the center of the country was the always-disputed seat of this ephemeral "Empire" of Kongo, the Kingdom of Kongo proper. In theory at least, the rulers of this kingdom were chosen alternately from Kinlaza and Kimpanzu lineages.[14] The kings maintained a fortress and a church at Kimbangu which served them as a refuge, just as it had earlier kings in 1700.[15] São Salvador had not re-established itself as a population center, however, although after Pedro IV's reign it had ceased to be abandoned altogether.[16] Since it was not well populated, the town remained as vulnerable as ever, and although the question of the succession of kings was handled by the alternation of Kimpanzu and Kinlaza, pretenders were common and often able to drive the king out of São Salvador. Indeed, just such a usurpation had occurred in 1764, while Cherubino da Savonna was in Kongo.[17] In any case, Kimpanzu and Kinlaza were no longer undiluted lineages in the sense that they had been a century before; more tightly knit houses derived from Kimpanzu and Kinlaza, such as the Houses of Agua Rosada, Romano Leite, and de Leão, had now come to the fore.

Kongo as a kingdom, or even an "empire," remained firmly fixed in the minds of the nobles who ruled it and its loose group of satellites. It was the center of their origin, and was endowed with mystical and religious significance even if it no longer had the political significance or economic power it once enjoyed. A respect for the hierarchy, and a willingness to obey superiors in symbolic ways, had substituted for real authority. Anton Felice Tommasi da Cortona, an Italian Capuchin, crossing Mbamba and Mpemba in 1734, described an elaborate ceremonial practiced by the Duke of Mbamba, various marquises, and the king.[18] However, it took several letters from the King of Kongo to get a minor marquis near Mpemba to allow the Capuchin to pass on to São Salvador.[19] Religion remained one of the links that kept the kingdom together, and the one real power that the king did enjoy was the right to bestow, for a fee, knighthoods in the Military Order of Kongo.[20] But although the knighthood might confer status on the holder, it surely did not render any income, for the king's income was minimal. Such a gift was therefore a shadow of the powers of former kings, who could just as quickly and easily bestow whole provinces on their favorites, or remove those who were out of favor from office.

Even the regional kingdoms described by Cherubino da Savonna were ephemeral. Cherubino da Savonna chose to emphasize the top-level structure of the country, and his description did not really cover the lower levels of political organization. Anton Felice Tommasi, in his travels of 1734–36, noted the petty splendor of the regional courts, each complete with titled officials and a well-developed set of courtly manners.[21] But the fundamental disunity is made clear by the account of the Portuguese missionary Rafael de Castello de Vide, who traversed Kongo in 1781 with a group of companions and lived in the country from 1781 to 1788.[22] It is clear from this account that the actual seat of sovereign power was a much smaller unit, ruled by a person bearing the title of marquis, which measured about a day's travel across and was in all real respects independent. The show of obedience to higher levels, like the obedience of the rulers of the regional kingdoms to the King of Kongo, was more symbolic and ideological than real in the political sense.[23] Thus the devolution of actual sovereignty from the level of the kingdom to local areas, each centered on an *mbanza* and encompassing an area whose limit was probably the distance from which agricultural surplus could be drawn, already easily visible in Luca da Caltanisetta's accounts of the 1690s, continued through the eighteenth century, and right on into the colonial era.[24]

The solidification of the new Kongo, which commenced—or rather began to commence, since social history never recognizes sharp breaks— with the sack of São Salvador in 1666–78, appears to have been nearly complete by the reign of Pedro IV. Unlike his predecessors, Pedro IV saw clearly that the restoration of Kongo into the old mould was impossible.

Although he was probably not the first to recognize the limitations of the new Kongo, he was the first king clearly to build his policy around that recognition. Thus it was during his reign that ideological recognition of the new Kongo commenced for all levels of society. Since legal and ideological forms are often the last social forms to change in any new era, the reign of Pedro IV can properly be seen as marking the end of the period of transition from the centralized, town-centered Kongo of Garcia II to the decentralized, village-centered Kongo of the later period.

The Kongo that Pedro IV founded is the Kongo known by the modern ethnographers who have described it since the late nineteenth century. A comparison of the accounts of various eighteenth-century travellers and missionaries with those of the nineteenth century and in early precolonial era make it fairly clear that the institutional structure of Kongo changed very little over this period, although of course individual regions may have changed and various circumstances no doubt altered some of the forms. It is an image of this period that the modern researcher finds by studying Kongo's present-day social structure, oral tradition, art, and religion. In many cases there is a clear continuity between these modern forms and their predecessors, even in the seventeenth century, especially those aspects of Kongo society that pertained to the village sector, which was less changed than the urban sector by the alteration of Kongo social structure in the era of the civil wars. Even in those forms that underwent great transformation there is some continuity, and the student of the seventeenth-century documents will recognize in these many institutions described in modern ethnography. But there have been changes, and this is why attempts to understand the structure of seventeenth-century Kongo that make use of modern ethnography and twentieth-century oral tradition fail. The older system is familiar enough to encourage assumptions of total continuity, but in fact contains deep underlying differences.[25]

From a study of the subtle changes in Kongo's oral tradition, it is easy to see both how they reflect real historical changes in Kongo and how they can easily mislead modern scholars who rely on them to understand political structures. We have seen how Kongo oral tradition gradually changed even during the period under study. Initially the traditions described Nimi a Lukeni, a fierce conqueror who established São Salvador and ruled the Kongo directly from his capital, giving out the provinces to his followers for short terms. This tradition, the basic form of all the seventeenth-century accounts, was an excellent constitutional basis for the Kongo of Garcia II. It provided ideological and historical justification for the hierarchical Kongo based on the right of conquest, the division of Kongo into town and village sectors, and the power of the king to appoint and remove officials all over the country.[26] However, as the seventeenth

century drew to a close, and as the Kongo social system altered with the
destruction of São Salvador, this tradition changed. Now tradition came
to emphasize the first king as a conciliatory figure, a "wise blacksmith,"
which was much more fitting for the decentralized constitution of Kongo,
where power rested on conciliation, and the king was hardly even first
among equals.[27]

The same tendency is noticeable in the mature oral tradition of the
eighteenth century, the one written down for King José I in 1782.[28] This
document, once again, does not place any attention on the first king (now
Afonso I, not Nimi a Lukeni)[29] as conqueror. Here the first king was the
one who introduced Christianity, and who first exercised the important
role of dispenser of the Order of Christ—the most important source of
prestige and revenue for eighteenth-century kings in Kongo.[30] In all these
versions there are common threads and some of these threads are remarkable—for example, the kinglist attached to the 1782 version accords well
with the actual succession of kings, in so far as it is possible to check it.
Yet all give slightly different casts to Kongo's differences that can be
accurately explained only by turning to the exact historical situation in
which they were generated and the requirements of the social system
they legitimized and explained.

What has been said of royal oral traditions is likewise true of local
traditions. In the seventeenth century, as far as can be told, local traditions conformed to the model of the royal one, save for variations on the
general theme of Nimi a Lukeni as conqueror. For instance, Girolamo da
Montesarchio, recording a tradition in Mpemba Kazi just south of the
Zaire River, noted that its ruler controlled the area where Nimi a Lukeni
was supposed to have first crossed to conquer Kongo.[31] The founding
tradition of Kongo was thus known to nobles in the rural, local sectors as
in the towns. Modern oral traditions are specific to certain localities and
set about explaining the present-day (or at least recent) hierarchies, using
the idiom of clientage, seniority, and slavery.[32] Their only reference to
São Salvador is to note that all clans originated there, and migrated to
their present localities after a series of political and social upheavals.[33]
These "upheavals" of the modern tradition probably have no real basis in
fact, but serve the function of legitimizing the present order in each area.
The modern oral traditions appear to be the Kongo way of explaining the
dissolution of the centralized kingdom of the seventeenth century. Contemporary documents prove that households that were once based in São
Salvador came to be permanently resident in the provinces. The traditions of today represent this movement with fantastic stories of migration.
As the households of São Salvador gradually fitted into the rural society,

a "charter" in the form of a migration tradition evolved in which each social group in the modern region gets a place, either as migrants from São Salvador, clients, slaves, or the junior descendents of the original immigrants.

While the significance of these oral traditions is clear once the historical process is understood, attempting to work in the other direction is fraught with difficulties and hazards. A clear example of this is the attempt of Joseph van Wing to reconstruct Kongo history from these traditions. In his version, van Wing argues that the migration traditions of the modern Kongo refer to the period of the original formation of Kongo in the thirteenth or fourteenth century, or before the arrival of the Portuguese, probably because the better-documented later period clearly contains no mass movement from São Salvador to the provinces.[34] In fact, it is quite clear that these events occurred not only after the arrival of the Portuguese, but after the sack of São Salvador in the period 1666–78.

How a literal reading of oral tradition might result in erroneous historical constructions can be seen also by looking at oral traditions in Nsoyo. The foundation of Nsoyo is traced by its modern-day inhabitants to a member of the court of Kongo's King Álvaro, "Pango a Luqueni,"[35] who is said to have settled in Nsoyo after being driven out of Kongo. The further details of this account resemble, in outline, the oral tradition of seventeenth-century Kongo more than that of modern Kongo—a resemblance that is not surprising inasmuch as Nsoyo's centralization in the eighteenth century was greater than Kongo's in the same period. In Nsoyo the various regional rulers are held by modern tradition to be descendents of the Count.[36] Once again the historical record explains the pattern of the tradition, but a literal reading might well give a misleading version of the actual events or structures.

The study of oral traditions of Kongo demonstrates how the ideological foundations of Kongo history, as seen by the Kongo themselves, changed over the three centuries that separate us from Pedro IV. A quick examination of another Kongo institution, that of slavery, shows how social forms as well as ideological forms altered with the changes in Kongo, but retained enough of their old appearances to confuse the reconstruction of Kongo history. As remarked earlier, the central and most important aspect of slavery in Garcia II's Kongo was not any particular labor performed by slaves, but rather the fact that for a time the status of slave was conferred on people after their capture to allow them to be transferred to one central location. The transferral of people to São Salvador kept the town in its central, and hence ruling position. What was important about seventeenth-century slavery was not the amount of work the slaves performed, or even the relationship that they had to land, tools, or other property, even though the slaves on seventeenth-century estates around the towns may have produced more surplus than their nineteenth-century equivalents.

In nineteenth-century rural Kongo, slaves were most often used to increase the strength of lineages. They were settled, left to unsupervised production, and charged dues in kind.[37] They formed in all sectors of Kongo society a minority. English observers of the early nineteenth century noted that slaves were the minority in all the settlements along the Zaire River, and they shared work in the fields with the wives of the nobility.[38] The same seemed to hold true even in São Salvador. Pietro Paolo da Bene, a Capuchin who visited São Salvador in 1819–20, noted that although the king had some 300 slaves in his service, he was required to pay them in cloth and wine for their services.[39] In the seventeenth century, they performed more than this. While they were still probably a minority in Kongo's population, they were centralized, and their demographic mass, if nothing else, provided for a large absolute surplus and the human resources to render the town both an economic center and invulnerable to attack. It was this integration, a conscious policy of Kongo kings and ruling strata, that made slavery (or rather the Kongo social institution based on labor rent and labor centralization) the mainstay of Kongo's seventeenth-century society.

It was the disintegration of Kongo's main town center that made slavery a secondary mode of labor control, and of little importance in Kongo's subsequent history. This understanding of Kongo's modern system has led such researchers as Kajsa Ekholm to reject slavery as an important force in Kongo's earlier history and to rely instead on complex and ingenious systems of marital exchange and control of trade to explain the power of the kings and the destruction of the kingdom.[40]

Another social institution whose place between the seventeenth century and today has given rise to considerable confusion is the Catholic Church. Modern researchers, basing their interpretation on a modern, missionary-oriented conception of Christianity, have argued that the religion either did not survive in Kongo or never genuinely took root there. This is not so much because Christianity has changed in Kongo as because the notion of what constitutes Christianity has changed in Europe and North America. The Christian faith in seventeenth-century Kongo was in all its essentials simply Kongo's own religious system renamed, while the people of the country identified themselves as Christians. Added to this were declarations made by kings that they were obedient servants of the Catholic Church, and the acceptance of these claims by the Papacy. Christianity's success and continuation in Kongo depended largely on the successful implantation in the country of a religious hierarchy based on ordained *nganga* under control by central authorities, and the suppression of all unauthorized ("non-Christian") *nganga*. If the self-identification of the people as Christians ceased, or the clerical apparatus—whether it was composed of ordained priests or (as developed in the seventeenth century) lay priests (in the guise of catechists) with ordained priests to perform the sacraments—dissolved, then the Christian religion was no longer operating.

In many parts of Kongo, the ecclesiastical organization did in fact begin to disappear in the eighteenth century. Mbula and Nsundi, both in the northern parts of the country, were not visited by members of the Capuchin order after the middle of the eighteenth century. In time, their local devotion to the idea of Christianity disappeared, and when modern missionaries entered this region, they found no one able to say that he was Christian. Since missionary and anthropological work in what is today Zaire has been the most influential in shaping our ideas of Kongo religion, the strong tendency has been to dismiss Christianity's influence altogether.

Such has not been the case in the regions farther south, in Angola, where both the nominal clerical hierarchy and some knowledge of the religion remained. The reports of the Castello de Vide mission at the end of the eighteenth century abound in references to Christian nobility who knew some Christian doctrine and could read and write.[41] Canons from Luanda continued to visit São Salvador from time to time, and church slaves continued the traditions well into the nineteenth century.[42] Indeed, if Christianity faded away, that was owing to changes in the attitudes of the European clergy that defined it out of existence. By the 1820s the cultural chauvinism that would later become racism was widespread in Europe, especially with regard to Africa, and it emerged in the reports of the last Capuchins to visit Kongo in the period 1814–20.[43] These reports show that what had been acceptably Christian to Girolamo da Montesarchio or Luca da Caltanisetta two centuries before was no longer acceptable.[44]

Pedro IV presided over the death of one Kongo and the birth of another, a transformation that was at least as radical and confusing to Kongo's citizens as to later historians. It is easy to assign too much significance, or the wrong significance, to events that mark deep structural changes in society. Pedro's reign did not, after all, occur in an historical vacuum, but was the point of convergence of many distinct movements. Its significance is that it occupied (and contributed to) a moment when some salient historical cycles, associated with the old centralized Kingdom of Kongo, came to rest. As such it seems a fitting end to the study of the centralized Kingdom of Kongo.

Reference Matter

Note on Sources

IN A study based almost entirely on contemporary written documents, it is absolutely necessary to build up as large and varied a collection of material as possible. Thus it is important to insure that no witnesses to the events in Kongo are excluded from the collection, and to do this it is vital to identify all the various types of people who were likely to report on events in Kongo. Thus, for example, it would not be correct to base the research solely on the reports of Capuchin missionaries, even though they provide almost all of the documentation for the period after 1645. A complete search must include others who were in a position to see what was happening in Kongo and wrote about what they saw.

Beyond the problem of simply identifying possible witnesses is the problem of locating their accounts. This can sometimes be accomplished easily, by visiting archives: the Archivo Histórico Ultramarino in Lisbon, for example, where routine reports of Portuguese government officials were filed, or the archives of the "Propaganda Fide" in Rome, where a good series of Capuchin reports is found. But unfortunately, a number of documents strayed from the direct path from writer to archive. Missionaries wrote reports, even books, that were never filed in the appropriate archive; traders wrote private memoirs; government officials kept private correspondence. Moreover, not all archives have survived to the present day. Wars, fires, and administrative reorganizations have scattered the material or destroyed it. Careful searching is necessary to gather together the material that remains intact.

It is safe to say that there were five major categories of literate witnesses to events in Kongo in 1641–1718: (1) literate Kongo; (2) missionaries sent from Europe; (3) secular clergy attached to the See of Congo and Angola; (4) private citizens and government agents in Angola; and (5) merchants who paid visits to the area. Taking each category in turn, then, we can trace the history of the documentation from its creation to its present-day home in a library, archive, or private collection.

LITERATE KONGO

Literacy has been widespread among the upper class of Kongo since the early sixteenth century, the correspondence of King Afonso I (1506–43) with Kings Manuel I and João III of Portugal being the best-known product of this local literacy.[1] No doubt a vast amount of this material was placed in Kongo's own archives, which are known to have existed as early as 1550, for documents written on that date were retrieved, copied, and sent to Europe in 1552.[2] Kongo kings in the seventeenth century complained that their archives were destroyed in 1568 by the Yaka invasions, and it is clear that archives were refounded after the re-establishment of that lost archive.[3] This archive probably suffered as well during the civil wars, especially inasmuch as São Salvador was totally destroyed between 1666 and 1678, although not all the material may have been lost. In 1856, when Alfredo de Sarmento, a Portuguese official, visited São Salvador, he met with the royal archivist, who allowed him to see the documents collected there. Although this archive was subsequently destroyed by fire in the 1890s,[4] Sarmento did describe documents which appeared to date from the seventeenth century.[5]

Therefore, it seems that for the present, most documentation of local authorship has been lost, although a few documents may still be in private hands in Angola or Zaire. We must therefore rely on that documentation which has survived outside of Kongo, in the archives of the the recipients of correspondence. The most useful of these collections for the seventeenth century is the correspondence of Álvaro III and Pedro II with Juan Bautista Vives, Kongo's permanent ambassador in Rome, which is maintained in the Vatican Library, MS 12 516.[6] There is no convenient series of documents from Kongo for later years, although relevant correspondence was fairly regularly sent to the Arquivo Histórico Ultramarino, where almost all dealings with the lands outside Portugal were housed after about 1630. Similarly, after the early 1630s, most overseas correspondence with Rome ended up in the archives of the Propaganda Fide, and letters from literate Kongo are found scattered there as well as in Portugal.[7]

MISSIONARIES

The Kongo mission was dominated by two orders of clergy, the Capuchins and the Jesuits.[8] Members of both orders serving on the mission were required to report on their activities, and these reports are the solid base for any history of Kongo. The Capuchins were required to report annually to the prefect of the mission, and were also required to write a report upon their return to Europe.[9] Some, like Alessandro da Popi, wrote only a single folio as a report, while others, like Bernardo da Gallo, wrote reports of dozens of pages.[10] Most of these reports were filed in the archives of the Propaganda Fide in Rome, as were other occasional reports, or requests for information or clarification of doctrinal points.[11] However, it is clear that Capuchins also wrote reports and memoirs for the local (home) chapters upon their return to Europe, and some of these longer reports were published, either in their lifetimes or in modern times. Giovanni Francesco da Roma, Giovanni Antonio Cavazzi, and Dionigio Carli da Piacenza all wrote and published book-length memoirs shortly after their return from Africa, while Girolamo da Montesarchio, Andrea da Pavia, and Luca da Caltanisetta's memoirs were not published until recently, and Antonio de Teruel's are not published at all.

The Capuchin provincial archives that have survived and kept their early records have yielded a great quantity of such material. The provincial archive of Florence contains Girolamo da Montesarchio's report, while the archives at Venice and Valencia have lengthy chronicles including letters from missionaries to the superior of the mission and reminiscences of the missionaries. The Florentine provincial archives also have a very extensive series of letters from Serafino da Cortona and Lorenzo da Lucca addressed to the head of the province. However, when the regular orders in Italy were suppressed during the nineteenth century, many of the archives of the provinces were dispersed, destroyed, or transferred to the public archives. The State Archives of Milan, Modena, and Parma all contain material which was probably transferred from the Capuchin provincial archives, including collections of letters (in Parma), chronicles (in Milan), and other documents (in Modena). Similarly, such material is found in the National Libraries in Rome and in Florence.[12] In addition to reaching the state archives, some of the documentation that was formerly in missionary archives found its way into private hands—Giacinto Brugiotti's long report on the Kongo mission, now lost, was last seen in private hands, while the Este Library in Modena has Giuseppe Monari's account of his travels in Nsoyo, and the Araldi family, also of Modena, has over the years acquired early drafts of Cavazzi's material.[13]

Finally, some missionaries wrote personal letters to members of their families, and although these are often less informative than the letters to officials in the church, they also prove useful. The Tommasi family's collection of letters by their ancestor Anton Felice Tommasi da Cortona, addressed to his brother and mother, is an important source for Kongo's history in the 1730s.[14]

The Jesuit missionaries had somewhat different procedures from those of the Capuchins, although their material has survived in much the same way. Normally the Jesuit superior in one region would write a single report to Rome to give account of the entire province each year. These annual letters are very important sources on the Jesuit activities in Kongo. Most seem to have been sent originally to the General Jesuit archives in Rome, where many are still filed. However, the Jesuit archives have suffered badly since the seventeenth century, and much of their original contents have been lost. Some documents may be found in Portuguese archives, where copies were evidently filed with the Provincial; others are known only from published chronicles of the order, such as that of António Franco, which made use of the annual reports which have now been lost.[15]

Like the Capuchins, Jesuits also kept private correspondence and correspondence with the provincial headquarters. In Portugal the provincial material has come to rest, after the suppression of the order in the eighteenth century, in the archives at Torre de Tombo and in the Biblioteca da Ajuda in Lisbon. In Italy, some material has come into the hands of the State archives; Parma, for example, having a short chronicle which might have been housed originally in one or another local Jesuit archive.[16]

CLERGY OF THE SEE OF CONGO AND ANGOLA

The See was originally founded in 1596 in São Salvador, and after 1624 the Bishop resided in Luanda. Local secular clergy, whether residing in a parish or on "visit," do not seem to have been required to file any report; if they did, no evidence of it has survived. Much of the local documentation was filed in Luanda, and of that, great amounts were lost during the Dutch occupation of the city (1641–48), although two *códices* of late seventeenth-century documentation still remain in Luanda.[17] Appointments to the cathedral staff were normally conferred by the Portuguese king in his capacity as Master of the Order of Christ, and a certain amount of information on the personnel of the cathedral (though little else) can be found in the main registers of appointments in the chancellery records of the order at the Torre de Tombo archive in Lisbon.

The bishops of Angola and Congo were formally appointed in Rome, although nomination came from Portugal, and the processes by which the candidates were considered are recorded in Rome in the Vatican Archives. These processes normally included reports on the state of the diocese, which provide considerable information, usually submitted by eyewitnesses or people with long experience in the area. Moreover, the bishop was expected to provide Rome with regular reports of the state of the diocese, and to make visits to the major points in it periodically. These reports, also in the Vatican Archives, are only available up to 1640, when the last visit to Kongo was made.

Finally, since the bishop had a regular part in the administration of Angola, his correspondence often included reports of a more or less administrative nature to the Overseas Council in Lisbon. These reports, like other administrative material from Portugal's overseas possessions, were filed in the Arquivo Histórico Ultramarino in Lisbon.

PRIVATE CITIZENS AND GOVERNMENT AGENTS IN ANGOLA

Certainly the most important single document written by witnesses of this sort is António de Oliveira de Cadornega's *História Geral das Guerras Angolanas* (completed in 1681). Not commissioned for any purpose—apparently the work of a curious local resident—it survived in manuscript form until the early twentieth century, when printed versions were put together.[18] Most material of this sort, however, is found in the Angolan National Archives (the Centro de

Documentação e Investigação Histórica) and at the Arquivo Histórico Ultra-marino in Lisbon. After the Overseas Council took over administration of Portuguese possessions outside of Portugal, almost all administrative reports, correspondence, and orders were filed there. These include the *códices*, which are normally summaries of incoming or outgoing correspondence and orders, and the *caixas* and *maços*, which are boxes of loose original material (some of which can be traced through the *códices*, but most of which is simply stored in a disorderly chronological box or bundle). The Angolan material was probably richer originally, but time has worn heavily on it, and there are very few documents in Luanda which predate 1726 outside of the episcopal archives.[19]

The habit that senior Portuguese administrators in the seventeenth century had of keeping their own archives in their private possession has led to considerable losses. Some important administrative documents are probably still in private hands in Portugal,[20] and others are now on deposit in public archives. The records of Governor Fernão de Sousa (1624–31), now housed in the Biblioteca da Ajuda in Lisbon, are perhaps the most famous of these private collections now in public deposit.[21]

MERCHANTS WHO VISITED KONGO AND ANGOLA

The slave trade brought merchants from many nations to Kongo, but Dutch merchants probably ranked second in number to those of Portugal before the end of the seventeenth century. The Dutch records, a valuable source of information, were retained in the archives of the Oude West Indische Compagnie, now in the Algemeen Rijksarchive in the Hague.[22] For the later part of the period, the records of the Second Dutch West India Company are important as well.[23]

Fewer French and English merchants came to the country, and only in the late seventeenth century. In both countries, commercial records of the slave-trading companies have found their way into the national archives, the English in the T/70 series of the Public Records Office, and the French in the Archives de la Marine, Series 4JJ, B[3] and B[7], and the Archives des Colonies, Series F[2] and C[6].[24]

Notes

ABBREVIATIONS

ACA	Louis Jadin, *L'ancien Congo el l'Angola d'après les archives romaines, espagnoles, portugaise et néerlandaise,* 3 vols. (Memoires de L'Institute historique belge de Rome, vols. 39–41, 1974).
AHU	Arquivo Histórico Ultramarino, Lisbon.
AHU: PA	Papeis Avulsos section of AHU.
ANTT	Arquivo Nacional do Torre de Tombo, Lisbon.
APC	Provincial Archives of the Capuchin Order, various cities.
APF	Archivio "De Propaganda Fide," Rome.
APF: SOCG	Series Scritture Originale in Congregazioni Generali of APF.
APF: SRC	Series Scritture riferite nelle Congressi of APF.
ARSI	Archivum Romanum Societas Iesu, Vatican City.
AS	Archivio di Stato, various Italian cities.
ASV	Archivio Segreto Vaticano, Vatican City.
BE	Biblioteca Estense, Modena.
BIHBR	*Bulletin de L'Institute historique belge de Rome.*
BN	National Library, various Romance languages.
BPE	Biblioteca Pública e Arquivo Distrial de Evora.
MMA	António Brásio, *Monumenta Missionaria Africana,* 11 vols. (Lisbon, 1953–71).

INTRODUCTION

1 Álvaro VI has not left us his full titles. These are extracted from the titles of Álvaro IV (d. 1636) contained in a letter to the Jesuit Generalate, 25 October 1632, *MMA* 8:199.

2 F. Capelle to J.-M. de Nassau, March, 1642, in Louis Jadin, "Rivaltés luso-néerlandaise au Soyo, Congo . . . ," *BIHBR,* 37 (1699): 225; BN Madrid, MS 3533, Antonio de Teruel, "Descripcion narrativa de la mission serafica

des los padres capuchinos . . . en el Reyno del Congo" (ca. 1664), introduction (n. p.) and fol. 124; Giovanni Antonio Cavazzi da Montecuccolo, *Istorica descrizione de' tre regni Congo, Matamba ed Angola* (Bologna, 1687), book 2, no. 122.

3 APF: SOCG 250, fols. 198v–99, Giacinto Brugiotti da Vetralla, "Alcuni appuntamenti notabili circa la missione del Congo . . ." (ca. 1659); BN Madrid, MS 3533, de Teruel, "Descripcion narrativa," fol. 124; BE, MS Italicus 1380, alpha N-9-7, Giuseppe Monari da Modena, "Viaggio al Congo" (1723), fol. 221 (p. 434). Monari's account reproduces an earlier chronicle of the mid-seventeenth century, which Francisco Leite da Faria attributes to Giacinto Brugiotti, in Graziano Maria de Leguzzano, ed. and trans., *Descrição dos três reinos Congo, Matamba e Angola*, 2 vols. (Lisbon, 1965), 1:xxvi, note 42. Garcia's earlier history is reconstructed from the exploits of "Garcia Guipaucus" in António Franco, *Synopsis annalium societatis Jesu in Lusitania ab anno 1540 usque ad annum 1725* (Augsburg, 1726), pp. 263–64, 296. Guipaucus, in this Latin text, is seen as a deformation of "Quipaco," Garcia's nickname reported in António de Oliveira de Cadornega, *História geral das guerras angolanas, 1680*, ed. José Matias Delgado and Manuel Alves da Cunha, 3 vols. (1972; Lisbon, 1940–42), 1:217.

4 Matheus Cordoso, "Relação da morte del Rej del Congo, e da eleição que se fez em Dom Pedro, Duque de Bamba" (June, 1622), in António Brásio, "O problema da eleição e coroação dos reis do Congo," *História e missiologia: ineditos e esparsos* (Luanda, 1973), p. 232.

5 The spatial and demographic dimensions of mid-seventeenth-century Kongo are given in John Thornton, "Demography and History in the Kingdom of Kongo, 1550–1750," *Journal of African History*, 18 (1977): 526.

6 Alessandro Zorzi, "Relazione che Io, Alessandro havuto . . ." (1517), published in Francisco Leite de Faria and Avelino Teixeira da Mota, *Novidades náuticas e ultramarinas numa informação dada em Veneza em 1517* (Lisbon, 1977), pp. 16, 20.

7 John Thornton, "The Kingdom of Kongo, ca. 1390–1678: History of an African Social Formation," *Cahiers d'études africaines*, forthcoming.

8 For the state of Christianity in the eighteenth and nineteenth centuries, see Louis Jadin, "Survivances chrétiennes au Congo and XIXe siècle," *Études d'histoire africaine*, 1 (1970): 137–85.

9 On general foreign relations see the introduction to Jean Cuvelier and Louis Jadin, *L'ancien Congo d'après les archives romaines* (Brussels, 1954). Relations with the Holy See have been traced in detail by Teobaldo Filesi, "Le relazioni tra il regno del Congo e la Sede Apostolica nel prima meta del XV secolo," *Africa (Rome)*, 22 (1967): 247–85; "Le Relazioni tra il regno del Congo e la Sede Apostolica nel prima meta del XVI secolo," ibid., pp. 413–60; "Duarte Lopez ambasciatore del Rè del Congo presso Sisto V nel 1588," ibid., 23 (1968): 44–83; and "Nuove testimonianze sulla missione congolese a Roma del 1608," ibid., pp. 431–69.

10 The letter to the Negus Neghast was written on Kongo's behalf by their

permanent representative in Rome, Mons. Juan Bautista Vives, 18 April 1617, *MMA* 6:277–78.

11 Afonso I to Manuel I, 5 October 1514, *MMA* 1:295–314 *passim*, which gives a good idea of the goods the Portuguese obtained in Kongo in the early sixteenth century.

12 Ibid., p. 313 for a good idea of the Portuguese methods in Kongo.

13 David Birmingham, *Trade and Conflict in Angola* (London, 1966), pp. 49–63; John Thornton, "Early Kongo-Portuguese Relations, 1483–1575: A New Interpretation," *History in Africa*, 8 (1981): 183–204.

14 Thornton, "Early Kongo-Portuguese Relations."

15 João III to Afonso I, ca. 1531, *MMA* 1:526; Manuel Pacheco to João III, 28 March 1536, *MMA* 1:57–60.

16 Thornton, "African Social Formation."

17 Olifert Dapper, *Umbeständliche und Eigentliche Beschreibung von Africa* (Amsterdam, 1670), pp. 556–57. This is the German edition, much expanded, of Dapper's original description of West Africa, published in 1668.

18 Anne Wilson, "The Kongo Kingdom to the Mid-Seventeenth Century" (Ph.D. dissertation, University of London, School of Oriental and African Studies, 1977), pp. 142–45, 193–96. Wilson has changed her surname to Hilton.

19 Jan Vansina, *Kingdoms of the Savanna* (Madison, 1966), p. 154.

20 To take two excellent examples, Antonio da Serravezza was known as the "father of seven languages," for he knew both Kikongo and Kimbundu as well as five European languages. Giovanni Maria da Barletta preached in such fluent Kikongo that he was said to have reached native proficiency. Cavazzi, *Istorica descrizione*, book 7, no. 15; Luis de Mendonça wrote of da Barletta that he "preached in the language of Congo to the blacks as if he were a native of their land." APF: SOCG 651, fol. 339, de Mendonça, 18 May 1723. Paulo Generoso da Silva, the Prince of Nsoyo, wrote of this same Father da Barletta that he "worked a thousand miracles by means of our language." Da Silva to Capuchin Prefect, 28 August 1708, in Levy Maria Jordão de Paiva Manso, *História do reino de Congo (documentos)* (Lisbon, 1877), p. 348.

21 On the social background of the clerical staff, see pp. 65–67 below.

22 Biographies of various Capuchins can be found in APC Toscana, Filippo Bernardi da Firenze, "Ragguagli del Congo, cioè viaggi fatti da' missionarij . . . a' regni del Congo . . ." (1711), *passim;* and BPE, códice CXVI/2–1, Cavazzi, "Vite de frati minori cappuccini . . . morti nelle missioni d'Etiopia dall'anno 1645 fino all'anno 1677"; and Cavazzi, *Istorica descrizione, passim.*

23 Georges Balandier, *Daily Life in the Kingdom of the Kongo: Sixteenth to Eighteenth Century,* trans. Helen Weaver (London, 1965).

24 Alexander Ihle, *Das Alte Königreich Kongo* (Leipzig, 1929); Joseph van Wing, *Études Bakongo,* 2nd ed. (Brussels, 1959).

25 Balandier, *Daily Life;* W. G. L. Randles, *L'ancien royaume du Congo des origines à la fin du XIXe siècle* (Paris, 1968); Kajsa Ekholm, *Power and Prestige: The Rise and decline of the Kongo Kingdom* (Uppsala, 1972).

26 Afonso de Albuquerque Felner, *Angola* (Coimbra, 1933).
27 James Duffy, *Portuguese Africa* (Cambridge, Mass., 1959), pp. 12–16; Basil Davidson, *Black Mother: The Years of the Atlantic Slave Trade* (Boston, 1961), pp. 118–47.
28 The French translation, *L'ancien royaume du Congo* (Brussels, 1946), is much better known and more widely available.
29 Jadin has attempted a synthesis, "Aperçu de l'histoire du royaume du Congo (1482–1718)," *Bulletin du Faculté des Lettres de Strasbourg* (March, 1964).
30 Filesi's work has been concentrated in the journal *Africa (Rome)*. His attempt at a synthesis is a curious semifictional work, *San Salvador: Croniche dei rè di Congo* (Florence, 1974), which borrows heavily from Balandier for its interpretative approach. Bontinck has translated two major sources: Giovanni Francesco da Roma, *Brève relation de la fondation de la mission des Frères mineurs Capuchins . . . au royaume de Congo (1648)* (Louvain, 1964); and Lucca da Caltanisetta, *Diaire congolaise, 1690–1701* (Louvain, 1971). His other work consists of a host of short articles, published in Zairean journals for the most part, such as *Ngonge Kongo* or *Études d'histoire africaine*.
31 English edition published Madison, 1966.
32 For example, *Kingdoms*, pp. 41–45, where reconstruction of the rural economy and social structure of the Kongo is done by way of van Wing and other anthropologists.
33 Jan Vansina, "Anthropologists and the Third Dimension," *Africa*, 39 (1969): 62–68.
34 Birmingham, *Trade and Conflict, passim;* and "Central Africa from the Cameroons to the Zambezi," in *Cambridge History of Africa*, (in progress, 1975———), vols. 3 and 4.
35 Wilson, "Kongo Kingdom." Hilton's synthesis has much in common with Birmingham's contributions to the *Cambridge History of Africa*.

CHAPTER 1: THE NATURAL SETTING

1 An excellent discussion of the interaction of humans and nature can be found in Georges Bertrand's provocative introduction to the environment of rural France, "Pour une histoire écologique de la France rural," in Georges Duby and Armand Wallon, eds., *Histoire de la France rurale*, 4 vols. (Paris, 1975–76), 1:37–113.
2 L. Cahen and J. J. Snelling, *The Geochronology of Equatorial Africa* (Amsterdam, 1966), pp. 122–36, provides the background to the geological history of the Kongo region. Although the discussion is not cast in terms of current plate tectonic theory, it clearly establishes the stability of the region for many thousands of years.
3 ARSI, Lusitania, 55, fol. 116v, Matheus Cordoso, "Relação do alevamento de Dom Afonso, irmão del Rey Dom Álvaro III de Congo" (January, 1622).

4 Lorenzo da Lucca's annual letters, edited and translated by Jean Cuvelier, *Relations sur le Congo du Père Laurent de Lucques* (Brussels, 1954), pp. 259–60.

5 Physical features of eastern Kongo are clearly visible on "Carta da colonia de Angola" (Junta das Missões Geographicas e de Investigações Colonais, Lisbon, 1949), on a scale of 1:250,000.

6 Da Caltanisetta, *Diaire,* pp. 169–70.

7 Cavazzi, *Istorica descrizione,* book 1, nos. 8–10, where the river is called the Barbela.

8 ARSI, Lusitania, 56, fols. 216–24 *passim,* "Carta da missão que fizerão o P. Manuel Ribeyro . . . de anno 1672 para o de 1673" provides a detailed description of the lay of the land in this region.

9 BN Madrid, MS 3533, de Teruel, "Descripcion narrativa," fol. 148.

10 ARSI, Lusitania, 56, fols. 216–24 *passim,* Manuel Ribeyro, "Carta," on the varying degrees of sovereignty possessed by the rulers of the Ndembu region, despite formal claims of their overlords in both Angola and Kongo.

11 Da Caltanisetta, *Diaire,* p. 194.

12 Contemporary descriptions of Kimbangu when it was the seat of a royal line: da Lucca, ed. Cuvelier, *Relations,* p. 273; da Caltanisetta, *Diaire,* pp. 194–95.

13 Pedro Mendes to Governor of Angola, 2 December 1710, Paiva Manso, *História,* p. 355.

14 Matheus Cordoso, *História do reino de Congo,* ed. António Brásio (Lisbon, 1969), p. 17. On the author and date of composition of this document, see François Bontinck's introduction to the French translation, "Histoire du royaume de Congo," *Études d'histoire africaine,* 4 (1972).

15 BN Madrid, MS 3533, de Teruel, "Descripcion narrativa," fols. 103, 136.

16 Ibid., fol. 88.

17 Ibid., fol. 116

18 Da Lucca, ed. Cuvelier, *Relations,* pp. 269–76.

19 Da Caltanisetta, *Diaire,* p. 188.

20 Da Roma, *Relation,* pp. 40–41.

21 Dapper, *Beschreibung,* pp. 545–46.

22 Da Lucca, ed. Cuvelier, *Relations,* pp. 47, 186.

23 Ibid., pp. 90, 96–97, 100–101; da Roma, *Relation,* p. 27.

24 Girolamo Merolla da Sorrento, *Breve e succinta relatione del viaggio nel Congo* (Naples, 1692), pp. 310–12.

25 APC Toscana, Girolamo da Montesarchio, "Viaggio dal Gongho" (1669), fols. 27–54, describes the relative political independence of the lands along the south bank of the Zaire, especially Mpemba Kazi, whose ruler was held to be the "Mother of the King of Kongo." On the other hand, Nsevo, one of the most defensible of the river-made mountains, was firmly under royal control in Garcia II's time, and these regions never really possessed the independence of the eastern mountains or the Ndembu region of southern Kongo.

26 Da Roma, *Relation,* p. 27; Dapper, *Beschreibung,* pp. 546–47.

27 Serafino da Cortona to the Superior of Tuscany, 22 November 1651, *MMA* 9:117–18. He baptized 1,846 people on an island with an area of about 100 square kilometers. On the validity of such calculations, see Thornton, "Demography and History." I have assumed there were no baptized people on the island prior to his visit.

28 Da Lucca, ed. Cuvelier, *Relations*, p. 341. A detailed modern study of soil types in Angola is António Castanho Diniz, *As carateristicas mesologicas de Angola* (Nova Lisboa, 1973), pp. 16–101.

29 Da Lucca, ed. Cuvelier, *Relations*, p. 208; Dionigio Carli da Piacenza, "Relation nouvelle et curieuse d'un voyage au Congo, fait ès années 1666 et 1667" (sic: the voyage was made in 1667–68), in Jean-Baptiste Labat, *Relation historique de l'Ethiopie occidentale*, 5 vols. (Paris, 1732), 5:157.

30 ARSI, Lusitania, 55, fol. 116v, Cordoso, "Relação do alevamento."

31 Carli, "Relation nouvelle," in Labat, *Relation*, 5:168.

32 On erosion caused by agriculture in a nearby, similar area, see John Desmond Clark, "Observations on Forest Destruction in the Congo Basin in Prehistoric Times, with Special Reference to Northeast Angola," in *Further Paleo-Anthropological Studies in Northern Lunda* (Lisbon: Companhia de Diamantes de Angola, Publicações Cultureis, no. 78, n.p., 1968), pp. 125–47.

33 Giacinto Brugiotti da Vetralla, "Infelicità felice o vero mondo alla roversa . . . ," a lost manuscript summarized, with quotations, in Giuseppe Simonetti, "P. Giacinto Brugiotti e la sua missione al Congo," *Bolletino della Società Geografica Italiana*, 4th ser., 8 (1907): 315; Cavazzi, *Istorica descrizione*, book 1, nos. 43–45. On modern Angolan rainfall, see *O clima de Angola* (Luanda: Servicos Meteorológicos, 1955).

34 BE, MS Italicus 1380, alpha N-9-7, Monari, "Viaggio," fol. 97v (p. 186), gives the liturgical calendar observed in Nsoyo in the early years of the eighteenth century.

35 Dapper, *Beschreibung*, p. 558; da Lucca, ed. Cuvelier, *Relations*, p. 99; BE, MS Italicus 1380, alpha N-9-7, Monari, "Viaggio," fols. 76v–77 (pp. 144–46); Antonio Zucchelli da Gradisca, *Relazione del viaggio e missione di Congo nell' Etiopia inferiore occidentale* (Venice, 1712), pp. 214–19.

36 Cavazzi, *Istorica descrizione*, book 1, no. 275; MS Araldi, Cavazzi, "Missione evangelica al regno del Congo . . ." (1667), fol. 604.

37 APC Toscana, da Montesarchio, "Viaggio," fols. 42–43, 64, 90–94, and fol. 7 of the renumbered folios at the end of the manuscript.

38 Da Lucca, ed. Cuvelier, *Relations*, p. 219.

39 BN Madrid, MS 3533, de Teruel, "Descripcion narrativa," fol. 130.

40 APC Toscana, da Montesarchio, "Viaggio," fols. 45, 70; BN Madrid, MS 3533, de Teruel, "Descripcion narrativa," fol. 160 (marginal note).

41 Garcia Mendes de Castello Branco, "Relação tocante ao Reyno de Congo," 16 January 1620, *MMA* 6:437, 440.

42 Thornton, "Demography and History," p. 529 and note 116.

43 APF: SOCG 457, fols. 371–72, Andrea da Buti to Propaganda Fide, 1 July 1674; APF: SOCG 464, fol. 379, Giuseppe Maria da Busseto to Capuchin

Superior, 18 April 1674 (for the drought of 1673). APC Toscana, Bernardi, "Ragguagli," fols. 622–25 (on drought of 1691–92).

44 Thornton, "Demography and History," p. 529.

45 APC Toscana, da Montesarchio, "Viaggio," fol. 45. For a similar incident in 1700, see da Caltanisetta, *Diaire,* pp. 205–6.

46 APC Toscana, Bernardi, "Ragguagli," fols. 622–25; Merolla, *Relatione,* pp. 112–23.

47 See note 43 (above) for evidence.

48 APF: SOCG 457, fol. 347, Prince Paulo III da Silva to Giuseppi Maria da Busseto, 29 May 1674; APF: SRC Congo, 1, fol. 14–4v, report of da Busseto, 1676.

49 Serafino da Cortona to Capuchin Superior, 12 May 1653, *MMA* 11:306.

50 APC Toscana, da Montesarchio, "Viaggio," fol. 11.

51 Cavazzi, *Istorica descrizione,* book 5, nos. 23–27. Secular clergy had such faith in the efficacy of the Pope's intervention that they even credited to it a cessation of locust infestations in Kongo. Testimony of Manuel Robrerdo, MS Araldi, Cavazzi, "Missione evangelica," fols. 225–30.

52 Cavazzi, *Istorica descrizione,* book 1, no. 295.

53 Thornton, "Demography and History," pp. 518–19.

54 APC Toscana, da Montesarchio, "Viaggio," fols. 83–85.

55 APC Toscana, Bernardi, "Ragguagli," fol. 341.

56 Da Lucca, ed. Cuvelier, *Relations,* pp. 96–97.

57 Clark, "Forest Destruction," pp. 125–26.

58 Ibid., p. 125; BN Madrid, MS 3533, de Teruel, "Descripcion narrativa," fol. 137.

59 Dapper, *Beschreibung,* p. 544; BN Madrid, MS 3533, de Teruel, "Descripcion narrativa," fol. 26.

60 APC Toscana, da Montesarchio, "Viaggio," fols. 35, 117–20.

61 Giacinto Brugiotti to Superior, 20 August 1652, *MMA* 11:216–17.

62 Carli, "Relation nouvelle," in Labat, *Relation,* 5:157.

63 Dapper, *Beschreibung,* pp. 551–52, cites various wild animals that provided meat, as does Cavazzi in *Istorica descrizione,* book 1, nos. 99–153. BN Madrid, MS 3533, de Teruel, "Descripcion narrativa," fols. 90–91 shows how travellers used wild crops to survive. Also see Carli, "Relation nouvelle," in Labat, *Relation,* 5:150–55.

64 MS Araldi, Cavazzi, "Missione evangelica," fols. 584–604 *passim.*

65 BN Madrid, MS 3533, de Teruel, "Descripcion narrativa," fol. 138; APC Toscana, da Montesarchio, "Viaggio," fol. 98.

66 Cavazzi, *Istorica descrizione,* book 7, no. 19.

67 Andrea da Pavia, "Voyages apostoliques aux missions du Afrique" (ca. 1692), in Louis Jadin, "Andrea da Pavia au Congo, à Madère, à Lisbonne. Journal d'un missionaire capuchin," *BIHBR,* 41 (1970): 432.

68 Carli, "Relation nouvelle," in Labat, *Relation,* 5:142, 150, 161.

69 APC Toscana, Bernardi, "Ragguagli," fol. 675; Carli, "Relation nouvelle," in Latat, *Relation,* 5:194; Brugiotti, "Infelicità felice," cited in Simonetti, "Brugiotti," p. 379.

70 APC Toscana, da Montesarchio, "Viaggio,"fols. 99–107.
71 APF: SOCG 495, fol. 168, Paolo da Varezza (1682).

CHAPTER 2: THE SOCIAL ENVIRONMENT OF KONGO

1 Cadornega, *História*, 3:193–94 provides a listing of various ethnic and linguistic groups in Kongo in mid-century, before the civil wars cut the Portuguese traders of Luanda off from markets in Kongo. On the linguistic divisions within Kikongo visible in various linguistic exercises of the Capuchins, see François Bontinck, "Les premiers travaux linguistiques kikongo des missionaries Capuchins," *Ngonge Kongo*, 15 (1963).

2 APF: SOCG 576, fol. 335v, Bernardo da Gallo, "Conto delle villacazione missionale, ò sia relazione delle Miss^ini di Congo et Angola dovè missionò ij anni"(12 December 1712).

3 Cadornega, *História*, 3:188.

4 Cordoso, *História*, ed. Brásio pp. 43–44; Cavazzi, *Istorica descrizione*, book 2, nos. 84–90. On possible authorities for Cavazzi's traditions, see John Thornton, "New Light on Cavazzi's Seventeenth Century Description of Kongo,"*History in Africa*, 6 (1979):259.

5 Cadornega, *História*, 3:193. On the importance of "fidalgos moxicongos" in eastern Kongo, where they controlled important positions but were ethnically different, see ARSI, Lusitania, 55, fol. 117, Cordoso, "Relação do alevamento."

6 Wyatt MacGaffey, "Oral Tradition in Central Africa,"*International Journal of African Historical Studies*, 7 (1974): 422–25; Ekholm, *Power and Prestige*, p. 157; Laurent Monnier, "Note sur les structures politiques de l'ancien royaume de Kongo avant l'arrivée des portugais," *Génève-Afrique*, 5 (1966): 26–27.

7 APF: SOCG 576, fol. 335v, da Gallo, "Conto." Louis Jadin's rendition of this passage into French in his edition of this document in "Le Congo et la secte des Antoniens . . . ," *BIHBR*, 33 (1961): 481, is incorrect, as he has mistranscribed "Abhata"as "Akkata"and "Abumba"as "Alumbu."

8 BN Centrale, Rome, Fundo Minori 1896, MS Varia 274, "Vocabularium Latinum, Hispanicum et Congoense, ad usum missionariorum transmit orum ad Regni Congo missiones." Teobaldo Filesi has established the original author of this dictionary (the extant copy is that made by Joris van Gheel) as Bonaventura da Sardegna in collaboration with the Afro-Portuguese canon Manuel Roboredo and assisted by José de Pernambuco and Francisco de Veas. See Teobaldo Filesi and I. Villapardiena, *La 'Missio Antiqua' dei Cappuccini nel Congo (1645–1835)* (Rome, 1978), pp. 182–83. It was completed in mid-1648. On the use of the root *-bhata* as "barbarian,"see fol. 15, where "barbarus"is *múbhata*, "barbarè"is *yaúbhata*, and "barbaries"is *ubhata*.

9 This translation was suggested to me by Wyatt MacGaffey in a personal communication, 5 December 1978.

10 Da Roma, *Relation*, p. 115.
11 This conception of the economics of "rent" is taken from Karl Marx, *Capital*, 3 vols. (1867; New York, 1967), 3:790–803. Marx's definition of rent as a form of surplus production includes the taxation of producers by the state, as in examples he chooses from Asia. A useful and interesting modern commentary on this conception in Marx is found in Barry Hindess and Paul Hirst, *Pre-Capitalist Modes of Production* (London, 1975), pp. 221–55.
12 Carli, "Relation nouvelle," in Labat, *Relation*, 5:168; Dionigio Carli da Piacenza, *Il Moro trasportado nell'inclita città di Venezia* (Bassano, 1687), p. 67. This second work of Carli's, not nearly as well known as the first one, describes the same missionary voyage (of 1667–68), often in the same words. However, it contains considerable new information, presumably from the same notes or diary.
13 APF: SOCG 249, fol. 337, Buenaventura de Cerolla, "Relasion de los ritos gentilicos, ceremonias diabolicas y supersticiones destos infelicissimos Reynos de Congo" (1653).
14 For example, tolls, extracted by the *nkuluntu* from passing travellers: Cadornega, *História*, 1:217, and 3:274.
15 Wilson, "Kongo Kingdom," p. 23.
16 Carli, "Relation nouvelle," in Labat, *Relation*, 5:131–33; and Carli *Moro*, pp. 43–45, based on his experience in Mbamba province in 1667, give us our best eyewitness account of life in rural villages. This description is part of the passages dealing with a larger village, the seat of a minor marquis, whom Carli, however, calls an *nkuluntu* ("Macolonte"). It is, however, as much an ideal description of many rural villages which Carli and his travelling companion, Michelangelo Guattini da Reggio, visited during their stay in Africa as of any particular village.
17 The question of the role of elders and juniors in African societies is currently much discussed in literature, especially (but not entirely) the Marxist anthropology of the last twenty years, beginning with Claude Meillassoux's "The 'Economy' in Agricultural Self-Sustaining Societies: A Preliminary Analysis," in David Seddon, ed., *Relations of Production: Marxist Approaches to Economic Anthropology* (London, 1978), pp. 127–58 (first published in French in 1960); criticized and expanded by Emmanuel Terray, "Historical Materialism and Segmentary and Lineage-Based Societies," in his *Marxism and 'Primitive' Societies* (New York–London, 1972) and Pierre-Phillipe Rey, *Colonialisme, néo-colonialisme, et transition au capitalisme* (Paris, 1971), pp,. 32–71. Wyatt MacGaffey has applied some of those concepts to nineteenth-century Kongo society, in "The Economic and Social Dimensions of Kongo Slavery (Zaire)," in Suzanne Meiers and Igor Kopytoff, eds., *Slavery in Africa: Historical and Anthropological Perspectives* (Madison, 1977), pp. 235–57. Several attempts have been made to extend this analysis more generally to past society in Kongo, such as Ekholm, *Power and Prestige*, pp. 65–145, or Monnier, "Structures politiques," but these generally use modern anthropological materials instead of historical material as evidence.

18 Carli, "Relation nouvelle," in Labat, *Relation*, 5:131–33; and Carli, *Moro*, pp. 43–45.

19 Thornton, "Demography and History," *passim*.

20 Settlement inventories made by Antonio Maria da Firenze and Giuseppe Monari da Modena at the end of the seventeenth century list some 134 settlements within the region called "Mbanza Nsoyo." Of these, the ruler's place was only somewhat larger that the others. An earlier Dutch source of the 1640s confirms this notion. Thornton, "Demography and History," pp. 518, 520.

21 We lack a good physical description of São Salvador. See Dapper, *Beschreibung*, pp. 545–46, and da Roma, *Relation*, pp. 40–41 for the best ones. On the plank houses of Mbanza Nsoyo, see da Lucca, ed. Cuvelier, *Relations*, p. 55.

22 Cordoso, *História*, ed. Brásio, pp. 43–47; Cavazzi, *Istorica descrizione*, book 2, no. 87. On the mechanisms of the slave trade in the sixteenth century, see Afonso I to Manuel I, 5 October 1514, *MMA* 1:314.

23 Brugiotti, "Infelicità felice," cited in Simonetti, "Brugiotti," p. 374.

24 APF: SOCG 250, fol. 28, "Delli schiavi che si cõprano e vendero nel Regno di Congo" (ca. 1659).

25 Wilson, "Kongo Kingdom," pp. 173–74, on various means used to obtain slaves.

26 APF: SOCG 495, fol. 182v, Giuseppe Maria da Busseto to Propaganda Fide, 13 February 1685.

27 Da Pavia, "Voyages apostoliques," p. 450.

28 Álvaro II to Pope Paulo V, 13 February 1613, *MMA* 6:129.

29 Thornton, "Demography and History," pp. 520–21, 523–24. Thirty-five kilometers represents just about the distance that a loaded porter could travel in a single day, at least in the nineteenth century (Jan Vansina, personal communication).

30 An excellent discussion of slavery as an economic institution (that is, as a form of surplus production), as opposed to a legal and social institution, is in Hindess and Hirst, *Modes of Production*, pp. 109–76.

31 Merolla, *Relatione*, pp. 155–56.

32 Ibid., p. 161.

33 Da Lucca, ed. Cuvelier, *Relations*, p. 159.

34 Pedro II to Juan Bautista Vives, 23 June 1622, *MMA* 7:36.

35 For the full semantics of the word in Kikongo: François Bontinck, "Les Quimbares: Note sémantique," *Africa (Rome)* 31 (1976): 47–48.

36 See Jean Cuvelier's note on the term in his French translation of this same document, Cuvelier and Jadin, *L'ancien Congo*, p. 426, note 1.

37 Da Roma, *Relation*, p. 115.

38 Cavazzi, *Istorica descrizione*, book 3, no. 47 on the market, Polangola.

39 See the studies in Claude Meillassoux, ed., *Esclavage en Afrique précoloniale* (Paris, 1975); and Meiers and Kopytoff, *Slavery*.

40 Matheus Cordoso, *Doutrina Christãa* (Lisbon, 1624), modern edition edited and translated by François Bontinck and D. Ndembe Nsasi, *Le caté-*

chisme kikongo du 1624: Réédition critique (Brussels, 1978), pp. 58–59. Those who are not Christian remain "escravo do demonio" (slave of the devil), *mubica ancariampemba*. Also see BN Centrale, Rome, Fundo Minori 1896, MS Varia 274, "Vocabularium," fols. 9v, 92v, where the Latin *servus* and *ancilla* (male and female slave) are rendered as *mubica*.

41 BN Centrale, Rome, Fundo Minori 1896, MS 274, "Vocabularium," fols. 9v, 92v, where *muai* is given as a second definition of *servus* and *ancilla*. On the derivation of the term (also taken from the dictionary of 1648), see Wilson, "Kongo Kingdom," p. 55.

42 For a fully documented discussion of the *nleke* in the missionary economy, see Hildebrand de Hooglede, *Le martyr Georges de Gheel et les debuts de la mission de Congo (1645–52)* (Antwerp, 1940), pp. 200–204. For the use of the term *nleke* as child, see its use in Cordoso, *Doutrina*, ed. Bontinck and Nsasi, *passim*.

43 Cavazzi, *Istorica descrizione*, book 5, no. 58; da Roma, *Relation*, p. 119.

44 APF: SOCG 250, fol. 28, "Schiavi."

45 Carli's village is perhaps atypical (see note 16, above), since it was larger than normal, but the model suggests at least one household for the *nkuluntu* and one for the *kitomi*, plus three others for the "assistants" of the *nkuluntu*. It is also probable that each of these households included more than one adult woman as wives of the head of the household, perhaps as many as three or four. Taking children into account, fifteen to twenty consumers of surplus for every hundred people seems reasonable.

46 Angel de Valencia, "Relacion," 8 June 1645, *MMA* 9:278; Cavazzi, *Istorica descrizione*, book 1, no. 51.

47 Cavazzi, *Istorica descrizione*, book 1, no. 51.

48 Filippo Pigafetta, *Relatione del Regno di Congo et delle circonvince contrade tratta dalli scritti e ragionamenti di Oduarte Lopez Portoghese* (Rome, 1591), p. 40.

49 Da Lucca, ed. Cuvelier, *Relations*, p. 90; F. Capelle to J.-M. de Nassau, March 1642, in Jadin, "Rivaltés," p. 224.

50 On the European analogy: Fernand Braudel, *Capitalism and Material Life, 1400–1800*, trans. Miriam Koch (New York, 1973), pp. 92–95.

51 Barry Hindess and Paul Hirst, in *Mode of Production and Social Formation* (Atlantic Highlands, N.J., 1977), pp. 67–72, have argued that the degree to which nonproducers involve themselves, as managers or planners, in the process of production is crucial to economic relations. The two types of rent here can be distinguished by the degree of involvement of the nonlaboring class in the technical operations of production.

52 Dapper, *Beschreibung*, p. 558; "Relação da costa da Guiné" (ca. 1607), *MMA* 5:386.

53 The existence of a single, dominant class which benefits from varying productive enterprises and conditions the integration of all the diverse means of surplus creation into one economic system under their control fits the definition of a social formation given by Hindess and Hirst, *Social Formation*, pp. 55–62.

54 For example, Pero Saldanha, writing in 1611, explains how money from Kongo sources could be used to buy slaves in the Mpumbu region, in *MMA* 6:52–54, 106–7. Also see Wilson, "Kongo Kingdom," pp. 126–30, on *nzimbu* in the east. This book presents a different interpretation of the facts presented by Hilton, however.

55 "Description de Congo," extracts published in French translation in Cuvelier and Jadin, *L'ancien Congo*, p. 131. The manuscript was written after 1628 and is in one hand. The first part of the text is clearly based on second-hand sources, either from the Carmelite mission of 1583–86 or Pigafetta's book. However, there is an addition to this, with new material not drawn from any other source and including information on the economic and social structure of Kongo, which postdates 1608. It was probably added to the first account by the author of the entire manuscript as he set it to writing, so its information probably dates from the period around 1625–30. Cuvelier suggests, with good reason, that the author of the manuscript was either Juan Bautista Vives or one of his secretaries (pp. 8–9). As Vives was Kongo's permanent representative in Rome, he would have had access to considerable information about Kongo, which he probably kept as up-to-date as possible.

56 Da Pavia, "Voyages apostoliques," p. 450.

57 Dapper, *Beschreibung*, p. 558. Dapper gives the king's income in terms of a European money, as "16 less than 400 Reichsthaler" (384 Reichsthaler). His informants, probably Dutch representatives of the West India Company visiting São Salvador after the fall of Luanda in 1641, were simply converting a sum stated in *nzimbu* into Portuguese *reis*, for which there was a regular custom of conversion. According to Réné Sedilliot, *Toutes les monnaies du monde* (Paris, 1955), p. 437, one Reichsthaler in 1641 was equal to 103.5 grams of silver, while one *rei*, according to Frédéric Mauro, *Le Portugal et l'Atlantique au 17e siècle* (Paris, 1960), p. 421 (4,000 *reis* per *mark* of silver), was equal to .0058 grams of silver. Thus, 384 Reichsthaler were equal to seven million *reis*, and since the *rei*, in the 1640s, was held to be more or less equal to twenty *nzimbu* (according to Cuvelier, *L'ancien Congo*, p. 309), this sum was equal to 140 million *nzimbu*, which if placed in standard bags, called *kofu*, of 20,000 *nzimbu* each, would equal 7,000 *kofu*.

58 Kongo's total income, stated in silver at the exchange rate noted above, would come to four metric tons of silver. For comparison, see the state incomes of European countries calculated by Fernand Braudel, in *The Mediterranean and the Mediterranean World in the Age of Phillip II*, trans. Siân Reynolds, 2 vols. (New York, 1972), 2:680–86.

59 Dapper, *Beschreibung*, p. 558; Cavazzi, *Istorica descrizione*, book 2, no. 75. On the *mani mbembo*, see Cuvelier and Jadin, *L'ancien Congo*, p. 426, note 2.

60 Cavazzi, *Istorica descrizione*, book 2, no. 75.

61 BN Madrid, MS 3533, de Teruel, "Descripcion narrativa," fols. 125–26; "Description," in Cuvelier and Jadin, *L'ancien Congo*, p. 131.

62 Dapper, *Beschreibung*, p. 536.

63 Cadornega, *História*, 2:268.

64 Merolla, *Relatione*, p. 138; BE, MS Italicus 1380, alpha N-9-7, Monari, "Viaggio," fol. 112 (p. 215); da Pavia, "Voyages apostoliques," p. 434.

65 The sources in note 64, above, give its level, stated sometimes in papal *scudi* and other times in *mabongo*, the cloth money of Kongo. A conversion for the relevant time period (late seventeenth century) is possible, from Merolla, *Relatione*, p. 235, which gives the value of one *scudo* as fifteen *mabongo*. Merolla put average bridewealth at 135 *mabongo*, Monari at 120, and da Pavia at eighty. Of course, the amount one would have to pay fluctuated widely.

66 Wilson, "Kongo Kingdom," *passim* gives substantial data on Kongo's trade with the east; see especially pp. 126–30.

67 A list of typical trade items available through Dutch sources is given in Capelle, March, 1642, in Jadin, "Rivaltés," p. 228.

68 Cavazzi, *Istorica descrizione*, book 1, no. 000. Many writers, most recently Ekholm (*Power and Prestige*, pp. 117–30) and Wilson ("Kongo Kingdom," *passim*), have emphasized the role of foreign trade and redistribution by the rulers as fundamental both to Kongo's strength, and, as European merchants circumvented royal control of trade in foreign goods, to its weakness and decline. In this book, however, trade and redistribution are seen as much less important than rent, and with it local productive activities, in Kongo's centralization.

69 Da Roma, *Relation*, p. 115; "Description" (ca. 1625–30), in Cuvelier and Jadin, *L'ancien Congo*, p. 135.

70 BN Madrid, MS 3533, de Teruel, "Descripcion narrativa," fols. 125–26. Cadornega, *História*, 3:195 mentions salaries paid to Portuguese living in Kongo (as a "moradia"). They were paid in *mpusu* (a larger unit of the *lubongo*, monetary cloth), which would permit them to trade in Portuguese Angola, where such cloth also circulated as money, and where it could be freely converted to *nzimbu* as well.

71 De Hoogleede, *Martyr*, pp. 307–9, on the Dutch at São Salvador and Ngongo Mbata; AHU: PA, Angola, Caixa 4, Consulta of 3 August 1656, with enclosed letter of Sousa Chicorro to Conselho Ultramarino, 26 January 1655.

72 APF: SOCG 249, fol. 343, Antonio da Monteprandone to Propaganda Fide, ca. 1656; AHU: PA, Angola, Caixa 4, Consulta of 19 January 1656.

73 De Hoogleede, *Martyr*, pp. 307–8, on Joris van Gheel's conversion of Dutch "heretics"; APF: SOCG 249, fol. 343, da Monteprandone, ca. 1656, on the conversion of "36 houses" of Vili at São Salvador.

74 AHU: PA, Angola, Caixa 4, Consulta of 25 February 1656, enclosure of Sousa Chicorro, 26 January 1655.

75 See pp. 39–42, below.

CHAPTER 3: VILLAGES AND PRODUCTION IN KONGO

1 Antonio Maria da Firenze's enumeration of settlements of the rural districts east of Mbanza Nsoyo forms the basis for these assertions. APF: SRC,

Congo, 3, fols. 127–7v, "Nota delle missione che jo Fr. Antonio Maria da Fiorenza . . . nel Contea di Sogno . . . 1704." Allowing 225 people per *lubata* and 1,000 per *mbanza*, the ratio of *mbanza* to *lubata* gives us between 67 and 77 percent of the rural residents as living in *lubata*. Assuming 75,000 as the combined population of São Salvador and Mbanza Nsoyo (the two major town centers of 1650) and the population of the country as 500,000, then 80 percent of the population lived in rural areas. For the demographic basis for these estimates, see Thornton, "Demography and History," pp. 518–22.

2 Thornton, "Demography and History," p. 518; Cavazzi, *Istorica descrizione*, book 1, no. 154.

3 Dionigio Carli, "Relation nouvelle," in Labat, *Relation*, 5:131, 139, 155; da Lucca, ed. Cuvelier, *Relations*, p. 169. For northern Nsoyo, with a more spread-out pattern, see BN Madrid, MS 3533, de Teruel, "Descripcion narrativa," fol. 27; for the center of east, Olifert Dapper, *Beschreibung*, p. 555.

4 Da Roma, *Relation*, pp. 112–14; Carli, *Moro*, p. 43.

5 See the various definitions of "evata" in C. Penders and J. van Wing, eds. and trans., *Le plus ancien dictionnaire Bantu* (Louvain, 1928), p. 29. This dictionary is a translated, reorganized, and retranscribed version of BN Centrale, Rome, Fundo Minori 1896, MS Varia 274, "Vocabularium." The original text takes Latin words as its base and provides Kikongo equivalents (and occasionally Spanish reglosses where Latin is inadequate or ambiguous), while the edition of Penders and van Wing takes the Kikongo words as the base and provides French and Flemish equivalents, drawn from the Latin text. Thus it is much easier to consult Penders and van Wing to get all Latin terms which once might have been rendered into the same Kikongo term. Obviously, such an approach must be used with caution.

6 Thornton, "Demography and History," p. 518.

7 Carli, "Relation nouvelle," in Labat, *Relation*, 5:168; Carli, *Moro*, p. 67.

8 There is insufficient data to allow any further speculation on questions concerning household size, composition, or cycles, although such questions raised by historians of the family, especially in Europe, make it clear that many complexities can occur in peasant settings.

9 Da Lucca, ed. Cuvelier, *Relations*, p. 76, on the evening meal. Also Brugiotti, "Infelicità felice," in Simonetti, "Brugiotti," p. 316.

10 Da Lucca, ed. Cuvelier, *Relations*, p. 78.

11 Merolla, *Relatione*, p. 140.

12 Brugiotti, "Infelicità felice," in Simonetti, "Brugiotti," p. 316; da Lucca, ed. Cuvelier, *Relations*, p. 76; Serafino da Cortona to Prefect of Tuscany, 20 March 1648, *MMA* 10:98; Merolla, *Relatione*, pp. 140–41.

13 On *nfundi* in general: da Roma, *Relation*, p. 90; Cavazzi, *Istorica descrizione*, book 1, no. 286; da Lucca, ed. Cuvelier, *Relations*, pp. 76–77; Merolla, *Relatione*, p. 140. On *nfundi* as "our daily bread" in the Lord's prayer, see Cordoso, *Doutrina*, ed. Bontinck and Nsasi, pp. 80–81: *enfundi etu*

yaquilumbuyaquilumbu (*nfundi etu ya kilumbu ya kilumbu*) is translated as *o nosso pão de cada dia* (our daily bread). Also BN Centrale, Rome, Fundo Minori 1896, MS Varia 274, "Vocabularium," fol. 71v.

14 Da Roma, *Relation*, p. 114; da Lucca, ed. Cuvelier, *Relations*, pp. 76–78; Cavazzi, *Istorica descrizione*, book 1, no. 287.

15 Between them, Cavazzi and Monari list more than thirty useful varieties of trees and their products. Included were fruit and wine, bark cloth, medicine, poison, and even the incense used by priests in ecclesiastical functions. Cavazzi, *Istorica descrizione*, book 1, nos. 54–84; BE, MS Italicus 1380, alpha N-9-7, Monari, "Viaggio," fols. 197–83v (pp. 349–58); Merolla, *Relatione*, pp. 184–89.

16 Cavazzi, *Istorica descrizione*, book 1, no. 52, for one such comment among many. The relative importance of men's and women's work in societies both past and present has sparked considerable anthropological writing: Ester Boserup, *Women's Role in Economic Development* (London, 1970); and various discussions arising out of the feminist movement on women's work in some societies: Special Woman's issue in *Critique of Anthropology*, 3 (1977); and Rayna Reita, ed., *Towards an Anthropology of Women* (New York, 1975).

17 These calculations, and their results, are obviously not based on firm data, and must be considered as speculation. It should be noted, however, that the gradual intrusion of foreign manufactured products and the labor policies of the colonial economies have undermined traditional men's work far more than women's work (e.g., ironwork, cloth production, and aboriculture in general). As a result, modern calculations would underestimate the contributions of men.

18 Merolla, *Relatione*, p. 141. The children, at least until adolescence, fell into the women's world. On the notion of separation of the two worlds of men and women in African and other societies, see Susan Carol Rogers, "Woman's Place: A Critical Review of Anthropological Theory," *Comparative Studies in Society and History*, 20 (1978): 123–62.

19 Manuel Bautista, "Relação dos costumes, Ritos e usos do R^no do Congo, que o Bp̄o deu a V Mg^da," 7 September 1619, *MMA* 6:375; Dapper, *Beschreibung*, p. 555.

20 See chapter 2, note 17, above.

21 On bridewealth see chapter 2, note 65, above.

22 Most sources speak of the payment as being in money, and hence without special "prestige goods"—for example, Merolla, *Relatione*, p. 138; or BE, MS Italicus 1380, alpha N-9-7, Monari, "Viaggio," fol. 112 (p. 215). Da Pavia, "Voyages apostoliques," p. 434 does mention special hoes used only for the purpose of bridewealth, suggesting that perhaps an earlier system of special bride goods was surviving into the seventeenth century.

23 Da Lucca, ed. Cuvelier, *Relations*, p. 136. Balandier, *Daily Life*, p. 173, in quoting this passage, notes that the statement of da Lucca that the prospective bridegroom approaches the girl's father is an error, and that it was the

maternal uncle who was approached. Balandier's criticism is not itself un-
assailable, however; owing to the considerable flexibility of the lineage, any
one of several males might have been approached, including the father.
Wyatt MacGaffey in particular has been critical of anthropologists who, in
studying Kongo, have created hard and fast rules about behavior based on
ideal models about what ought to be done: *Custom and Government in the
Lower Congo* (Berkeley and Los Angeles, 1970).

24 Da Lucca, ed. Cuvelier, *Relations,* pp. 136–38 is one of many missionary
accounts of the institution of marriage in Kongo that, in spite of their mainly
denunciatory intention, contain much useful descriptive information.

25 Today the word *dikanda* represents a lineage, which is not exogamous and
groups households in one or several villages. MacGaffey, *Custom and Government,* p. 18. In the seventeenth century the word *dikanda* translated
the Latin *familia,* which has a much more extended usage than its modern
cognates in European languages (BN Centrale, Rome, Fundo Minori 1896,
MS Varia 274, "Vocabularium," fol. 36v), while *domus,* which in Latin can
mean either a physical structure ("house") or a social unit, was rendered as
nzo (ibid., fol. 32), which is not surprising since *nzo* is both a social and
physical item in modern Kikongo (MacGaffey, *Custom and Government,*
pp. 18–21). MacGaffey notes that the term *ekanda* today is used for two
levels of social organization, but this confusion might result from the historical circumstance (pp. 118–19, below) of noble lineages moving into the
rural areas. On *dikanda* as *republic,* see Cordoso, *Doutrina,* ed. Bontinck
and Nsasi, pp. 140–41, where the Fourth Commandment (Honor thy father
and thy mother) is extended to include *nossos prelados e aos que governão
a Republica* (our prelates and those who govern the republic), which comes
out in Kikongo as *Aculuntuêtu anganga yoâna aludica edicanda. Dicanda*
here translates as *republic,* but in a familial context.

26 Joris van Gheel's travels in eastern Kongo in 1652, and their reconstruction
by Hildebrand de Hoogleede, show the overall stability of Kongo's lower
district structure, even if the villages can no longer be located. "Oud plaatsnamen in Kongo," *Kongo-Overzee,* 4 (1938): 105–26; *Martyr,* pp. 294–311.

27 BE, MS Italicus 1380, alpha N-9-7, Monari, "Viaggio," fols. 97–98v (pp.
186–88); and APF: SRC, Congo, 3, fol. 127, Antonio Maria da Firenze,
1704, both provide lists of villages arranged into districts. Only by examining a map and seeing how closely packed the districts are is it possible to
distinguish the sprawling group of villages in rural areas from the districts
around the *mbanza.*

28 See chapter 2, note 17, above. The *kitomi* also seems to have obtained a
share, either directly, from gifts of villagers, or (as one source suggests) as a
portion given him by the *nkuluntu.* APF: SOCG 249, fol. 337, de Cerolla,
"Relasion de los ritos." The *kitomi* does not seem to have been related to
the *nkuluntu,* since they did not legally marry (and hence have legal off-
spring), and were recruited by some other system, which is not stated in
the sources. Hilton quotes sources suggesting a trusted disciple succeeded
him, or that the position was hereditary. Wilson, "Kongo Kingdom," p. 25.

29 The question of the right of conquest in Kongo's ideology is discussed at greater length in chapter 5, below.

30 On noble households and their pattern of distribution, see chapter 4, below.

31 Dapper, *Beschreibung*, p. 556 (with markets on a seven-day cycle: a variant or simply an error?); da Caltanisetta, *Diaire*, p. 100; Merolla, *Relazione*, p. 141. Merolla says only women went to market; da Caltanisetta says both sexes went. Regional variation? (Merolla was in Nsoyo, da Caltanisetta in Nsundi.) Cyclical market weeks are common in Africa: Paul Bohannan and George Dalton, eds., *Markets in Africa* (New York, 1962).

32 Da Caltanisetta, *Diaire*, pp. 110, 112, 114.

33 Da Caltanisetta was the first priest that anyone there could remember visiting the region, although Girolamo da Montesarchio had crossed the area about a half-century earlier. I have assumed that there were no baptized people in the area, save for the inhabitants of the *mbanza*, and hence that his figures for baptisms performed at the markets are a census of all these who were attending. These figures vary, but the variation is probably the result of the resistance to baptism he says he met in some of the markets. I have taken his high figure, 200, to be typical; if the figures are in error, they err on the low side.

34 Binza seems to have been a district about thirty kilometers on a side, or about 1,000 square kilometers in all, which, if the estimate of average population densities for this area of four per square kilometer ("Demography and History," p. 525) is correct, would have a population of some 4,000 people. Da Caltanisetta mentions baptizing adults, but if there were many children present, there may have been fewer households represented than this analysis suggests.

35 Da Caltanisetta, *Diaire*, p. 100.

36 Cadornega, *História*, 3:195–96; Cordoso, *História*, ed. Brásio, p. 24; Dapper, *Beschreibung*, p. 558.

37 BN Centrale, Rome, Fundo Minori 1896, MS Varia 274, "Vocabularium," fol. 139v, as interpreted by de Hoogleede, *Martyr*, p. 388. Van Gheel probably figured the value of his money in chickens, and likewise collected iron bars, probably for use in trade.

38 A good summary of exchange rates between *nzimbu* and European money is found in Cuvelier and Jadin, *L'ancien Congo*, pp. 308–11. The big fall occurred in the late sixteenth century, between 1540 and 1575. Local production of *nzimbu* was estimated by Domingos Abreu e Brito in 1592, probably based on records kept on Luanda Island by the clerk in the service of the King of Kongo, as about 80,000 *kofu* per annum, roughly the same as a similar estimate reported by Dapper, *Beschreibung*, p. 596 (assuming the value reported by Dapper, of 22,000 Reichsthaler, is in fact a misprint for 2,200 Reichsthaler—otherwise production had increased tenfold since 1575). The weight of this, at thirty kilograms per *kofu*, would be 2,400 metric tons, far more than European shipping could carry.

39 Wilson, "Kongo Kingdom," pp. 130–31, 203–5, *passim*, presents the most clearly stated case that Portuguese meddling with Kongo's money supply

helped to bring the kingdom down. Although the seizure of Luanda after 1649 might have deprived Kongo's upper classes of revenue, only by increasing production could they cause inflation—had they decreased it, Kongo's money supply (and prices) would have declined.

40 Dapper, *Beschreibung*, p. 548; Cavazzi, *Istorica descrizione*, book 1, nos. 5–6; da Lucca, ed. Cuvelier, *Relations*, p. 171.

41 Da Caltanisetta, *Diaire*, pp. 50–51, 70; Cavazzi, *Istorica descrizione*, book 1, no. 8; Carli, "Relation nouvelle," in Labat, *Relation*, 5:175; Capelle to Nassau, 1642, in Jadin, "Rivaltés," p. 226; Dapper, *Beschreibung*, p. 547. The antiquity of ironworking in eastern Kongo is attested to by the excavations of several Belgian archaeologists in what was once Nsundi province: M. Baequart, "Foulles à Thysville du Musée royale du Congo belge en 1938," *Actes du Ve Congrès Panafricain de Préhistoire et de l'étude du Quaternaire* (Brussels: Mémoires du Musée royale de l'Afrique Centrale, vol. 40, 1962), pp. 468–69.

42 Cavazzi, *Istorica descrizione*, book 1, no. 53; da Roma, *Relation*, p. 93; Capelle to de Nassau, 1642, in Jadin, "Rivaltés," p. 227.

43 Capelle to Nassau, 1642, in Jadin, "Rivaltés" p. 227. Jan Vansina, in a personal communication to me, suggested the possibility of *mboma* being made from sugarcane.

44 James Barbot and John Casseneuve, "Abstract of a Voyage to the Kongo River and Kabinda in 1700," in Thomas Astley, *A New General Collection of Voyages and Travels . . .* (London, 1747), 3:208–9.

45 Ibid., 3:208.

46 Carli, "Relation nouvelle," in Labat, *Relation*, 5:175; Carli, *Moro*, p. 68.

47 John Thornton, "An Eighteenth Century Baptismal Register and the Demographic History of Manguenzo," in Christopher Fyfe and David McMaster, eds., *African Historical Demography* (Edinburgh, 1977), pp. 411–12. This somewhat late (1774–75) document represents monogamy as the prevalent household form, and leads us to suspect that political leaders tended to have plural marriages. That must remain a suspicion only, since information covering the entire population is not available; but it is at any rate clear that some men were able, while still young, to take several wives.

48 Thornton, "Baptismal Register," pp. 411, 415, and note 25: the only man to have four wives in this eighteenth-century Nsoyo community was Salvador Vemba, who was "dominus loci"(*nkuluntu*) of Ganza Village.

49 Cavazzi, *Istorica descrizione*, book 1, no. 338; da Lucca, ed. Cuvelier, *Relations*, p. 140; BE, MS Italicus 1380, alpha N-9-7, Monari, "Viaggio," fol. 128 (p. 247).

50 Bautista, "Relação," *MMA* 6:375, for one of many such complaints.

51 BN Madrid, MS 3533, de Teruel, "Descripcion narrativa," fol. 79.

52 Da Caltanisetta, *Diaire*, p. 75. Also see *ibid.*, p. 24; and APC Toscana, da Montesarchio, "Viaggio," fol. 28.

53 BN Madrid, MS 3533, de Teruel, "Descripcion narrativa," fol. 80. Fidalgos, he noted, had up to thirty wives, but in the villages it was, at most, "2, 4 or 6."

54 Gianuario da Nola to Giovanni Battista da Napoli, 16 June 1645, *MMA* 9:306.

55 Carli, "Relation nouvelle," in Labat, *Relation*, 5:131–32, 155.

56 Cavazzi, *Istorica descrizione*, book 1, nos. 260–62; Brugiotti, "Infelicità felice," in Simonetti, "Brugiotti," p. 318; da Roma, *Relation*, p. 107; Merolla, *Relatione*, p. 170; da Lucca, ed. Cuvelier, *Relations*, pp. 78–79.

57 Carli, "Relation nouvelle," in Labat, *Relation*, 5:187.

58 Cavazzi, *Istorica descrizione*, book 1, nos. 275–76. A more favorable report is in da Roma, *Relation*, p. 114, BE, MS Italicus 1380, alpha N-9-7, Monari, "Viaggio," fol. 179v (p. 349). For detail on furnishings, see da Caltanisetta, *Diaire*, pp. 79–80.

59 On food crops: Cavazzi, *Istorica bescrizione*, book 1, no. 51; Merolla, *Relatione*, pp. 181–83; BE, MS Italicus 1380, alpha N-9-7, Monari, "Viaggio," fols. 184–4v (pp. 359–60); da Roma, *Relation*, pp. 95–96. Meat: Carli, "Relation nouvelle," in Labat, *Relation*, 5:152, da Roma, *Relation*, p. 114; Cavazzi, *Istorica descrizione*, book 1, no. 287 (small wild game) and nos. 99–105 (various wild game); also for wild game, Dapper, *Beschreibung*, pp. 551–52. Fish: Dapper, *Beschreibung*, p. 552; da Roma, *Relation*, p. 102; da Caltanisetta, *Diaire*, p. 70. A useful discussion of peasant nutrition and the ill effects of overspecialization on it is found in Maurice Aymard, "Pour une histoire de l'alimentation: Quelques remarques de method," *Annales: Économies, Sociétés, Civilisations*, 25 (1975): 431–34.

60 Thornton, "Demography and History," pp. 517–19; and "Baptismal Register," pp. 410–11. On the significance of infant mortality rates in assessments of nutrition, see Aymard, "Alimentation," p. 442.

61 Cavazzi, *Istorica descrizione*, book 1, nos. 50–52; da Roma, *Relation*, p. 88; and APF: SOCG 250, Giacinto Brugiotti da Vetralla, "Alcuni appuntamenti circa la missione del Congo" (ca. 1659), among others.

62 Eric Wolf, *Peasants* (Englewood Cliffs, N.J., 1966), pp. 18–59.

63 Da Roma, *Relation*, p. 88; Merolla, *Relatione*, p. 140; da Caltanisetta, *Diaire*, pp. 41–42.

64 No seventeenth-century source provides data on long-term use of the soil, but the characteristics of central African agriculture today may be of some guidance. Marvin Miracle, *Agriculture in the Congo Basin: Tradition and Change in African Rural Economics* (Madison, 1966).

65 Da Roma, *Relation*, p. 89—an assertion repeated in most Capuchin desciptions of Kongo agriculture. The claim that there were abundant yields in Kongo must be considered in the context of agriculture of the missionaries' home countries at the time, of course, and not by the standards of modern Europe. Italy was not a particularly productive country, as demonstrated in Aldo de Maddalena, "Il mondo rurale italiano nel cinque e nel seicento," *Rivista storica italiana*, 76 (1964): 378–80.

66 Carli, *Moro*, p. 78.

67 Da Roma, *Relation*, pp. 88–89; Carli, *Moro*, pp. 60, 64; Cavazzi, *Istorica descrizione*, book 1, no. 52. Luca da Caltanisetta often had to suspend missionary activities in the last month of the dry season due to "famine,"

possibly as a result of the old crop running out before the new harvest was taken in. Da Caltanisetta, *Diaire*, pp. 56–57, 76, 204.

68 Carli, "Relation nouvelle," in Labat, *Relation*, 5:167; Carli, *Moro*, p. 67.

69 APF: SOCG 250, fol. 77v, "Sitio."

70 APF: SOCG, fol. 42, "Punta di trovare nella risposta di Papa al Ré di Congo" (ca. 1652).

CHAPTER 4: ECONOMY AND POLITICS IN THE TOWNS

1 Cavazzi, *Istorica descrizione*, book 1, no. 154; Thornton, "Demography and History," pp. 520–24.

2 BN Madrid, MS 3533, de Teruel, "Descripcion narrativa," fol. 78.

3 Ibid., fol. 84.

4 Dapper, *Beschreibung*, p. 558.

5 Cavazzi, *Istorica descrizione*, book 2, nos. 73–83; da Roma, *Relation*, pp. 84–86; BN Madrid, MS 3533, de Teruel, "Descripcion narrativa," fol. 148; APF: SOCG 250, fols. 76–6v, "Sitio"; fol. 154, anonymous report of ca. 1659; 198v, Brugiotti, "Alcuni appuntamenti."

6 Cavazzi, *Istorica descrizione*, book 1, no. 326; Brugiotti, "Infelicità felice," in Simonetti, Brugiotti," p. 374.

7 Da Roma, *Relation*, p. 53.

8 Cavazzi, *Istorica descrizione*, book 1, no. 326. A similar situation was observed in Nsoyo in the 1680s: Merolla, *Relatione*, pp. 155–56.

9 BN Madrid, MS 3533, de Teruel, "Descripcion narrativa," fol. 102.

10 Dapper, *Beschreibung*, pp. 557–58. See the graphic account of the fall from power of one titled noble in the 1620s, "Description," in Cuvelier and Jadin, *L'ancien Congo*, pp. 133–34.

11 BN Madrid, MS 3533, de Teruel, "Descripcion narrativa," fol. 130.

12 Da Roma, *Relation*, pp. 116–17.

13 BN Madrid, MS 3533, de Teruel, "Descripcion narrativa," fol. 101.

14 APF: SOCG 250, fols. 27–28, "Schiavi"; fols. 198–8v, Brugiotti, "Alcuni appuntamenti."

15 Da Roma, *Relation*, p. 117.

16 Ibid.

17 Cavazzi, *Istorica descrizione*, book 2, no. 78; Dapper, *Beschreibung*, p. 558.

18 Ibid.

19 Cavazzi, *Istorica descrizione*, book 2, no. 78.

20 Cordoso, "Relação da morte," in Brásio, "Problema," p. 232.

21 Relative musketeer strength: in 1668 the Marquis of Dande, Captain General of Mbamba, had twenty-four musketeers—Carli, "Relation nouvelle," in Labat, *Relation*, 5:145–46; and in 1655 the Marquis of Nsevo had an equal number—APC Toscana, da Montesarchio, "Viaggio," fol. 59; BN Madrid, MS 3533, de Teruel, "Descripcion narrativa," fols. 99–100. Larger dis-

tricts may have had twice as many. São Salvador, on the other hand, brought 360 musketeers to the battle of Mbwila, the effective strength of a force of some 500, in all probability: "Relação do mais gloriosa victória que alançarão as armas del Rei D. Affonso VI," in C. R. Boxer, "Uma relação inedita e contemporanea da batalha de Ambuíla em 1665," *Boletim Cultural do Museu de Angola*, 2 (1960): 69, note 1. In 1595 the king was said to have a permanent armed force of 20,000 men, mostly Teke slaves ("De Statu Regni Congi," *MMA* 5:508). Anne Hilton has argued that the large number of musketeers found in areas outside the capital was indicative of declining centralization. However, surely no single province, or even group of provinces, could raise a larger musketeer force than that in São Salvador, and all still faced the problem of lack of concentration: Wilson, "Kongo Kingdom," pp. 170–71.

22 Population estimates based on Thornton, "Demography and History," pp. 522–25.

23 Franco, *Synopsis annalium*, pp. 263–64. The Jesuit author of this account probably exaggerated Daniel da Silva's force, which he placed at 20,000.

24 Cavazzi, *Istorica descrizione*, book 4, nos. 224 and 423 (Mbata); and BN Madrid, MS 3533, de Teruel, "Descripcion narrativa," fol. 103 (Wandu).

25 BM Madrid, MS 3533, de Teruel, "Descripcion narrativa," fol. 148.

26 Ibid., fol. 78.

27 Ibid., fol. 102.

28 Matheus Cordoso to Manuel Rodrigues, 1624, *MMA* 7:291.

29 BN Madrid, MS 3533, de Teruel, "Descripcion narrativa," fol. 84.

30 Ibid., fols. 132 and 103, for a similar situation in Wandu.

31 ARSI, Lusitania, 55, fols. 115–17, Matheus Cordoso, "Relação do alevamento"; and Cordoso, "Relação da morte," in Brásio, "Problema," *passim*.

32 BN Madrid, MS 3533, de Teruel, "Description narrativa," fols. 103, 136.

33 Cavazzi, *Istorica descrizione*, book 2, no. 73; Gastão Sousa Dias, *A batalha de Ambuíla* (Lisbon, 1942).

34 BN Madrid, MS 3533, de Teruel, "Descripcion narrativa," fols. 181–84.

35 Cavazzi, *Istorica descrizione*, book 2, no. 78; Dapper, *Beschreibung*, p. 558.

36 BN Madrid, MS 3533, de Teruel, "Descripcion narrativa," fols. 181–84.

37 ARSI, Lusitania, 55, fols. 115–17, Cordoso, "Relação do alevamento"; Cordoso "Relação da morte," in Brásio, "Problema" *passim;* Cordoso to Rodrigues, 1624, *MMA* 7:291.

38 Extracts of letters of Álvaro III to Juan Bautista Vives, 1616–20, *MMA* 6:252–53.

39 Capelle to Maurice de Nassau, 1642, in Jadin, "Rivaltés," p. 228.

40 APF: SOCG 250, fols. 198–199, Brugiotti, "Alcuni appuntamenti," on the canon's timely warning; Brugiotti to Propaganda Fide, 1655, *MMA* 11:441–42, on the congregations as recruiting grounds.

41 "Description du Congo," in Cuvelier and Jadin, *L'ancien Congo*, p. 134. Hilton has suggested that the traditional twelve council members represented interests of *kanda* or original kinship units (Wilson, "Kongo Kingdom,"

p. 36). The case is without any supporting documentation, however, and in the mid-seventeenth century, in any case, the positions were completely the king's gift.

42 Álvaro III to Philip II, 24 October 1615, *MMA* 6:236.

43 Extracts of letters, 1616–20, *MMA* 652–53; BN Madrid, MS 3533, de Teruel, "Descripcion narrativa," fols. 181–84.

44 ARSI, Lusitania, 55, fols. 115–17, Cordoso, "Relação do alevamento," *passim.*

45 "Description du Congo," in Cuvelier and Jadin, *L'ancien Congo,* pp. 133–34.

46 Cadornega, *História,* 3:194–95.

47 Ibid.; de Hoogleede, *Martyr,* pp. 294–311.

48 Matheus Cordoso, "Relação da 2ª ida que eu . . . fez ao Reino de Congo," 1625, *MMA* 7:377.

49 This conversion is based on data in da Pavia, "Voyages apostoliques," p. 450.

50 Dapper, *Beschreibung,* p. 558.

51 Merolla, *Relatione,* p. 161.

52 Pedro II to Juan Bautista Vives, 23 June 1623, *MMA* 7:36.

53 Álvaro II to Juan Bautista Vives, 25 October 1617, *MA* 6:292–93.

54 Cavazzi, *Istorica descrizione,* book 2, no. 83.

55 Cordoso, "Relação," 1625, *MMA* 6:381.

56 Da Lucca, ed. Cuvelier, *Relations,* p. 97; BN Madrid, MS 3533, de Teruel, "Descripcion narrativa," fol. 148; APC Toscana, da Montesarchio, fol. 39.

57 Cavazzi, *Istorica descrizione,* book 2, no. 76.

58 BN Madrid, MS 3533, de Teruel, "Descripcion narrativa," fol. 184.

59 Manuel Bautista, "Relação dos costumes," *MMA* 6:375.

60 See chapters 7–8, below.

61 Cavazzi, *Istorica descrizione,* book 1, no. 328.

62 Ibid.

63 Ibid.

64 ANTT, Miscelaneas Manuscritas, vol. 1115, fol. 141, anonymous MS of about 1740. The sections of Kongo date from the mid-seventeenth century. A second, nineteenth-century copy is found in BN Lisbon, Secção dos MSS, Caixa 206, no. 145.

65 Cavazzi, *Istorica descrizione,* book 1, nos. 275–76; da Roma, *Description,* pp. 114–15.

66 Cordoso, *História,* ed. Brásio, p. 81.

67 APC Toscana, da Montesarchio, fol. 85 (António); Cavazzi, *Istorica descrizione,* book 2, no. 12 (Afonso).

68 ANTT, Chancelleria do Ordem de Christo, book 45, fols. 438–8v; AHU: PA, Angola, Caixa 8, Consulta of 20 May 1673, "Relação dos successos do Reyno de Congo, e suas alterações começa do anno de 1641 . . ." has the canons of São Salvador as Garcia's cousins, while AHU, códice 275, fol 366v has Miguel de Castro as one of Garcia's sons. The salaries are given in AHU: PA, Angola, Caixa 3, chapter of São Salvador to João IV, 13 October 1651.

69 BN Madrid, MS 3533, de Teruel, "Decripcion narrativa," fol. 78.

70 Ibid., fol. 119.

71 APC Toscana, da Montesarchio, "Viaggio,"fols. 67–68.

72 Brugiotti to Propaganda Fide, 1655, *MMA* 11:441–42.

73 BN Madrid, MS 3533, de Teruel, "Descripcion narrativa,"fol. 119.

74 Cordoso, *História*, ed. Brásio, p. 81, gives a list of minor family surnames. Other examples: Miguel de Castro, ambassador of Nsoyo to Brazil and the Low Countries, 1643–45, J. Nieuhof, *Gedenkweerdige Brasilianse Zee en Land-Reise*, 1682, in *ACA* 1:373–74; Gabriel Afonso de Menezes (the "Afonso" element indicates marriage into the royal house), secretary major of Kongo, 1625, Cordoso, "Relação," *MMA* 7:381; Bernardo de Menezes, a criado of Garcia II who served as his ambassador to the Dutch in Luanda in 1643— Garcia II to Rector of the Jesuits, 23 February 1643, *MMA* 9:17, and J. Nieulandt and Hans Mol to XIX, 10 June 1643, *ACA* 1:427; Antonio Martinez de Barreiros and Baltassar Veiria, major and minor secretaries of Kongo for Pedro II—Pedro II to Juan Bautista Vives, 23 June 1622, *MMA* 7:38; Domingos Fernandes and Diogo Fernandes de Santa Maria, ambassadors of Garcia II to Luanda in 1642, Report of Pieter Moortamer, 14 October 1642, *ACA* 1:339–40.

75 The most widely utilized names of the Kongo houses of Garcia's time are only known from the later seventeenth century and early eighteenth century. Names fluctuated: in 1624 Matheus Cordoso reported two houses, the "House of Sundi" and the "House of Coilo" (*História* ed. Brásio, p. 81). Given the situation at the time, the House of Sundi must have been the house headed by Pedro II, probably the House of Nsundi, as Pedro II's immediate ancestor had been a Duke of Nsundi. The house of Coilo (Kwilu) was that of Álvaro III, since Cavazzi (*Istorica descrizione*, book 1, no. 234) gives the province as Álvaro III's birthplace. The later, and more famous, names for the houses are given by Bernardo da Gallo (APF: SOCG 576, fol. 331), who lists three houses: Kimpanzu, Kinlaza (not in existence in 1624 when Cordoso wrote, at least not as a major force), and Kinkanga a Mvika. The the names seem to derive from the names of founders or important members—Pedro II's name was Nkanga a Mvika, while Álvaro V, the last Kimpanzu to rule undisputed, was named Mpanzu a Nimi, according to BN Madrid, MS 3533, de Teruel, "Descripcion narrativa," introduction. Some writers on Kongo history have been misled by Jadin's incorrect transcription and translation of da Gallo's report, which rendered *Kikanga a Mvika* as another name for the *Kinlaza*, rather than another branch, as is written in the original text. Jadin, "Secte des Antoniens,"p. 474.

76 Wilson, "Kongo Kingdom," Appendix A, on the kinship reckoning as constructed from seventeenth-century vocabularies. Hilton's work suggests subtle changes in kinship reckoning which altered succession to the throne and political systems in Kongo. However, the making of a state apparatus, the creation of an appointive system of status and income, and the vesting of offices and land in the state freed the rulers of Kongo from the necessity of adherence to kinship systems to determine succession or power. Hence the older kinship system could be retained without altering politics.

77 Well documented in Wilson, "Kongo Kingdom," pp. 79–80.
78 Ibid., pp. 226–28.
79 Judicial inquest into the treason of Pedro Canga Mobemba, 10 April 1550, *MMA* 2:261.
80 Extracts of letters, 1616–20, *MMA* 6:252–53.
81 Pigafetta, *Relatione*, pp. 57–58.
82 Pierre du Jarric, *Histoire des choses plus memorables advenues tant ez Indes Orientales, que autres pais de la desccouverte des Portugais*, 3 vols. (Bordeaux, 1608–10), 3:69–75.
83 Traceable in Álvaro III's correspondence, published in *MMA* 6, *passim*.
84 Cavazzi, *Istorica descrizione*, book 2, no. 125; MS Araldi, Cavazzi, "Missione evangelica," fols. 592–93; Merolla, *Relatione*, pp. 324–25; APF: SOCG 576, fol. 3, da Gallo, "Conto."
85 Judicial inquiry, 1550, *MMA* 2:248–62 *passim*. In his letter to D. Rodrigo, one of the plotters, Pedro Nkanga a Mvemba mentions "a geração de Quybala" (house of Kibala) as the name of his house, which leads us to suppose that his opponent, King Diogo I, was of a different house.
86 On the rise and fall of the House of da Silva in Mbamba, 1614–20, see extracts of letters, 1616–20, *MMA* 6:252–53. Álvaro III's ally Pedro later became Pedro II of the House of Kinkanga a Mvika. On Jordão, see ARSI, Lusitania, 55, fols. 115–17, Cordoso, "Relação do alevamento," and Cordoso, "Relação da morte," in Brásio, "Problema," *passim*.
87 Cordoso, "Relação da morte," in Brásio, "Problema," p. 239.
88 Franco, *Synopsis annalium*, pp. 247–48.
89 Ibid., pp. 263–64.
90 BN Madrid, MS 3533, de Teruel, "Descripcion narrativa," fols. 123–25.
91 Capelle to Maurice de Nassau, 1642, in Jadin, "Rivaltés," p. 228.
92 Franco, *Synopsis annalium*, pp. 263–64; AS Parma, Conventi e Confraternite, Collegio dei Gesuiti di S. Rocco, busta 90, anonymous, "Breve relatione della vita e morte del P. Lattantio Leonardi . . . ," n.d. (seventeenth-century hand).
93 Robrerdo was a son of Álvaro V's daughter, Eva. BN Madrid, MS 3533, de Teruel, "Descripcion narrativa," fols. 125–26; Simão de Medeiros and Miguel de Castro were brothers and related to Garcia II or Álvaro VI (Kinlaza in any case)—see note 66 above. Estevão Castanho was a half brother to the other two. APF: SOCG 250, fol. 178, Brugiotti to Propaganda Fide, ca. 1659.
94 Daniel da Silva, ruler of Nsoyo, was the brother of Garcia II's wife. Cavazzi, *Istorica descrizione*, book 3, no. 317. Therefore some Kinlaza would naturally be found in Nsoyo. Also BN Madrid, MS 3533, de Teruel, "Descripcion narrativa," fol. 98; and APC Toscana, da Montesarchio, "Viaggio," fol. 9, on the other Kinlaza in Nsoyo.
95 BN Madrid, MS 3533, de Teruel, "Descripcion narrativa," fol. 13; BE, MS Italicus 1380, alpha N-9-7, Monari, "Viaggio," p. 557.
96 BN Madrid, MS 3533, de Teruel, "Descripcion narrativa," fols. 125–26; BE, MS Italicus 1380, alpha N-9-7, Monari, "Viaggio," pp. 347–48.

97 BN Madrid, MS 3533, de Teruel, "Descripcion narrativa," fols. 125–26; Cavazzi, *Istorica descrizione*, book 7, nos. 139–41; BE, MS Italicus 1380, alpha N-9-7, Monari, "Viaggio," pp. 547–48; AHU; PA, Angola, Caixa 7, Consulta of 9 July 1666.

98 The Kinlaza and Kinkanga were closely related, connecting themselves to Afonso I (d. 1543) by the same women, but diverging a generation later. The Kinlaza descent is revealed through their list of names in BN Madrid, MS 3533, de Teruel, "Descripcion narrativa," introduction. The genealogical significance of such name lists is explained by Matheus Cordoso in giving them for Pedro II in his letter to Manuel Rodrigues, 1624, *MMA* 7:292. The meaning of Kinlaza is not clear, but perhaps it came from the title "Mani Mulaza" borne by António I (d. 1665). Cadornega, *História*, 3:304, 306. There is no substance, however, to Cadornega's theory that the name derived from the province of Kongo dia Nlaza.

99 BN Madrid, MS 3533, de Teruel, "Descripcion narrativa," fols. 151–52.

100 Ibid., fol. 151; BN Paris, Founds espagnoles, 324, fol. 150, Brugiotti, "Osservationi del Regno de Congo dell'anno 1656"; APF: SOCG 250, fols. 198–8v, Brugiotti, "Alcuni appuntamenti"; BE, MS Italicus 1380, alpha N-9-7, Monari, "Viaggio," fols. 221–1v (pp. 434–35).

101 APF: SOCG 576, fol. 331, da Gallo, "Conto."

102 BN Madrid, MS 3533, de Teruel, "Descripcion narrativa," fol. 119.

103 Franco, *Synopsis annalium*, pp. 247–48, 296.

104 Inquiry of Diogo I, 12 November 1548, *MMA* 2: 197–206.

105 Wilson, "Kongo Kingdom," p. 141.

106 Thornton, "Demography and History," p. 520.

107 Extracts of letters, 1616–20, *MMA* 6:252–53. Franco, *Synopsis annalium*, pp. 247–48.

108 See chapter 7, below.

109 Wilson, "Kongo Kingdom," p. 160. Hilton claims that the king of Kongo imposed the de Sousa house on Nsoyo, but the evidence she cites does not prove it. In fact, Nsoyo under the de Sousas does not seem to have been any more loyal to Kongo that it was under the da Silvas.

110 Franco, *Synopsis annalium*, pp. 263–64.

111 BN Madrid, MS 3533, de Teruel, "Descripcion Narrativa," fol. 26; Dapper, *Beschreibung*, p. 544.

112 Cordoso to Rodrigues, 1624, *MMA* 7:291.

113 BN Madrid, MS 3533, de Teruel, "Descripcion narrativa," fols. 125–26; BE, MS Italicus 1380, alpha N-9-7, Monari, "Viaggio," pp. 552–55, 558; AHU: PA, Angola, Caixa 5, Consulta of 24 September 1659.

114 See note 94, above.

CHAPTER 5: THE MENTAL WORLD OF KONGO

1 On the notion of the separate histories and development of superstructure and base in African societies, see Maurice Bloch, "The Disconnection be-

tween Power and Rank as a Process: An Outline of the Development of Kingdoms in Central Madagascar," *Archives européens de sociologie*, 18 (1977): 107–48.

2 We have little information from seventeenth-century sources on the ideological basis which permitted the *nkuluntu* to exercise power.

3 Cordoso, *História*, ed. Brásio, pp. 44–47; and Cavazzi, *Istorica descrizione*, book 2, no. 86, are the best examples of the founding myths of Kongo in the seventeenth century.

4 Cordoso, "Relação da morte," in Brásio, "Problema," describes the coronation ceremony with the proclamation of historical traditions. Brásio's editorial comments are generally good in this article as well.

5 We have already suggested that slaves were integrated into the family structure of their owners, perhaps as permanent juniors. If this were the case, then the use of terms of kinship as an ideological representation of relations of power and hierarchy so prominent in other African societies, as well as in later Kongo society, may have played a part.

6 Cordoso, *Doutrina*, ed. Bontinck and Nsasi, pp. 140–41. The Portuguese text reads "nossos prelados e aos que governão a Republica," which the Kikongo makes "Akuluntu eetu a nganga yo aana aludika e dikanda."

7 BN Madrid, MS 3533, de Teruel, "Descripcion narrativa," fols. 101, 130.

8 Da Roma, *Relation*, p. 117.

9 APC Toscana, da Montesarchio, "Viaggio," fols. 64–65.

10 Ibid. Da Montesarchio calls the wife of the *kitomi Chitomessa*, but other sources make it clear that the *kitomi* did not marry, but only took a female companion: APF: SOCG 249, de Cerolla, "Relasion de los ritos," fol. 237.

11 Wilson, "Kongo Kingdom," pp. 229–65.

12 Wyatt MacGaffey, "The Religious Commissions of the Bakongo," *Man*, New Series, 5 (1970): 28–36. Because MacGaffey's work reflects the ideology of the modern Kongo, use of it to infer past ideology is speculative—although, of course, the speculation can be supported to some extent.

13 Cavazzi, *Istorica descrizione*, book 1, nos. 174–80, provides an excellent description of the two roles, complete with an explanation of the confusion as to precisely where each fit.

14 Ibid., book 1, no. 179.

15 APR: SOCG 249, fol. 336v, de Cerolla, "Relasion de los ritos"; APC Toscana, da Montesarchio, "Viaggio," fol. 64.

16 APF: SOCG 249, fol. 337, de Cerolla, "Relasion de los ritos"; BN Madrid, MS 3574, de Teruel, "Descripcion narrativa," fol. 199. (MS 3574 is a second copy of MS 3533, the original version of "Descripcion narrativa." It is incomplete and for the most part simply a copy of MS 3533, but in some instances, as in this reference, it contains information not contained in the original. Since MS 3574 is also written by de Teruel, these additions must be considered as editorial emendations).

17 Cavazzi, *Istorica descrizione*, book 1, no. 180.

18 APF: SOCG 249, fol. 337, de Cerolla, "Relasion de los ritos"; Cavazzi, *Istorica descrizione*, book 1, no. 179.

19 Ibid. MacGaffey, "The Cultural Roots of Kongo Prophetism," *History of Religion*, 17 (1977): 184–86, identifies the *kitomi* as a mediator with the *simbi* spirits. See also Wilson, "Kongo Kingdom," pp. 239–62.

20 Cavazzi, *Istorica descrizione*, book 1, nos. 183–97, provides a detailed list of typical functions of *nganga*, which clearly shows the extreme specialization of some. It was probably provided to Cavazzi from notes of Girolamo da Montesarchio in eastern Kongo in the period 1648–68 (Thornton, "New Light"). Hilton identifies the *nganga's* role as mediating with sky spirits, while the *kitomi* mediated with earth spirits, so that there was a cosmological as well as social distinction between the two. In any case, as this example shows, roles and categories of belief did not fit into a rigid system—Kongo religious life was characterized by substantial flexibility and innovation. Wilson, "Kongo Kingdom," pp. 254–60.

21 Da Caltanisetta, *Diaire*, pp. 99, 154. This entire section of da Caltanisetta's notes is replete with references to the activities of *nganga*, and is a mine of casual but acute observation on their activities and the ideology that motivated them.

22 Ibid., pp. 152–53.

23 Cavazzi, *Istorica descrizione*, book 1, nos. 182, 212; Brugiotti, "Infelicità felice," in Simonetti, "Brugiotti," p. 372; da Caltanisetta, *Diaire*, p. 103.

24 Da Caltanisetta, *Diaire*, p. 83.

25 Ibid., p. 83. Hilton claims that *nganga a ngombo*, as mediators with sky spirits, were not possessed ("Kongo Kingdom," p. 258). In this source, and elsewhere in his travels, da Caltanisetta encountered *nganga a ngombo* who were possessed (normally, da Caltanisetta believed, by the devil, whom Hilton also identifies as a sky spirit in the combination of Christianity with Kongo's religion; see "Kongo Kingdom," p. 254). It is important to stress, once more, that the beliefs of the Kongo, in the seventeenth century as today, should not be too rigidly defined. Personal initiative and revelation are important aspects of the religion of Kongo.

26 APF: SOCG 576, fol. 326, da Gallo, "Conto."

27 Cavazzi, *Istorica descrizione*, book 1, no. 198; APC Toscana, da Montesarchio, "Viaggio," fols. 122–23; APF: SOCG 249, de Cerolla, "Relasion de los ritos," fol. 336.

28 Cavazzi, *Istorica descrizione*, book 1, no. 198; APC Toscana, da Montesarchio, "Viaggio," fols. 122, 128; APF: SOCG 249, fol. 336v, de Cerolla, "Relasion de los ritos."

29 APC Toscana, Bernardi, "Ragguagli," fol. 140. Serafino da Cortona, author of this translation of de Cerolla's "Relasion de los ritos," has added to the original description of the "carnal mixing" of initiates of the *kimpasi*, "even those in the first degree, in fact, fathers with daughters, mothers with sons, etc." Since da Cortona also worked in the Kongo mission, these elaborations must be considered to have some authority.

30 APC Toscana, da Montesarchio, "Viaggio," fol. 132.

31 Ibid., fol. 131. The *kimpasi* also appears to have a connection with the *simbi* cults: MacGaffey, "Roots," pp. 184–85; Wilson, "Kongo Kingdom,"

pp. 245–53. Hilton finds the seventeenth-century *kimpasi* different from modern ones.

32 APC Toscana, Bernardi, "Ragguagli," fol. 142. Here da Cortona again extends the comments of de Cerolla (APF: SOCG 249, fol. 337) to include a description of the staff of office.

33 Da Caltanisetta, in *Diaire*, pp. 95, 112–13, 184, notes regional differences in the use of these devices—in Nsundi people wore *nkisi* or *iteke* regularly, while in Nsonso they did not, but regularly kept such devices in the house. Also see da Montesarchio to Bonaventura da Sorrento, 20 March 1650, *MMA* 10:486; BN Madrid, MS 3533, de Teruel, "Descripcion narrativa," fol. 99.

34 Cavazzi, *Istorica descrizione*, book 1, nos. 192, 196; da Lucca, ed. Cuvelier, *Relations*, pp. 131–32, 147–48.

35 Ibid.

36 Cavazzi, *Istorica descrizione*, book 1, no. 183; BN Madrid, MS 3533, de Teruel, "Descripcion narrativa," fols. 121–22. Often a successful *nganga* would be surrounded by students: Cavazzi, *Istorica descrizione*, book 1, no. 191.

37 APF: SOCG 249, fol. 337, de Cerolla, "Relasion de los ritos"; APC Toscana, Bernardi, "Ragguagli," fol. 142. In his translation, da Cortona implies that the *nkuluntu* provided revenue; the original does not specify.

38 Cavazzi, *Istorica descrizione*, book 1, no. 181.

39 Note the reaction of the King of Kongo when the Capuchins refused to accept his generous offerings: BN Madrid, MS 3533, de Teruel, "Descripcion narrativa," fols. 33–34.

40 BN Centrale, Rome, Fundo Minori 1896, MS Varia 274, "Vocabularium," fols. 17, 107. *Templus* is rendered as *nzo amquissi* and *Bibblia* as *Muquissi mucanda*.

41 For a view that the destruction of *nkisi* was a source of resentment, see Sigbert Axelson, *Culture Conflict on the Lower Congo* (Uppsala, 1970).

42 Cavazzi, *Istorica descrizione*, book 2, no. 89; Cordoso, *História*, ed. Brásio, pp. 18–19, 45.

43 Dapper, *Beschreibung*, pp. 560–62.

44 Da Lucca, ed. Cuvelier, *Relations*, pp. 111–12; BE, MS Italicus 1380, alpha N-9-7, Monari, "Viaggio," fols. 116–21 (pp. 223–32).

45 MacGaffey, "Roots," pp. 184–86; Wilson, "Kongo Kingdom," pp. 267–90.

46 Cavazzi, *Istorica Descrizione*, book 5, para. 58.

47 Charles R. Boxer, *The Portuguese Seaborn Empire, 1415–1825* (London, 1969), pp. 238–45.

48 Robert Ricard, *The Spiritual Conquest of Mexico*, trans. Lesley Byrd Simpson (Los Angeles and Berkeley, 1966), esp. pp. 15–128. Conquest was crucial to the definition of Christianity—for example, contrast the suppression of Hinduism in Portuguese Goa in the sixteenth and seventeenth centuries with the blending of Hinduism and Christianity on the Malabar Coast at the same time period. Boxer, *Portuguese*, pp. 66–76, 244–45.

49 Merolla, *Relatione,* pp. 143–44.

50 Thornton,, "Demography and History," pp. 510–12.

51 Wilson, "Kongo Kingdom," pp. 288–90.

52 Pierre Chaunu, "Sur la fin des sorciers au XVIIe siècle," *Annales: Économies, Sociétés, Civilisations,* 24 (1969).

53 Da Caltanisetta, *Diaire, passim;* APF: SOCG 576, da Gallo, "Conto," *passim.* When reading da Caltanisetta, one gains the distinct impression that he did not doubt their ability to do what they said they did, but he only attributed this ability to the Devil.

54 Da Caltanisetta, *Diaire,* pp. 152–53.

55 The term *fetish,* now largely used in the context of African religions, and elevated in the late nineteenth and early twentieth centuries to a religious concept in anthropological literature, was used in seventeenth-century Portuguese and Italian to designate sorcerers, healers, and witches in Europe, and during the witch craze specifically to indicate those who worked with the devil. Thus, the rendering of *fattuciero* or *feiticeiro* as "fetisher" is inaccurate—it should properly be "witch."

56 ANTT, Chancelleria do Ordem de Cristo, Book 45, fols. 438–8v; AHU, códice 275, fol. 366v; and AHU: PA, Angola, Caixa 8, Consulta of 20 May 1673, "Relação dos successos."

57 Bras Correia to Juan Bautista Vives, 10 December 1623, *MMA* 7:169; Capitols da Embaixador do Rei do Congo, 9 May 1648, *MMA* 10:140–41.

58 Pedro II to Juan Bautista Vives, 23 June 1623, *MMA* 7:169.

59 Wilson, "Kongo Kingdom," pp. 291–99.

60 Jadin, "Clergé seculier," pp. 208–23.

61 APF: SOCG 250, fol. 178, Brugiotti, ca. 1655; Bonaventura da Sorrento to Porpaganda Fide, 4 June 1645, *MMA* 9:272.

62 Decree of Propaganda Fide, 6 May 1653, *MMA* 9:297.

63 BN Madrid, MS 3533, de Teruel, "Descripcion narrativa," fols. 121, 138. One Capuchin-trained catechist, Francisco de Sousa, did become a secular priest and was eventually promoted to the cathedral staff in Luanda: APF: SRC Congo 1, fol. 356; ANTT, Chancelleria do Ordem de Cristo, book 63, fol. 283; Merolla, *Relatione,* p. 306. Also see Thornton, "Demography and History," p. 515.

64 Capitolos da Embaixador do Rei do Congo, 9 May 1648, *MMA* 10:139–42; François Bontinck, "Repurcussions du conflit entre le Saint-Siège et le 'Padroado' sur l'évangelisation de l'ancien Congo au XVIIe siècle," *Archivum historiae pontificiae,* 4 (1966): 197–218.

65 Brugiotti to Propaganda Fide, 1655, *MMA* 9:441–42.

66 Cavazzi, *Istorica Descrizione,* book 4, paras. 13–40; BE, MS Italicus 1380, alpha N-9-7, Monari, "Viaggio," fols. 221–224 (pp. 435–40).

67 BE, MS Italicus 1380, alpha N-9-7, Monari, "Viaggio," pp. 547–48; BN Madrid, MS 3533, de Teruel, "Descripcion narrativa," fols. 125–26.

68 APF: SOCG 651, fols. 330–1v, testimony on events in Mbamba province, 21 June 1723.

69 Serafino da Cortona to José de Grenada, March, 1653, in de Hoogleede, *Martyr*, p. 393.

70 AS Milano, Fundo de' Religione, 6491, "Annali," fols. 136, 139–40. Other accounts of this incident—the revolt of Nsevo which Dom Gregorio suppressed with the help of a troop of angels—do not mention the cause: APC Toscana, da Montesarchio, "Viaggio," fols. 48–51; BN Madrid, MS 3533, de Teruel, "Descripcion narrativa," fol. 99.

71 APC Toscana, da Montesarchio, "Viaggio," fols. 66–69.

CHAPTER 6: THE CIVIL WARS BEGIN

1 A good summary of current historiography is in David Birmingham, "Central Africa from Cameroun to the Zambezi," *Cambridge History of Africa*, 8 vols. in progress (London, 1975–), 4:328–42. Also Wilson, "Kongo Kingdom," pp. 102–228.

2 See the discussion of the battles of Mbwila and Kitombo, pp. 75–76 and 79–80 above.

3 Cavazzi, *Istorica descrizione*, book 2, no. 77.

4 On this raid, Bras Correa to Nuno Mascarenhas, 1623, *MMA* 7:178–79.

5 Joseph C. Miller, "The Slave Trade in Congo and Angola," in Martin Kilson and Robert Rotberg, eds., *The African Diaspora: Interpretative Essays* (Cambridge, Mass., 1976), pp. 79–83.

6 Pero Tavares to Provincial of Portugal, 29 June 1635, In Louis Jadin, "Pero Tavares, Missionaire jésuite, ses travaux apostoliques au Congo . . . ," BIHBR, 39 (1967): 329–38. For a later description of the same region, see ARSI, Lusitania, 56, fols. 215–6v, Manuel Ribeiro, "Carta."

7 Joseph C. Miller, "A Note on Kasanze and the Portuguese," *Canadian Journal of African Studies*, 6 (1972): 43–56.

8 John Thornton, "A Resurrection for the Jaga," *Cahiers d'études africaines*, 8 (1978): 225–26.

9 BN Madrid, MS 3533, de Teruel, "Descripcion narrativa," fols. 88–90, 116–17.

10 See various plans of Garcia Mendes Castello Branco, "Relação tocante ao reino de Congo," *MMA* 6:437–45; and Fernão de Sousa, various letters, 1624–30, *MMA* 7 and 8, *passim*.

11 See the writings of de Sousa, note 10 above. De Sousa, one of the few seventeenth-century governors whose private and official papers have survived (they are now housed in the Biblioteca da Ajuda), had a "forward policy" with regards to Kongo. Our knowledge of the policies of other governors is clouded by a great shortage of relevant primary sources.

12 F. Capelle to de Nassau, 1642, in Jadin, "Rivaltés," pp. 221–30.

13 Sources in note 10 above. Also see Wilson, "Kongo Kingdom," pp. 139–51 and 185–200, for a detailed examination of Kongo-Dutch-Portuguese activity in this period.

14 Bull of erection of the See of São Salvador, 20 May 1596, *MMA* 3:536–38. A

detailed account of the religious rivalry between Portugal and Kongo is found in Wilson, "Kongo Kingdom," pp. 291–99.

15 Bras Correia to Juan Bautista Vives, 23 June 1623, *MMA* 7:169; Capitolos da Embaixador do Rei do Congo, 9 May 1648, *MMA* 10:140–41.

16 For background on the Luso-Dutch struggle for the south Atlantic, see C. R. Boxer, *Salvador de Saa and the Struggle for Angola and Brazil* (London, 1952).

17 Pieter Moortamer to Brazil Council, 14 October 1642, *ACA* 1:339. The treaty was initially concluded on 28 March 1642. Minutes of the Luanda Council, 1 September 1641–28 March 1642, *ACA* 1:260. For the details of negotiations and the activities during the Dutch invasion of Angola, see Wilson, "Kongo Kingdom," pp. 185–201.

18 Pieter Moortamer to Brazil Council, *ACA* 1:229–40. Dutch troops helped to keep this route open; in fact, in 1646 they even suppressed a revolt on Garcia's behalf in the *ndembu* region of Nsala. Dapper, *Beschreibung*, p. 543.

19 J. Nieuhof, *Gedenkweerdige Brasilanese Zee en Lantreise* (1628), in *ACA* 1:373–74; Brazil Council to Daniel da Silva, Count to Nsoyo, 13 February 1643, *ACA* 1:392.

20 Dapper, *Beschreibung*, pp. 565–67; BN Madrid, MS 3533, de Teruel, "Descripcion narrativa," fols. 27–28.

21 *Ibid.*

22 On the death of the bishop, see António da Silva Rego, *A dupla restauração de Angola e Brasil* (Lisbon, 1948), p. 78. On his policies with regards to the Kongo church, see Wilson, "Kongo Kingdom," pp. 297–99.

23 For background on the arrival of the Capuchins, see de Hoogleede, *Martyr*, pp. 78–173.

24 Bontinck, "Repercussions."

25 Capitolos da Embaixador, *MMA* 10:139–42.

26 Nomination of Bishop, 8 June 1648, *MMA* 10:178–79. Also Wilson, "Kongo Kingdom," pp. 321–24, 327–28. The compromise bishop never took up his post, and as another compromise, Giacinto Brugiotti da Vetralla, a Capuchin, was sent to head the Capuchin mission to Kongo and act as a makeshift bishop. He was naturally widely opposed by secular priests and many of the Capuchins as well. His difficulties in Kongo may well explain the negative tone of his account of his travels in Africa, "Infelicità felice," which also deeply influenced Cavazzi's more widely available account. Thornton, "New Light," pp. 258–59.

27 Manuel Pacheco to Ambassador in France, 8 June, 28 June, and 26 July 1648, *MMA* 10:175–76, 186–87, 192; Nono da Cunha to Pope, July 1648, *MMA* 10:196–97.

28 On the restoration, Boxer, *Salvador de Saa*, pp. 253–69; da Silva Rego, *Restauração*, pp. 236–40.

29 Birmingham, *Trade and Conquest, passim*, for a description of Portuguese activities in this period.

30 Cadornega, *História*, 2:32.

31 Birmingham, *Trade and Conquest*, p. 112; and Wilson, "Kongo Kingdom," pp. 202–5, on the negotiations and effects of the treaty. Hilton's argument that the treaty was a disaster for Kongo must be balanced with the consideration that it remained a dead letter, never formally acknowledged by Portugal, and the dire effects of many of the clauses were never realized, as they were never put into force.

32 Cadornega, *História*, 2:131–34; AHU: PA, Angola, Caixa 5, Consulta of 24 September 1659; Caixa 14, Consulta of 18 September 1706, document dated 25 May 1658, Diogo Somez Morales; BN Madrid, MS 3533, de Teruel, "Descripcion narrativa," fol. 149.

33 Cadornega, *História*, 2:133–34.

34 Cavazzi, *Istorica descrizione*, book 2, no. 125.

35 Preposta de André Vidal de Negreiros, 27 September 1664, in Sousa Dias, *Ambuíla*, p. 72.

36 Vidal de Negreiros to António I, 15 March 1664; same to Cabido de Sé de Congo, 5 June 1655, in Sousa Dias, *Ambuíla*, pp. 75, 78; Wilson, "Kongo Kingdom," pp. 219–25.

37 Cadornega, *História*, 3:195–96.

38 AHU: PA, Angola, Caixa 4, Consulta of 19 January 1656.

39 Wilson, "Kongo Kingdom," opp. 207–9. Local Portuguese settlers in Angola were so concerned about the problems with *lubongo* as currency that they proposed converting Angola to the *nzimbu*, an attractive possibility since the Portuguese had seized the "mine" for the shell money on Luanda Island. "Requirimento do povo da cidade de Luanda, ao Senado da Camara, sobre a mundança de moedas para Zimbo e moeda de cobre cunhada"—5 March 1660, cited and quoted in Carlos Couto, *O Zimbo na historigrafia de Angola* (Luanda, 1973), pp. 25–29. The original document is in private hands, in the collection of Prof. D. Pedro de Melo da Cunha Mendonça e Menezes.

40 Sousa Dias, *Ambuíla*, pp. 119–37.

41 Wilson, "Kongo Kingdom," pp. 219–25. António's declaration of war, dated 13 July 1665, is in Paiva Manso, *História*, pp. 244–45.

42 "Victoria," in Boxer, "Relação inedita," pp. 65–73.

43 Ibid.

44 Cadornega, *História*, 2:525; "Victoria," in Boxer, "Relação inedita," p. 68. Given the size and age structure of the Kongo population as I have calculated it (Thornton, "Demography and History," pp. 525–26), a hundred thousand would represent every able-bodied man in the country. In fact, some regions sent only token detachments, and moreover, the campaign took place during the planting season, which would undoubtedly have limited recruitment considerably and encouraged desertion.

45 Regimento de André Vidal de Negreiros, 28 July 1665, in Sousa Dias, *Ambuíla*, pp. 96–100, gave special orders that troops be recruited from areas with military experience. On the Imbangala in Portuguese service and their military techniques, see Joseph C. Miller, *Kings and Kinsmen: The Imbangala Impact on the Mbundu of Angola* (Oxford, 1976), pp. 233–41.

46 The battle is described in several nearly contemporary sources, and many of their contradictions are worked out in Boxer, "Relação inedita," pp. 70–73. Also see Wilson, "Kongo Kingdom," p. 224, which gives the date of the battle as 30 October. I have also made use of MS Araldi, Cavazzi, "Missione evangelica," fols. 598–99, a source unknown to the other scholars who have studied the battle.

47 Ibid.

48 "Auto de Vassalagem de Dona Izabel, regente de Ambuíla," in Sousa Dias, Ambuíla, pp. 124–37. On the prospecting, see AHU: PA, Angola, Caixa 7, Consultas of 6 November 1666 and 24 July 1668.

49 Angola fought another full-scale war in the Ndembu region against Mbwila in 1692: AHU: PA, Angola, Caixa 11, Consultas of 23 September and 25 April 1693. Manuel Ribeiro noted the independence of the Ndembu region already when he crossed it in 1673–74: ARSI, Lusitania, 56, fols. 216–21, "Carta."

50 "Victoria," in Boxer, "Relação inedita," p. 72. His successor-designate was described as "one of his nephews, the son of one of his brothers." António's children, who might have succeeded him if he had lived longer, were all still minors.

51 APC Toscana, da Montesarchio, "Viaggio," fols. 136, 139; Pedro Mendes to Governor of Angola, 2 January 1710, in Paiva Manso, História, p. 350; Cadornega, História, 3:304 and note 172; MS Araldi, Cavazzi, "Missione evangelica," fol. 10; Cavazzi, Istorica descrizione, book 2, no. 124; AHU: PA, Angola, Consulta of 20 May 1673, "Relação." Afonso, the husband of Ana Afonso de Leão, is often represented as actually ruling in São Salvador at the later date than either Afonso II or Afonso III. See notes 60 and 64 below for what I believe to be the correct interpretation.

52 APC Toscana, da Montesarchio, "Viaggio," fol. 139; AHU: PA, Angola, Caixa 8, Consulta of 20 May 1673, "Relação," on Álvaro's victories over his rivals. On the flight of Afonso and his wife Ana, see Cadornega, História, 3:304; Pedro Mendes to Governor of Angola, Paiva Manso, História, p. 350.

53 Cadornega, História 3:304; Pedro Mendes in Paivo Manso, História, p. 350.

54 APC Toscana, da Montesarchio, "Viaggio," fols. 141–53.

55 AHU: PA, Angola, Consulta of 20 May 1673, "Relação"; Cadornega, História, 2:267; MS Araldi, Cavazzi, "Missione evangelica," fol. 10; Cavazzi, Istorica descrizione, book 2, no. 124. Álvaro VIII's African name, known only from an eighteenth-century compilation, "Factos memoraveis," Boletim official do Governo-Geral da Provincia de Angola, 642 (January 1858), may have given the name to the House of Kimpanzu, once the house of Kwilu.

56 AHU: PA, Angola, Caixa 8, Consulta of 20 May 1673, "Relação"; Cadornega, História, 3:301; Cavazzi, Istorica descrizione, book 2, no. 125.

57 Carli, "Relation nouvelle," in Labat, Relation, 5:124–26; and Carli, Moro, p. 6

58 AHU: PA, Angola, Caixa 8, Consulta of 20 May 1673, "Relação"; Cador-

nega, *História*, 3:302–3; Cavazzi, *Istorica descrizione*, book 2, no. 125. I have in all cases preferred the "Relação" from AHU for the details of these events over other sources, which contain contradictions. This document, apparently composed around 1671, was made, according to its title, "from news and information obtained at the camp of King D. Rafael." Since this Rafael was close to Pedro III, his information must be considered superior to that of Cadornega. Cavazzi also obtained first-hand information through correspondence with Capuchins in São Salvador, but in these passages he shows some confusion, and clearly misdates the events in 1670.

59 Cadornega, *História*, 2:267–84; AHU: PA, Angola, Caixa 7, Consulta of 15 March 1670.

60 AHU: PA, Angola, Caixa 8, Consulta of 20 May 1673, "Relação." It is also possible that Rafael did know that Pedro had survived the attack, and hoped that announcing the death of the king would strengthen his claims to the throne in the eyes of the Portuguese, to whom this account was clearly addressed. On Pedro's survival and flight, see Cadornega, *História*, 3:302–3. Note also that it is possible that the short-lived reign of Afonso, the husband of Garcia II's sister Ana, occurred at this time, and not (as I have indicated in the text) in 1665. No account establishes the chronology of his reign and flight to the Nkanda mountains firmly.

61 Cavazzi, *Istorica descrizione*, book 1, no. 154 (in which he discounts the rather low estimates of population he was receiving in correspondence; at the time, he was no longer living in Africa). ASV, Processi di Vescovi, 71, fol. 56, testimony of Domingos Erispinus Barreiros on the state of the diocese of Congo, 1672. See similar testimony in ASV, Processi de Vescovi, 74, fols. 28, 1675.

62 Cadornega, *História*, 2:359–61.

63 An excellent account, based almost solely on Portuguese sources, is Ralph Delgado, *História de Angola*, 4 vols. (Lisbon, 1970), 3:320–29. For the events from Nsoyo's perspective: Merolla, *Relatione*, pp. 121–27, and da Lucca, ed. Cuvelier, *Relations*, pp. 58–59.

64 Pedro Mendes in Paiva Manso, *História*, p. 350; Cadornega, *História*, 3:304.

65 Cadornega, *História*, 2:362.

66 APF: SRC, Congo, 1, fol. 9, "Come io, fra Giuseppe Maria da Busseto . . . lo stato delli Missioni di Congo . . ." (1675), on the wars of Pedro III, Afonso III, and Daniel I in 1674. Afonso II, here established by Nsoyo from the Kimpanzu lineage in 1672, is frequently confused with the husband of Dona Ana Afonso de Leão (see notes 51 and 60, above). The names of these kings and their succession is given, according to Miguel de Castro, secretary of King Daniel I, in Cadornega, *História*, 3:308–9. It is clear that the two Afonsos ruled after Rafael I and before Daniel I (thus between 1670 and 1674). It is also clear that the Afonsos were Kimpanzu, while Dona Ana's husband was a Kinlaza. Their history and descent are traced in part in Zucchelli, *Relatione*, p. 226, who obtained it from Dona Suzana de Nóbrega at Lobata in 1701. Dona Suzana was "figlia, sorella e madre di tre Re

successive di Congo . . ." in his account. From other parts of the same account, it seems that she was the mother of Daniel, sister of Afonso III, and daughter of Afonso II (note that mid-seventeenth century king numbering systems ignored a King Afonso II who ruled in the mid-sixteenth century). This would make Afonso III the son of Afonso II. Cuvelier, in *Biographie coloniale belge* (Brussels, 1954), col. 738, in a different interpretation of the same Italian passage quoted above, suggests that she was the daughter of one king (Álvaro II, 1587–1614), the sister of another one (Álvaro II, 1614–22), and the mother of three successive kings (Afonso II, Afonso III, and Daniel I), who would then all be brothers. Although this interpretation would require Dona Suzana to be quite old, it is consistent with the original text and with other accounts as well.

67 Pedro Mendes in Paiva Manso, *História*, p. 351; Merolla, *Relatione*, pp. 332–34; APF: SOCG 495, fols. 168, Paolo da Varezze.

CHAPTER 7: KONGO IN THE CIVIL WARS

1 APF: SOCG 576, fol. 335v, da Gallo, "Conto."

2 APF: SRC, Congo, 1, fol. 141, untitled, undated. The manuscript is a report to Propaganda Fide based on the information collected about 1701 (after the coronation of Pedro IV in 1699, before the reoccupation of São Salvador in 1702). The source of the information appears to be Francesco da Pavia, architect of the plan for Kongo's restoration presented in the memorandum, who visited Kimbangu in 1701.

3 APF: SOCG 579, fols. 218v–9, Columbano da Bologna to Nunzio of Portugal, 10 December 1710, quoted in the Nunce's letter to the Capuchin Protector in Rome, 20 December 1710.

4 Da Caltanisetta, *Diaire*, contains scattered mentions of various slave transactions and services.

5 This figure is derived from da Caltanisetta's baptismal statistics for the area in 1696. Thornton, "Demography and History," p. 525 and note 94. Even if we accept a hypothesis of maximum population density at the two towns in the area, Kimbangu and Mbula, and a totally empty countryside, the population of the two would number only 13,000 each, which would mean a density of thirty per square kilometer. However, it is perfectly clear from da Caltanisetta's notes that the rural countryside was well populated, and in all probability the town's immediate region scarcely exceeded the density of the remaining countryside.

6 Merolla, *Relatione*, pp. 317–20; and note 5, above.

7 Da Caltanisetta, *Diaire*, p. 46.

8 Ibid., pp. 214–20, *passim*. Compare da Caltanisetta's complaints with the observations of the first Capuchins on the speed of construction in São Salvador when they first arrived there; da Roma, *Relation*, pp. 109–11.

9 Pedro Mendes to Governor of Angola, in Paivo Manso, *História*, pp. 353–55; da Caltanisetta, *Diaire, passim.*

10 Da Caltanisetta, *Diaire*, p. 64.

11 Cadornega, *História*, 3:303.

12 Da Lucca, ed. Cuvelier, *Relations*, p. 259.

13 Ibid., p. 264.

14 Pedro Mendes to Governor of Angola, in Paiva Manso, *História*, p. 355 (Rafael); APF: SOCG 651, fol. 340, certificate of marrriage of Pedro IV (brother in Nzolo); da Lucca, ed. Cuvelier, *Relations*, p. 259 (female relative near Nkusu).

15 Da Caltanisetta, *Diaire*, pp. 64, 86, 89, 92 (da Paiva); 45, 50 (Deliciado).

16 Da Caltanisetta, *Diaire*, p. 53; da Lucca, ed. Cuvelier, *Relations*, pp. 42–43; APF: SRC, Congo, fols. 532–32v, Maestro Dom Francisco to Andrea da Pavia, 15 January 1692.

17 Da Caltanisetta, *Diaire*, p. 4; Pedro Mendes to Governor of Angola, in Paiva Manso, *História*, p. 352; da Pavia, "Voyages apostoliques," p. 477.

18 Da Lucca, ed. Cuvelier, *Relations*, pp. 269–71, 276.

19 Pedro Mendes to Governor of Angola, in Paiva Manso, *História* pp. 352–53.

20 APF: SOCG 651, fol. 340, certificate of marriage.

21 DA Caltanisetta, *Diaire*, p. 45.

22 Ibid., pp. 138, 163, 169.

23 Various missionaries commented on her age, and many believed her to be a centenarian when she died in 1710. APF: SOCG 579, fol. 217v.

24 Da Caltanisetta, *Diaire*, pp. 45–56.

25 Ibid., p. 45.

26 Pedro Mendes to Governor of Angola, in Paiva Manso, *História*, p. 353; APF: SOCG 579, fols. 217–7v, Columbano da Bologna to Nunzio of Portugal. Pedro IV, one of the brothers, was said to be a Kinlaza on his paternal side and a Kimpanzu on his maternal side.

27 APF: SRC, Congo, 2, fol. 153v, Manuel de Saa to Propaganda Fide, 2 November 1685, Cadornega, *História*, 3:304.

28 APF: SRC, Congo, 1, fol. 356, Miguel de Castro to Capuchins in Nsoyo, 1673; Merolla, *Relatione*, p. 306.

29 ANTT, Chancelleria do Ordem de Cristo, book 63, fol. 283, Appointment to See of Congo and Angola.

30 The successful commencement for Luanda-based clergy had to wait the death of the older generation of clergy that still operated as if Kongo were at its height. An example is the experience of Pedro Rebelo de Morais, who tried to seek a career in Kongo in 1680, but was blocked by Miguel de Castro. He returned successfully in 1687, after de Castro's death in 1685. MS of Canon Correia de Castro, Luanda, cited in António Brásio, "A promação sacerdotal do Africano," in *História e Missiologia*, p. 900. The opening up of Kongo to Luanda-based clergy had occurred for certain by 1687. AHU: PA, Angola, Caixa 10, Consulta of 15 June 1688; AHU, códice 554, fols. 102v–03.

31 APF: SOCG 651, fol. 339, testimony of Luis de Mendonça, 1726; da Caltanisetta, *Diaire*, pp. 53–54, 77, 104. Others who followed a similar pattern are related in the report of Domingos Botelho in Jadin, "Clergé seculier," pp. 438–40. One slight exception was Estevão Botelho, who was made a canon for São Salvador, but appointed in Luanda, ANTT, Chancelleria do Ordem de Cristo, book 60, fol. 295, 12 January 1697; APF: SOCG 651, fol. 339, Luis de Mendonça.

32 Da Caltanisetta, *Diaire*, p. 54.

33 APF: SOCG 490, fols. 140–40v, Lorenzo da Silva de Mendonça to Propaganda Fide, ca. 1684.

34 AHU: PA, Angola, Caixa 12, Consulta of 29 August 1697.

35 Thornton, "Demography and History," p. 520.

36 A contemporary description of Mbanza Nsoyo is in Merolla, *Relatione*, pp. 88–92.

37 Da Lucca, ed. Cuvelier, *Relations*, p. 114.

38 Cavazzi, *Istorica descrizione*, book 7, no. 124; Luis de Mendonça, 1672, in Paiva Manso, *História*, pp. 254–55. State structure is in da Lucca, ed. Cuvelier, *Relations*, p. 52. Also see the map in Thornton, "Demography and History," p. 521.

39 Merolla, *Relatione*, pp. 236–47.

40 The da Silva e Castros gave Nsoyo Princes Paulo II and Estevão in the 1660s and 1670s. By 1690 the Baretto da Silva line was prevailing. In 1708 another de Castro ruled as Paulo IV, but still later, in 1723, the prince was António IV Baretto da Silva. The lines never stayed completely separate; some documents show António III Baretto da Silva with "de Castro" as a final element—see da Lucca, ed. Cuvelier, *Relations*, pp. 180–81. Da Lucca gives the fullest account of the lines of descent of various houses from 1650 to 1710, to which we should add APF: SRC, Congo, 1, fol. 9v, da Busetto, "Come io" on earlier periods (prior to 1675); and da Lucca, ed. Cuvelier, *Relations*, p. 290. See also Paulo da Silva to Procurator of Capuchins, 28 August 1708, in Paiva Manso, *História*, pp. 348–49; APF: SRC, Congo, 4, fol. 257, Silvestro da Cassara to Propaganda Fide, 15 July 1723, for later princes.

41 Da Pavia, "Voyages apostoliques," pp. 446, 454; da Lucca, ed. Cuvelier, *Relations*, p. 54.

42 Da Lucca, ed. Cuvelier, *Relations*, p. 180.

43 Gil Machal, "Origem da raça solongo segunda a lenda," *Portugal em Africa*, 4 (1947): 86. The source for traditions was a nineteenth-century document written by an inhabitant of Nsoyo, probably a member of the hospice staff.

44 Cherubino da Savonna, "Breve ragguaglio del regno di Congo . . ." (1775), in Carlo Toso, "Relatione inedite di P. Cherubino Cassinis da Savonna," *L'Italia Francescana*, 45 (1974): 209, for a description of Nsoyo as it was in about 1765.

45 Zucchelli, *Relatione*, pp. 225–26 on the history of the da Nóbrega group.

46 Da Caltanisetta, *Diaire*, pp. 87–91.

47 See note 2 above for the text and its author.

48 On the later structure of Kongo see MacGaffey, *Custom and Government*, *passim*.
49 MacGaffey, "Slavery."
50 Da Caltanisetta, *Diaire*, pp. 205, 209, 217.
51 Ibid., p. 217.
52 Ibid., pp. 135–36.
53 Ibid., pp. 4, 27–28, 53; da Lucca, ed. Cuvelier, *Relations*, p. 266; Pedro Mendes to Governor of Angola, in Paiva Manso, *História*, pp. 351–53.
54 Da Lucca, ed. Cuvelier, *Relations*, p. 332.
55 Da Caltanisetta, *Diaire*, p. 212.
56 Thornton, "Demography and History," pp. 527–28.
57 Bernardo da Gallo, "Relazione dell'ultime guerre civili . . . 12 December 1710," in Teobaldo Filesi, "Nazionalismo e religione nel Congo all'inizio del 1700," *Africa (Rome)*, 37 (1971): 493.
58 Da Lucca, ed. Cuvelier, *Relations*, pp. 269–76, *passim*.
59 Da Caltanisetta, *Diaire*, p. 188.
60 Da Lucca, ed. Cuvelier, *Relations*, p. 213.
61 Ibid., p. 266.

CHAPTER 8: THE RESTORATION

1 On the limits of collection of rent in kind, see p. 20 above.
2 Cadornega, *História*, 2:416–19.
3 AHU: PA, Angola, Caixa 10, Consulta of 4 November 1678.
4 The plot was typical of the type of politics practiced in Kongo in the 1680s. The Prince of Nsoyo approached Pedro III with an offer of peace to be sealed by the marriage of one of his daughters to Pedro. But the "Princess" was in fact Manuel de Nóbrega, a bitter rival of Pedro III. When the two met, Manuel jumped up and shot Pedro to death with a pistol, while the army that accompanied the wedding train quickly routed the small force sent from Mbula to meet it. Despite this treachery, Mbula continued as a major force in Kongo and Pedro III was succeeded by his brother João II. Pedro Mendes to Governor of Angola, in Paiva Manso, *História*, p. 351; Merolla, *Relatione*, p. 118.
5 On the rule of the Yaka of the Niari in Kongo History, see Thornton, "Resurrection," pp. 525–26.
6 Da Caltanisetta, *Diaire*, *passim*.
7 Pedro Mendes to Governor of Angola, in Paiva Manso, *História*, p. 351; Merolla, *Relatione*, p. 118.
8 Da Caltanisetta, *Diaire*, pp. 73, 89, 96. Kimpese, on the west side of the Lukunga, was under the control of Mbula. Nsevo, located in the land above the Lukunga and protected on the east and south by steep bluffs, was ruled in 1700 by Duarte, a nephew of the Duke of Nsundi. Juan Mateo d'Anguiano, *Misiones Capuchinas en Africa*, ed. Buenaventura de Carrocera, 2

vols. (Madrid, 1950), 1:460. Anguiano's chronicle is largely a copy, rearranged, of Antonio de Teruel's manuscript of 1664, which Anguiano completed in 1705. This section, however, was an additional portion added by Anguiano to bring the manuscript up to date.

9 For the period around 1765, see da Savona, "Breve ragguaglio," p. 211.

10 Da Caltanisetta, *Diaire*, p. 23.

11 On Vili trading operations in general, see Phyllis Martin, *The External Trade of the Loango Coast* (Oxford, 1972), pp. 111–35.

12 On their family connections, see da Gallo, "Guerre civili," in Filesi, "Nazionalismo," p. 490. They were already independent by 1681 and were listed among the enemies of Garcia III in Cadornega, *História*, 3:303.

13 Da Caltanisetta, *Diaire*, pp. 93–94 (Magoa), 71–78 (Mpangu).

14 Ibid., *passim*.

15 Pedro Mendes to Governor of Angola, in Paiva Manso, *História*, pp. 352–53.

16 AHU: PA, Angola, Caixa 10, Consulta of 2 March 1689.

17 Birmingham, *Trade and Conflict*, p. 157. Around 1685 the rulers of Kina and Nkusu closed this route to the Portuguese, and it was not reopened until 1765. Document in Luanda archives, cited in Carlos Dias Coimbra, *Livros de 'Oficios para o Reino' do Arquivo Histórico Angolana (1726–1801)* (Luanda, 1959), p. 80.

18 Gonçalo da Costa e Meneses to King, 25 March 1692, Paiva Manso, *História*, p. 316. That this overthrow was of little benefit is demonstrated by the Role played by several southeast Kongo rulers (as well as Vili) in an anti-Portuguese war waged by Mbwila: AHU: PA, Angola, Caixa 11, Consulta of 25 April 1693, attachment, "Memória do Dembos, e sovas poderozso que Derão a Ambuíla socorro contro nos."

19 Da Lucca, ed. Cuvelier, *Relation*, pp. 170, 199, 279; Zucchelli, *Relatione*, pp. 226–27.

20 Pedro Mendes to Governor of Angola, in Paiva Manso, *História*, pp. 351–52; AHU: PA, Angola, Caixa 10, Consulta of 2 March 1689, cites a new king in Kongo who sent an embassy to Angola before 28 August 1688. This must have been King Manuel when he ruled in São Salvador. Another king, André I, was said to rule in Kongo after the death of Garcia III, but his reign was short and nothing is known of it, except that his death was due to illness.

21 Da Caltanisetta, *Diaire*, p. 71.

22 Ibid., pp. 41, 137.

23 Ibid., pp. 4, 27–28, 53; da Lucca, ed. Cuvelier, *Relations*, p. 266; Pedro Mendes to Governor of Angola, in Paiva Manso, *História*, pp. 351–53; APF: SOCG 579, fol. 218, da Bologna to Nunzio of Portugal.

24 Da Lucca, ed. Cuvelier, *Relations*, p. 270.

25 Da Pavia, "Voyages apostoliques," pp. 274–75. On Nsoyo's military strength: APC Toscana, Bernardi, "Ragguagli," fol. 602; BE, MS Italicus 1380, alpha N-9-7, Monari, "Viaggio," fol. 77v (p. 146).

26 Da Pavia, "Voyages apostoliques," pp. 461–75; various documents in Paiva

Manso, *História*, pp. 292–311; AHU: PA, Angola, Caixa 11, Consultas of 6 March 1690 and 25 April 1691.

27 AHU: PA, Angola, Caixa 11, Consultas of 6 March 1690 and 25 April 1691. The actual restoration of trade seems to have been a bit slower. In 1700 Nsoyo was still negotiating to have a factor of the Cacheu e India Company (AHU: PA, Angola, Caixa 12, Consulta of 12 February 1700). On the importance of the trade with northern European countries: APF: SRC, Congo, 3, fols. 288–8v, António Baretto da Silva to Propaganda Fide, 4 October 1701.

28 The Flemish mission is meticulously described with a full documentary appendix in Jadin, "Rivaltés," pp. 164–214 (text), 246–337 (documents). An account of the Flemish Recollets themselves in "De missione apostolica in principatu Soigno in Afroca . . . anno Domini 1673," in Marcellino da Civezza, *Missioni Francescane de Terra Santa*, vol. 2 (Florence, 1892), pp. 220–23, 274–81. The Italians Capuchins did not want to see Catholic slaves sold to heretics—thus they preferred the Dutch, whose trade was with Spanish America, to the English, who carried the slaves to Protestant lands. Merolla, *Relatione*, pp. 202–17; Barbot, "Voyage," in Astley, *Collection*, 3:204, 208 for details from the different sides on such negotiations.

29 Da Pavia, "Voyages apostoliques," pp. 458–61; Merolla, *Relatione*, pp. 274–75; APC Toscana, Bernardi, "Ragguagli," fol. 622.

30 APF: SOCG 567, fols. 62v–3, Columbano da Bologna to Propaganda Fide, 20 June 1708; Martin, *External Trade*, pp. 85–86.

31 Da Pavia, "Voyages apostoliques," pp. 475–76; Pedro Mendes to Governor of Angola, in Paiva Manso, *História*, p. 352; APC Toscana, Bernardi, "Ragguagli," fol. 620.

32 Pedro Mendes to Governor of Angola, in Paiva Manso, *História*, pp. 352–53; da Caltanisetta, *Diaire*, pp. 27–28.

33 Da Caltanisetta, *Diaire*, pp. 44, 53–54; APF: SOCG 579, fols. 217–8, da Bologna to Nunzio of Portugal.

34 APF: SRC, Congo, 1, fols. 141–42.

35 APF: SOCG 651, fol. 340, certificate of marriage.

36 Da Caltanisetta, *Diaire*, p. 196; AHU: PA, Angola, Caixa 12, Consulta of 23 February 1700.

37 Da Caltanisetta, *Diaire*, p. 220; APF: SOCG 558, fol. 337, Francesco da Pavia to Propaganda Fide, ca. 1702.

38 Da Caltanisetta, *Diaire*, pp. 45–56.

39 APF: SOCG 576, fols. 332–2v; da Gallo, "Conto"; da Gallo, "Guerre civili," in Filesi, "Nazionalismo," p. 475.

40 Ibid., both sources; APF: SOCG 558, fol. 337, da Pavia to Propaganda Fide.

41 APF: SOCG 576, fol. 332v, da Gallo, "Conto"; da Gallo, "Guerre civili," in Filesi, "Nazionalismo," pp. 475–76.

42 See his remarks quoted p. 000, above.

43 Lorenzo da Lucca to Clemenzio XIV, 5 October 1711, in Filesi, "Nazionalismo," p. 665.

44 From remarks in Lorenzo da Lucca and Bernardo da Gallo, she was twenty

years old at the time of her execution in 1, thus placing her birth in about 1686. Da Gallo, "Guerre civili," and da Lucca, "Lettera annua de 1706," in Filesi, "Nazionalismo."

45 Pedro IV was said to be twenty-eight years old in about 1700, thus putting his birthdate in about 1671. APF: SRC, Congo, 1, fol. 141.

46 MacGaffey, "Roots," pp. 184–85.

47 Da Gallo, "Guerre civili," in Filesi, "Nazionalismo," p. 495. The first line is also cited by da Lucca, in Filesi, "Nazionalismo," p. 651.

48 Da Gallo, "Guerre civili," in Filesi, "Nazionalismo," p. 482.

49 Ibid., p. 483.

50 Ibid., p. 498.

51 Ibid., pp. 495–96.

52 Da Lucca, ed. Cuvelier, *Relations*, here cited from the original in Filesi, "Nazionalismo," p. 649.

53 Da Gallo, "Guerre civili," in Filesi, "Nazionalismo," pp. 482–83.

54 Ibid., p. 483.

55 Da Pavia, "Voyages apostoliques," pp. 452–53. Although da Pavia notes that the Prince of Nsoyo told him this story, it probably originated with the party of Manuel I, whom Nsoyo supported for the throne.

56 Da Gallo, "Guerre civili," in Filesi, "Nazionalismo," p. 496. Viewed in the ideological context of Kongo, it should be apparent that those researchers who have seen in this nationalization of the main figures of Christian doctrine a movement of "Negritude" are in error. The same can be said of Beatrice's account of the origins of black and white people from the *nsanda* tree or from the clayey rock, called *fuma:* see MacGaffey, "Roots," pp. 186–87.

57 On this interpretation, see MacGaffey, "Roots," pp. 183–88. The current historiography has seen the Antonian movement as a cultural nationalist movement, placed in a "semi colonial" setting, and in reaction to supposed Portuguese/Christian control of Kongo's religion and politics. See Filesi, "Nazionalismo," pp. 268–80; Balandier, *Daily Life,* pp. 256–63; Randles, *L'ancien royaume,* pp. 157–60; Jadin, "Les sectes religieuses secretes des Antoniens au Congo (1705–09)," *Cahiers des religions africaines,* 2 (1968): 109–20. Hilton has proposed a definition in cosmological terms as well as in political terms that is exempt from this criticism; see Wilson, "Kongo Kingdom," p. 352.

58 Da Gallo, "Guerre civili," in Filesi, "Nazionalismo," p. 497.

59 Ibid., p. 495.

60 Ibid., p. 487.

61 Ibid., p. 497.

62 Da Lucca, in Filesi, "Nazionalismo," pp. 661, 645–47; Gabrielle da Bologna to Carlo da Massa di Carrara, 30 December 1705, printed in *Galleria di Minerva* (Venice 1706), p. 305.

63 Da Lucca, in Filesi, "Nazionalismo," pp. 645–48; da Gallo, "Guerre civili," ibid., p. 506.

64 Da Gallo, "Guerre civili," in Filesi, "Nazionalismo," pp. 490, 507; da Lucca,

      ed. Cuvelier, *Relations,* p. 228; APF: SOCG 594, fols. 441v–2, Francesco da Troyna to Clemenzio XIV.

65   Da Gallo, "Guerre civili," in Filesi, "Nazionalismo," p. 490; APF SOCG 594, fol. 443, da Troyna to Clemenzio XIV.

66   Da Gallo, "Guerre civili," in Filesi, "Nazionalismo," p. 490.

67   Ibid., p. 488. Da Gallo thought that the name "Santissimo Sacramento" was a corruption of one of the Pope's titles. The bull was perhaps the Pope's declaration in favor of Garcia II, and may have been brought along with a crown that was bestowed upon him in 1651. As such it would form part of the royal regalia in Kongo, and came into the hands of João II's brother and predecessor Pedro III when he ruled São Salvador in 1669.

68   Ibid., pp. 486–87.

69   Da Lucca, in Filesi, "Nazionalismo," p. 649.

70   Da Gallo, "Guerre civili," in Filesi, "Nazionalismo," p. 499.

71   Ibid., pp. 498–99.

72   Ibid., pp. 503–4; da Lucca, in Filesi, "Nazionalismo," pp. 652–55.

73   Da Lucca, in Filesi, "Nazionalismo," p. 665; da Gallo, "Guerre civili," ibid., p. 504.

74   Da Lucca, in Filesi, "Nazionalismo," p. 661.

75   Ibid., pp. 664–65; da Gallo, "Guerre civili," in Filesi, "Nazionalismo," pp. 505–6.

76   APF: SOCG 576, fol. 342v, Pedro IV to Bernardo da Gallo; da Gallo, "Guerre civili," in Filesi, "Nazionalismo," pp. 506–7.

77   APF: SOCG 576, fol. 342, Pedro IV to da Gallo, and fols. 332v–3, da Gallo, "Conto."

78   APF: SOCG 576, fol. 333, da Gallo, "Conto."

79   Pedro Mendes to Governor of Angola, in Paiva Manso, *História,* p. 355.

80   APF: SOCG 576, fol. 333, da Gallo, "Conto."

81   Pedro Mendes to Governor of Angola, in Paiva Manso, *História,* p. 355.

82   APF: SOCG 604, fol. 69, Lorenzo da Lucca to Propaganda Fide, 19 June 1715.

83   Ibid., fol. 69.

84   APF: SOCG 617, fols. 487–7v, Simpliciano da Borgia to Propaganda Fide, 4 April 1718.

EPILOGUE

1   I have searched APF: SRC, Congo to the end of volume 4 (1735), and SOCG by means of the Acta series, which forms an index until 1835. I have also examined the Papeis avulsos and códices of AHU to roughly 1730. It is apparent from this search that materials pertinent to Kongo fall off rapidly after 1720 in all the archival deposits. There is, however, considerable relevant material unpublished and as yet unused in studies of this period.

2   Da Savonna, "Breve ragguaglio," p. 207.

3 Ibid., p. 208.

4 Ibid.

5 Ibid.

6 Academia das Ciências, Lisbon, MS Vermelho 396, "Viagem do Congo do Fr. Rafael de Castello de Vide, hoje Bispo de S. Thomé," 1788, n.f. An Italian translation has been published: Marcellino da Civezza, *Storia universale delle Missioni Francescane*, 8 (1894).

7 Da Savonna, "Breve ragguaglio," p. 210.

8 Ibid., pp. 208, 211–13.

9 Ibid., p. 211.

10 Ibid., p. 212.

11 Ibid., p. 209.

12 Thornton, "Demography and History," p. 520.

13 Martin, *External Trade*, p. 85.

14 Da Savonna, "Breve ragguaglio," pp. 209, 212–14.

15 Ibid., pp. 207–8.

16 Ibid. His estimate that the resettled area of the capital had 35,000 people must be evaluated in the light of his other population estimates, which are too high by at least a factor of ten.

17 Ibid.

18 Anton Felice Tommasi da Cortona to his brother Annibale, 20 November 1734, letter in private collection of Tommasi family, Cortona, fols. 1v–2. My sincere thanks to Dr. Guido Tommasi Aliotti for kindly sending me photocopies of his family's documents and allowing me to use and cite the material. The essential parts of Tommasi's letters have been printed by D. Bruno Frescucci, *Pagine Cortonesi* (Cortona, 1968), pp. 58–69. The texts contain some errors of transcription in toponyms, however.

19 Tommasi to brother, 20 November 1734, fol. 2.

20 Raimondo da Dicomano, "Informação do reino do Congo," in António Brásio, "Informação do reino do Congo de Frei Raimondo da Dicomano," *Studia*, 34 (1972):32. Susan Herlin Broadhead recently discovered the original Italian version of this document (earlier editions by Jadin and Brásio were made from an eighteenth-century Portuguese translation in the BN Lisbon) in AHU, Angola, maço 823. On the political institutions of the restored Kongo, see Susan Herlin Broadhead, "Beyond Decline: The Kingdom of the Kongo in the Eighteenth and Nineteenth Centuries," *International Journal of African Historical Studies*, 12 (1979): 615–50. See pp. 624–30 on the role of Christianity.

21 Tommasi to brother, 20 November 1734, fols. 1–1v, 2v–3. See Broadhead, "Beyond Decline," pp. 622–23 on the political functions of these local groups of dignitaries.

22 De Castello de Vide, "Viagem," *passim*.

23 Ibid., *passim*.

24 Da Dicomano, "Informação", pp. 40–41; Vansina, *Kingdoms*, pp. 193–94.

25 Vansina, "Third Dimension," for a critical review of such methodologies.

26 See above, pp. 84–85 on changes in oral traditions.

27 APF: SRC, Congo, 1, fol. 141.
28 *Boletim do Governo-Geral de Angola*, 642 (1858), "Factos Memoraveis."
29 Nimi a Lukeni is cited in the kinglist which accompanies the document, however, as the first king. He is not mentioned in the traditions that accompany it.
30 *Boletim do Governo-Geral de Angola*, 642 (1858), "Factos memoraveis." In a partial tradition recorded by da Dicomano, "Informação," p. 42, the three families that regularly supplied kings in the 1792–94 period were said to be descended from Afonso, the first Christian king. See Broadhead, "Beyond Decline," pp. 630–32.
31 APC Toscana, da Montesarchio, "Viaggio," fol. 37.
32 MacGaffey, *Custom and Government*, pp. 17–33.
33 Ibid.; collections of modern Kongo traditions are found in van Wing, *Études*, pp. 77–98; Karl Laman, *The Kongo*, 3 vols. (Uppsala, 1953–68), 1:1–40.
34 Van Wing, *Études*, pp. 77–98.
35 Gil Machal, "Origem de raça Solongo (Zaire) segunda a lenda," *Portugal em Africa*, 4 (1947):78. Machal's source for the Nsoyo legends seems to be a nineteenth-century document of local authorship (written in "Português do preto"): Joaquim Martins, "As causas da emigração dos povos de S. Salvador do Congo segundo a tradição indigena," *Mensário Administrativa* (Angola), 6 (1948): 43. Álvaro Mpanzu a Lukeni is not the exact name of any Kongo king, although Mpanzu and Lukeni appear as elements in the names of several kings ruling in the 1630–50 period. In the dry season of 1980 the Laboratório Nacional de Antropologia of Angola conducted field work and recorded oral traditions in the area of Mbanza Nsoyo, and some preliminary analysis has been done on them by Cdas. Henriques Abranches and Simão Souindoula (publication pending).
36 Machal, "Origem," p. 86. The map on p. 84 shows the territorial divisions of Nsoyo, and corresponds well with the divisions of Nsoyo as represented in the titles of the Prince of Nsoyo about 1702. Da Lucca, ed. Cuvelier, *Relations*, p. 52.
37 The most systematic account of Kongo slavery in the nineteenth century is that of MacGaffey, "Slavery."
38 MacGaffey, "Slavery," pp. 234–48.
39 J. K. Tuckey, *Narrative of an Expedition to Explore the River Zaire* (London, 1818), pp. 120, 365–66.
40 Ekholm, *Power and Prestige*, pp. 92–94.
41 Axelson, *Culture Conflict*, is one of the most vigorous arguments based on assumptions of modern missionary work.
42 Academia das Ciênças, MS Vermelho 396, de Castello de Vide, "Viagem," *passim*.
43 Rosario dal Parco, "Information sur le Congo," in Louis Jadin, "Aperçu de la situation du Congo en 1760 et rite d'election des rois en 1775 d'après le P. Cherubino da Savonna . . ." *BIHBR*, 35 (1963): 370.
44 Teobaldo Filesi, "L'epilogo della 'Missio Antiqua' dei cappuccini nel regno del Congo (1800–1835)," *Euntes Docetes*, 23 (1970): 398–400.

NOTE ON SOURCES

1 Published in *MMA* 1–4, *passim.*

2 Auto de Devassa de D. Diogo I, *MMA* 2:248–62.

3 On the Kongo archives, see Wilson, "Kongo Kingdom," pp. 177–79.

4 Alfredo de Sarmento, *Os sertões d'Africa (apontamentos de viagem)* (Lisbon, 1880), pp. 58–65. On the destruction of the archives, see Birmingham, "The Forest and the Savanna of Central Africa," in *Cambridge History,* 5:261.

5 De Sarmento, *Os sertões d'Africa,* pp. 58–65. The documents that de Sarmento actually cites in this passage, however, would have already been known to him from their publication in other sources by either Paiva Manso or Francisco das Necessidades. We cannot know for sure, therefore, exactly what documents de Sarmento actually saw in the Kongo archives at the time.

6 Published by Cuvelier and Jadin, *L'ancien Congo, passim;* also in *MMA* 7–8, *passim,* in the original language.

7 Most of these up to 1655 are to be found in *MMA.*

8 The only other order to visit Kongo was the Recollets, who had a brief mission to Nsoyo in 1673–74.

9 Cf. Thornton, "Demography and History," pp. 509–10.

10 Da Poppi's report is in APF: SOCG 659, fols. 65–5v. Da Gallo's long accounts have been published in French in Jadin, "Secte des Antoniens."

11 These are filed into two sections, SRC (Congo) and SOCG, according to whether they were considered by an actual session of the Congregation or not. This administrative division is not important for the historian, since both series contain excellent source material.

12 Information on material contained in the state archives of Italy can be found in Richard Gray and David Chambers, *Materials for West African History in Italian Archives* (London: Ahtlone Press, 1965); Carlo Giglio and Elio Loddini, *Guida delle Fonti per la Storia dell' Africa esistenti in Italia* (Switzerland Inter Documentation AG, 1974), vols. 5 and 6; Teobaldo Filesi and I. Villapardiena, *La 'Missio Antiqua' dei Capuccini nel Conto (1945–1835)* (Rome, 1978).

13 Ibid. Also Leguzzano in *Descrição dos três reinos,* 2:488–90; and Thornton, "New Light."

14 These letters were partially published by Don Bruno Frescucci, *Pagine Cortonesi* (Cortona, 1968), pp. 58–70.

15 Franco, *Synopsis annalium, passim.* The amount of detail lost in this process of republishing can be guessed at by comparing extant annual reports, such as that of Matheus Cordoso, "Relação da morte," in Brásio, *Problema,* with the account of the same events in Franco.

16 As Parma, Conventi e confraternite, Collegio dei Gesuiti di S. Rocco, busta 90, "Breve relazione . . ."—where the route from the original holding to the state archives is clear from the classification.

17 Many of these documents were published in French translation by Louis Jadin, "Clergé seculier," *passim.*

18 The critical edition was finally published in 1940–42.
19 See Joseph C. Miller's rather gloomy account of the Angolan archives, "The Archives of Luanda, Angola," *International Journal of African Historical Studies*, 7 (1974): 551–90. The most important series of the official archives, "Oficios para o Reino," have been summarized up to the early nineteenth century in Dias Coimbra, *Livros*.
20 For example, the curious recommendation to the Camara Municipal of Luanda held by Prof. D. Pedro de Melo da Cunha Mandonça e Menezes and studied in Carlos Couto, *Zimbo*.
21 Large sections published in *MMA* 7–8, *passim*.
22 Many of the most important documents were published by Jadin in *ACA*.
23 I have not consulted this archive.
24 I have not consulted these archives.

Glossary of Kikongo Terms

isimbi (pl.; no singular) local spirits; territorial spirits.

kimpasi (pl. *impasi*) a special initiation cult.

kiteke (pl. *iteke*) a charm, used by *nganga*.

kitomi (pl. *itomi*) a religious figure, in charge of territorial spirits (*isimbi*).

kofu (no pl.) a unit of 20,000 *nzimbu* shells used as a monetary measure.

lubata (following seventeenth-century usage; in actual practice, *evata*, pl. *mavata*) a village.

lubongo (pl. *mabongo*) a cloth used as money.

mbanza (pl. same) a town; residence of a noble.

nganga (pl. same) a religious figure, ideally engaged in private activities for pay.

dikanda (pl. *makanda*) a lineage or a group of related households.

nkisi (pl. same) a charm used by *nganga*.

nkuluntu (pl. same) a village ruler.

nzimbu (pl. same) shell used as money.

Bibliography

UNPUBLISHED PRIMARY SOURCES

Italy

Archivio "De Propaganda Fide" (Archives of the Congregation for the Propagation of the Faith), Rome.
    a. Scritture riferite nelle Congressi, Africa, Congo. Volumes 1–4 (1669–1735).
    b. Scritture Originali in Congregazioni Generali. Volumes 1–659 (1622–1728).
    c. Acta. Volumes 39–100 (1669–1730).
Archivum Romanum Societas Iesu (Roman Archives of the Society of Jesus), Rome.
    a. Lusitania, Historia et Acta. Volumes 55–56 (1620–89).
    b. Epistolae Lusitania. Volumes 74–75 (1599–1699).
    c. Goana, Historia Aethiopia. Volumes 39–40 (1601–59).
Archivio Segreto Vaticano (Vatican Archives), Rome.
    a. Epistolae ad princeps.
    b. Nuziatura di Portogallo.
    c. Processi dei vescovi della S. Congregazione Consistoriale.
    d. Archivum Arcis.
Biblioteca Apostolica Vaticana (Vatican Library), Rome. Vaticana Latina. MSS 7210, 9565 and 13405.
Archivio Provinciale dei PP. Cappuccini, Toscana (Archives of the Tuscan Province of the Capuchin Order), Florence.
    a. Girolamo da Montesarchio, "Viaggio dal Gongho cioè relazione scritta da un nostro Cappuccino," 1669.
    b. Filippo Bernardi da Firenze, "Ragguagli del Congo, cioè viaggi fatti da' missionarij apostolici cappuccini della provincia di Toscana a' regni del Congo, Angola, Matamba, ecc . . . ," 1711.
Archivio Provinciale dei PP. Cappuccini, Venice. Emmanuele da Udine, "Annali."
Archivio di Stato (State Archives), Milan. Fundo de' Religione, MSS 6491, 6501.

Archivio di Stato, Modena. Busta Roma, 105 (Chancelleria Ducale).

Archivio di Stato, Parma. Raccolta dei MSS, "Viaggi," busta 49. Convente e Confraternite, Collegio dei Gesuitidi S. Rocco, busta 90, "Breve relatione della vita e morte del P. Lattanio Leonardi . . . dal Regno di Congo."

Biblioteca Estense (Este Family Library), Modena. MS Italicus 1380, alpha N-9-7, Giuseppe Monari da Modena, "Viaggio al Congo."

Biblioteca Nazionale Centrale (National Central Library), Rome.

    a. *Galleria di Minerva.*

    b. Fundo Minori 1896, MS Varia 274, "Vocabularium Congoese, Hispanicum et Latinum . . . ," ca. 1648.

Portugal

Arquivo Histórico Ultramarino (Overseas Historical Archive), Lisbon.

    a. Papeis avulsos: Angola section. Caixas 1–16 (to 1726). Maços 1–3 (eighteenth century).

    b. Códices: 15–18 (livros 3–6 of Consultas Mixtas, 1652–95); 275–6 (livros 1–2 of Cartas das conquistas, 1644–1727); 545 (livro 1 of Cartas que se escrivam aos governadores de Angola. 1673–1725); 554 (livro 1 of Cartas de Angola, 1673–1772).

Arquivo Nacional do Torre de Tombo (National Archive of the Tombo Tower), Lisbon.

    a. Cartórios das Jesuitas, maços 68–69 (seventeenth century).

    c. Chancellery documents for: João V; Pedro II; Afonso VI.

    d. Chancellery of the Order of Christ.

    e. Miscelaneas manuscritas.

Biblioteca Pública e Arquivo Distrial de Evora (Public Library and District Archives of Evora), Evora.

    a. Códice CXX/2–3.

    b. Códice CXVI/2–1, Giovanni Antonio Cavazzi da Montecuccolo, "Vite de Frati Minori Cappuccini . . . 1677."

Academia das Ciéncas (Academy of Sciences), Lisbon. MS Vermelho 396, "Viagem do Congo do missionario Fr. Raphael de Castello de Vide . . . ," 1788.

Biblioteca do Palácio da Ajuda (Library of the Palace of Ajuda), Lisbon.

Spain

Biblioteca Nacional (National Library), Madrid. Ms 3533 and 3574, Antonio de Teruel, "Descripcion narrativa de la mission serafica de los Padres Capuchinos . . . en el reyno de Congo," ca. 1664.

Archivio de los Padres Capuchinos (Capuchin Provincial archives), Valencia. Joseph de Alicante, MS, "Segunda parte de las cronicas de los Capuchinos de la Provincia de Valencia desde 1650 hasta 1722."

France

Bibliothèque Nationale (National Library), Paris Fonds espagnoles.

Private Documents

Araldi Family, Modena, Giovanni Antonio Cavazzi da Montecuccolo, "Missione evangelica al regno del Congo, et altri circonvinci . . ." MSS Collection, 1665–67.

Tommasi Family, Cortona. Letters of Anton Felice Tommasi da Cortona.

PUBLISHED PRIMARY SOURCES

Anguiano, Juan Mateo d'. *Misiones Capuchinas en Africa*. Buenaventura de Carrocera, ed. 2 vols. Madrid: Consejo superior de investigaciones científicas, Instituto Santo Toribio de Mogrovejo, Biblioteca "Missionalia hispánica," 7, 1950.

Barbot, James, and John Casseneuve. "Abstract of a Voyage to the Kongo River and Kabinda in 1700." Thomas Astley, *A New General Collection of Voyages and Travels Comprehending Everything Remarkable in Its Kind in Europe, Asia, Africa and America*. 3 vols. London: 1747, 3:200–209.

Boxer, C. R. "Uma relação inedita e contemporanea de batalha de Ambuíla em 1665." *Boletim Cultural do Museu de Angola* 2 (1960):65–73.

Brásio, Antonia, ed. *Monumenta missionaria Africana*. 1st series. 11 vols. Lisbon: Agência Geral do Ultramar, 1953–71.

Brugiotti da Vetralla, Giacinto. "Infelicità felice o vero mondo alla roversa . . ." Giuseppe Simonetti, "P. Giacinto Brugiotti e la sua missione al Congo." *Bolletino della Società Geografica Italiana*. 4th series, vol. 8 (1907):305–22, 369–81.

Cadornega, António de Oliveira de. *História geral das guerras Angolanas, 1680*. José Matias Delgado and Manuel Alves da Cunha, eds. 3 vols. Lisbon: Agência Geral das Colonias, 1940–42.

Caltanisẹtta, Luca da. *Diaire congolaise, 1690–1701* François Bontinck, ed. and trans. Louvain: Editions Nauwelaerts, 1970. Original Italian published in Romain Rainero, *Il Congo agli inizi del settecento nella relazione di P. Luca da Caltanisetta*. Florence: La Nuova Italia, [1974].

Carli, Dionigio da Piacenza. *Il moro transportado nell'inclita città di Venezia*. Bassano: G. A. Remondini, 1687.

Carli da Piacenza, Dionigio. "Relation nouvelle et curieuse d'un voyage au Congo, fait ès années 1666 et 1667." In Jean-Baptiste Labat, *Relation historique de L'Ethiopie occidentale*. Vol. 5 of 5 vols. Paris: J. B. Delespine le fils, 1732.

Castello de Vide, Rafael. "O Congo." In Marcellino da Civezza, ed. and trans., *Storia universale delle missioni Francescana*. Vol. 7 of 7 vols. Rome: Typografia Tiberina, 1894.

Cavazzi, Giovanni Antonio da Montecuccolo. *Istorica descrizione de' tre regni Congo, Matamba ed Angola*. Bologna: Giacomo Monti, 1687. Portuguese translation, *Descrição histórico dos três reinos Congo Matamba e Angola*.

Graziano Maria da Legguzzano, trans. and ed. 2 vols. Lisbon: Junta de Investigações do Ultramar, 1965.

[Cordoso, Matheus.] *História do reino de Congo.* António Brásio, ed. Lisbon: Junta de Investigações do Ultramar, 1969.

Cordoso, Matheus. *Doutrina christãa.* Modern re-edition and French translation, *Le catéchisme kikongo du 1624: Réédition critique.* François Bontinck and D. Ndembe Nsasi, eds. and trans. Brussels: Académie Royale des sciences d'outre-mer, 1978.

Cuvelier, Jean, and Louis Jadin, eds. *L'ancien Congo d'après les archives romaines.* Brussels: Memoires de l'academie royale de science coloniale 36 (1954).

Dapper, Olifert. *Umbeständliche und Eigentliche Beschreibung von Africa.* Amsterdam: Jacob von Moers, 1670. Reprinted, New York: Johnson Reprint Corp. 1967.

"De missione apostolica in Principatu Soigno in Africa . . . anno Domini 1674." Marcellino da Civezza, ed. *Missione Francescane de Terra Santa* 2 (1892).

Dicomano, Raimondo da. "Informação do reino de Congo." In António Brásio, ed., "Informação do reino de Congo de frei Raimondo da Dicomano." *Studia* 34 (1972).

"Factos memoraveis da história de Angola." *Boletim official do Governo-Geral da Provincia de Angola* 642 (1858).

Filesi, Teobaldo. "Nazionalismo e religione nel Congo all'inizio del 1700." *Africa (Rome)* 9 (1971):267–303, 463–508, 645–68.

Franco, António. *Synopsis annalium societatis Jesu in Lusitania ab anno 1540 usque ad annum 1725.* Ausburg: P. M. and J. Veith, 1726.

Jadin, Louis. "Le Congo et la secte des Antoniens. Restauration du royaume sous Pedro IV et la 'Saint Antoine' congolaise (1694–1718)." *Bulletin, Institute historique belge de Rome* 33 (1961):411–615.

Jadin, Louis. "Aperçu de la situation du Congo en 1760 et rite d'élection des rois en 1775, d'après le P. Cherubino da Savona, missionaire au Congo de 1759 à 1774." *Bulletin, Institute Historique belge de Rome* 35 (1963):343–419.

Jadin, Louis. "Le Clergé séculier et les Capuchins au Congo et d'Angola aux XVIᵉ et XVIIᵉ siècles, conflits de jurisdiction, 1700–1725." *Bulletin, Institute historique belge de Rome* 36 (1964):185–483.

Jadin, Louis. "Rivaltés luso-néerlandaise au Soyo, Congo, 1600–1675." *Bulletin, Institute historique belge de Rome* 37 (1966):137–359.

Jadin, Louis. "Pero Tavares, missionaire jésuite, ses travaux apostoliques au Congo, Bamba et l'Angola." *Bulletin, Institute historique belge de Rome* 39 (1967):271–402.

Jadin, Louis. *L'ancien Congo et Angola d'après les archives romaines espagnoles, portugaise et néerlandaise.* 3 vols. Rome: Memoires de l'Institute historique belge de Rome 39–41 (1974).

Leite da Faria, Francisco, and Avelino Texeira da Mota, eds. *Novidades náuticas e ultramarinas numa informação dada em Veneza em 1517.* Lisbon: Centro de Estudos de Cartografia Antiga, Serie Separata 99 (1977).

Lucca, Lorenzo da. *Relations sur le Congo du Père Laurent de Lucques.* Jean Cuvelier, ed. and trans. Brussels: Memoires, Institute royale colonial belge 32 (1954).

Merolla da Sorrento, Girolamo. *Breve e succinta relatione del viaggio nel Congo.* Naples: F. Mollo, 1692.

Monari, Giuseppe da Modena, "La missione del Soyo (1713–16) nella relazione inedita di Giuseppe da Modena, O.F.M. Cap." Calogero Piazza, ed. *L'Italia Francescana* 48 (1977):209–92, 347–73.

Montesarchio, Girolamo da. *La prefettura apostolica del Congo alla metà del XVII secolo. La Relazione inedita di Girolamo da Montesarchio.* Calogero Piazza, ed. Milan: A. Giuffrè, 1976.

Paiva Manso, Levy Maria Jordão de. *História do reino de Congo . . . (documentos).* Lisbon: Typographía da Academia, 1877.

Parco, Rosario dal. See Jadin, "Aperçu de la situation . . ."

Pavia, Andrea da. "Voyage apostoliques aux missions du Afrique." Louis Jadin, ed. and trans. "Andrea da Pavia au Congo, à Madère, à Lisbonne. Journal d'un missionaire capuchin." *Bulletin, Institute historique belge de Rome* 41 (1970).

Penders, C., and J. van Wing. *Le plus ancien dictionnaire Bantu.* Louvain: J. Kuyl-Otto, 1928.

Pigafetta, Filippo. *Relatione del Regno di Congo et delle circonvince contrade tratta dalli scritti e ragionamenti di Oduarte Lopez Portoghese.* Rome: B. Grassi, 1591. Facsimile edition, ed. Rosa Capeans. Lisbon: Agência Geral das Colónias, 1949.

Roma, Giovanni Francesco da. *Brève relation de la fondation de la mission des frères mineurs Capuchins . . . au royaume de Congo.* François Bontinck, ed. and trans. Louvain: Editions Nauwelaerts, 1964.

Sarmento, Alfredo de. *Os sertões d'Africa (apontamentos de viagem).* Lisbon: F. A. da Silva, 1880.

Savonna, Cherubino da. "Breve regguaglio del regno di Congo . . ." In "Relatione inedite di P. Cherubino Cassinis da Savona," edited by Carlo Toso. *L'Italia.Francescana* 45 (1974).

Sousa Dias, Gastão. *A batalha de Ambuíla.* Luanda: Museu de Angola, 1942.

Tuckey, J. K. *Narrative of an Expedition to Explore the River Zaire.* London: J. Murray, 1818.

Zucchelli, Antonio da Gradisca. *Relatione del viaggio e missione di Congo nell'Etiopia inferiore occidentale.* Venice: Bartolameo Giavarina, 1712.

SECONDARY SOURCES

Aymard, Maurice. "Pour une histoire de l'alimentation: Quelques remarques de method." *Annales: Économies, Sociétés, Civilisations* 25 (1975).

Axelson, Sigbert. *Culture Conflict on the Lower Congo.* Uppsala: Studia missionalia upsaliensia, 1970.

Baequart, M. "Foulles à Thysville du Musée royale du Congo belge en 1938." *Actes du ve Congrès Panafricain de Préhistoire et de l'étude du Quarternaire.* Brussels: Memoires du Musée royale de l'Afrique Central 40 (1962).

Balandier, Georges. *Daily Life in the Kingdom of the Kongo: Sixteenth to Eighteenth Century.* Helen Weaver, trans. London: George Allen and Unwin, 1968.

Birmingham, David. *Trade and Conflict in Angola.* London: Oxford University Press, 1966.

Bohannan, Paul, and George Dalton. *Markets in Africa.* New York: Natural History Press, 1965.

Bloch, Maurice, "The Disconnection between Power and Rank as a Process: An Outline of the Development of Kingdoms in Central Madagascar." *Archives européens de sociologie* 18 (1977):107–48.

Bontinck, François. "Les Premiers travaux linguistiques kikongo des missionaires Capuchins." *Ngonge Kongo* 15 (1963).

Bontinck, François. "Repurcussions du conflit entre le Saint-Siège et le 'Padroado' sur l'évangelisation de l'ancien Congo au XVII^i siècle." *Archivum historiae pontificiae* 4 (1966):197–218.

Boserup, Ester. *Women's Role in Economic Development.* London: George Allen and Unwin, 1970.

Boxer, Charles R. *Salvador de Saa and the Struggle for Angola and Brazil.* London: University of London Press, 1952.

Boxer, Charles R. *The Portuguese Seaborn Empire, 1415–1825.* London: Hutchinson, 1969.

Brásio, António. *História e missiologia: Ineditos e esparsos.* Luanda: Instituto de Investigação Científica de Angola., 1973.

Braudel, Fernand. *The Mediterranean and the Mediterranean World in the Age of Phillip II.* Siân Reynolds, trans. 2 vols. New York: Harper and Row, 1972.

Braudel, Fernand. *Capitalism and Material Life, 1400–1800.* Miriam Koch, trans. New York: Harper and Row, 1973.

Cahen, L., and J. J. Snelling. *The Geochronology of Equatorial Africa.* Amsterdam: North Holland Publishing Company, 1966.

Cambridge History of Africa. 8 vols. London: Cambridge University Press, 1975–present.

Castanho Diniz, António. *As caracteristicas mesologicas de Angola.* Nova Lisboa: Missão de Inqueritos Agrícolas de Angola, 1973.

Clark, John Desmond. *Further Paleo-Anthropological Studies in Northern Lunda.* Lisbon: Companhia de Diamentes de Angola. Publicações cultureis 78 (1963).

Chaunu, Pierre. "Sur la fin des sorciers au XVIIe siècle." *Annales: Économies, Sociétés, Civilisations* 24 (1969).

Coquery-Vidrovitch, Catherine. "Towards an African Mode of Production." In David Seddon, ed., *Relations of Production: Marxist Approaches to Economic Anthropology.* London: Cass, 1978.

Couto, Carlos. *O Zimbo na historiografia de Angola.* Luanda: Instituto de Investigação Científica de Angola, 1973.

Critique of Anthropology 3 (1977). Special Women's Issue.

Cuvelier, Jean. *L'ancien royaume du Congo.* Brussels: Desclee de Brouwer, 1946.

Davidson, Basil. *Black Mother: The Years of the African Slave Trade.* Boston: Little, Brown and Company, 1961.

Davidson, Basil. *A History of East and Central Africa.* Garden City, N.Y. Anchor Books, 1969.

Delgado, Ralph. *História de Angola,* 2nd rev. ed. 4 vols. Lobito, Angola: Gráficas da Livraria Magalhães, 1972.

Duby, Georges, and Armond Wallon, eds. *Histoire de la France rurale.* 4 vols. Paris: Editions seuil, 1975–76.

Duffy, James. *Portuguese Africa.* Cambridge, Mass.: Harvard University Press, 1959.

Duffy, James. *Portugal in Africa.* Cambridge, Mass.: Harvard University Press, 1962.

Ekholm, Kajsa. *Power and Prestige: The Rise and Fall of the Old Kongo Kingdom.* Uppsala: Skriv Service AG, 1972.

Felgas, Hélio. *História do Congo Português.* Carmona, Angola: Emprensa Gráfica do Uige, 1958.

Felner, Afonso de Albuguerque. *Angola.* Coimbra: Imprensa da Universidade 1933.

Filesi, Teobaldo. "Le relazioni tra il regno del Congo e la Sede Apostolica nel prima meta del XVI secolo." *Africa* (Rome) 22 (1967):247–85, 413–60.

Filesi, Teobaldo. "Duarte Lopez ambasciatore del Rè del Congo presso Sisto V nel 1588." *Africa (Rome)* 23 (1968):44–83.

Filesi, Teobaldo. "Nuove Testimonianze sulla missione congolese a Roma del 1608." *Africa (Rome)* 23 (1968):423–69.

Filesi, Teobaldo. "L'epilogo della 'Missio Antiqua' dei Cappuccini nel regno del Congo (1800–1835)." *Euntes Docetes* 23 (1970).

Filesi, Teobaldo. *San Salvador: Croniche dei rè di Congo.* Bologna: E.M.I., 1974.

Frescucci, Don Bruno. *Pagine cortonesi.* Cortona: privately printed, 1968.

Godelier, Maurice. "Structure, system et contradiction dans 'Le Capital.'" *Horizon: Trajets marxistes en anthropologie.* Paris: F. Maspero, 1973.

Godelier, Maurice. "The Object and Method of Economic Anthropology." David Seddon, ed. *Relations of Production: Marxist Approaches to Economic Anthropology.* London: Cass, 1978.

Gray, Richard, and David Birmingham, eds. *Pre-Colonial African Trade: Essays on Trade in East and Central Africa before 1900.* Oxford: Clarendon Press, 1970.

Henige, David. *The Chronology of Oral Tradition: Quest for a Chimera.* Oxford: Clarendon Press, 1974.

Hilton, Anne. See Wilson, Anne.

Hindess, Barry, and Paul Hirst. *Pre-Capitalist Modes of Production.* London: Routledge and Kegan Paul, 1975.

Hindess, Barry, and Paul Hirst. *Mode of Production and Social Formation* Atlantic Highlands, N.J.: Humanities Press, 1977.

Hooglede, Hildebrand de. "Oud Plaatsnamen in Kongo." *Kongo-Overzee* 4 (1938):15–26.

Hooglede, Hildebrand de. *Le martyr Georges de Gheel et les debuts de la mission de Congo (1645–52).* Antwerp: Archives des capuchins, 1940.

Ihle, Alexander. *Das Alte Königreich Kongo.* Leipzig: E. and E. Vogel, 1929.

Jadin, Louis. "Aperçu de l'histoire du royaume du Congo (1482–1718)." *Bulletin du Faculté des Lettres du Strasbourg* (March, 1964).

Jadin, Louis. "Les sectes religieuses secretes des Antoniens au Congo (1705–09)." *Cahiers des religions africaines* 2 (1968):109–20.

Laman, Karl. *The Kongo.* 3 vols. Uppsala: Studia ethnographica upsaliensa 4, 1953–68.

MacGaffey, Wyatt. *Custom and Government in the Lower Congo.* Los Angeles and Berkeley: University of California Press, 1970.

MacGaffey, Wyatt. "Oral Tradition in Central Africa." *International Journal of African Historical Studies* 7 (1974):417–26.

MacGaffey, Wyatt. "The Cultural Roots of Kongo Prophetism." *History of Religion.* 17 (1977):177–93.

MacGaffey, Wyatt. "The Economic and Social Dimensions of Kongo Slavery (Zaire)." Suzanne Meiers and Igor Kopytoff, eds. *Slavery in Africa: Historical and Anthropological Perspectives.* Madison: University of Wisconsin Press, 1977.

Machal, Gil. "Origem da raça solongo (Zaire) segunda a lenda." *Portugal em Africa* 4 (1947).

Maddalena, Aldo de. "Il mondo rurale italiano nel cinque e nel seicento." *Rivista storica italiana* 76 (1964).

Martin, Phyllis. *The External Trade of the Loango Coast.* Oxford: Clarendon Press, 1972.

Martins, Joachim. "As causas da emigração dos povos de S. Salvador do Congo segundo a tradição indigena." *Mensário Administrativo* (Angola) 6 (1948):41–44.

Marx, Karl. *Capital.* 3 vols. 1867–94; New York: International Publishers, 1967.

Mauro, Frédéric. *L'expansion européen (1600–1870).* Paris: Presses universitaires de France, 1967.

Meillassoux, Claude. "The 'Economy' in Agricultural Self-Sustaining Societies: A Preliminary Analysis." In David Seddon, ed., *Relations of Production: Marxist Approaches to Economic Anthropology.* London: Cass, 1978.

Meillassoux, Claude, ed. *Esclavage en Afrique pré-coloniale.* Paris: François Maspero, 1975.

Miller, Joseph C. "A Note on Kansanze and the Portuguese." *Canadian Journal of African Studies* 6 (1972):43–56.

Miller, Joseph C. *Kings and Kinsmen: The Imbangala Impact on the Mbundu of Angola.* Oxford: Clarendon Press, 1976.

Miller, Joseph C. "The Slave Trade in Congo and Angola." Martin Kilson and Robert Rotberg, eds. *The African Diaspora: Interpretative Essays.* Cambridge, Mass.: Harvard University Press, 1976.

Miracle, Marvin. *Agriculture in the Congo Basin: Tradition and Change in African Rural Economics.* Madison: University of Wisconsin Press, 1966.

Monnier, Laurent. "Note sur les structures politiques de l'ancien royaume de Kongo avant l'arrivée des portugais." *Génève-Afrique* 5 (1966).

Morais Martins, Martin de. *Contacto de culturas no Congo portugues.* Lisbon: Junta de Investigações de Ultramar, 1958.

Movemento Popular de Liberação de Angola. *História de Angola.* Porto, Portugal: Afrontamento, 1975.

Randles, W. G. L. *L'ancien royaume du Congo des origines à la fin du XIXe siècle.* Paris: Mouton, 1968.

Reita, Rayna, ed. *Towards an Anthropology of Women.* New York: Monthly Review Press, 1975.

Rey, Pierre-Phillipe. *Colonialisme, néo-colonialisme, et transition au capitalisme.* Paris: François Maspero, 1971.

Ricard, Robert. *The Spiritual Conquest of Mexico.* Translated by Lesley Byrd Simpson. Berkeley and Los Angeles: University of California Press, 1966.

Rodney, Walter. "European Activity and African Response in Angola." In T.O. Ranger, ed., *Aspects of Central African History.* London: Heinemann, 1968.

Rogers, Susan Carol. "Woman's Place: A Critical Review of Anthropological Theory." *Comparative Studies in Society and History* 20 (1978):123–62.

Seddon, David, ed. *Relations of Production: Marxist Approaches to Economic Anthropology.* London: Cass, 1978.

Sedilliot, Réné. *Toutes les monnaies du monde.* Paris: Recueil Sivey, 1955.

Silva Rego, António da. *A dupla restauração de Angola e Brasil.* Lisbon: Agência Geral das Colónias, 1948.

Terray, Emmanuel. *Marxism and "Primitive" Societies.* New York and London: Monthly Review Press, 1972.

Thornton, John. "Demography and History in the Kingdom of Kongo, 1550–1750." *Journal of African History* 18 (1977):507–30.

Thornton, John. "An Eighteenth Century Baptismal Register and the Demographic History of Manguenzo." In Christopher Fyfe and David McMaster, eds., *African Historical Demography.* Edinburgh: Centre of African Studies, 1977.

Thornton, John. "A Resurrection for the Jaga." *Cahiers d'études africaines* 18 (1978):223–28.

Thornton, John. "Early Kongo-Portuguese Relations, 1483–1575: A New Interpretation." *History in Africa* 8 (1981):183–204.

Thornton, John. "The Kingdom of Kongo, ca. 1390–1678: History of an African Social Formation." *Cahiers d'études africaines* (forthcoming).

Vansina, Jan. *Kingdoms of the Savanna.* Madison: University of Wisconsin Press, 1966.

Vansina, Jan. "Anthropologists and the Third Dimension." *Africa* 39 (1969): 62–68.

Wilson, Anne. "The Kongo Kingdom to the Mid-Seventeenth Century." Ph.D. Dissertation, University of London, School of Oriental and African Studies, 1977.

Wing, Joseph van. *Études Bakongo*. 2nd ed. 2 vols. Brussels: Desclée de Brouwer, 1959.

Wolf, Eric. *Peasants*. Englewood Cliffs, N.J.: Humanities Press, 1966.

GUIDES TO SOURCE MATERIAL

Biographie coloniale belge. Brussels: Institute royale coloniale belge, 1954.

Cuvelier, Jean. "Note sur la documentation de l'histoire du Congo." *Bulletin des séances, Académie Royale des sciences d'outre mer* 34 (1953):443–70.

Dias Coimbra, Carlos. *Livros de 'Oficios para o Reino' do Aquivo Histórico Angolana* (1726–1801). Luanda. Instituto de Investigação Científica de Angola, 1959.

Filesi, Teobaldo, and I. Villapardiena. *La "Missio Antiqua" dei Cappuccini nel Congo (1645–1835)*. Rome: Instituto Storico dei Cappuccini, 1978.

Giglio, Carlo, and Elio Loddini. *Guida delle fonti per la storia dell' Africa esistenti in Italia*. Zug: Inter Documentation, 1973–74.

Gray, Richard, and David Chambers. *Materials for West African History in Italian Archives*. London: Athlone, 1965.

Jadin, Louis. "Recherches dans les archives et bibliotheques d'Italie et du Portugal sur l'ancien Congo." *Bulletin des séances, Académie Royale des sciences coloniales* 2 (1956):951–80.

Lopes da Silva Junior, António Joaquim. *Os reservados da Biblioteca Pública de Evora*. Coimbra: Imprensa da Universidade, 1905.

Miller, Joseph C. "The Archives of Luanda, Angola." *International Journal of African Historical Studies* 7 (1974):551–90.

Ryder, Alan F. C. *Materials for West African History in Portuguese Archives*. London: Athlone, 1964.

Simar, Théofile, and Eduard de Jonghe, *Archives congolaises*. Brussels: Vromont, 1919.

Streit, Robert, and Johannes Dindinger. *Biblioteca Missionum*. 33 vols. Aachen: Veröffentlichungen des International Instituts für Missionswissenschaftliche Forschung, 1916–present.

Thornton, John. "New Light on Cavazzi's Seventeenth Century Description of Kongo." *History in Africa* 6 (1979):253–64.

Thornton, John. "A Note on the Archives of the Propaganda Fide and the Capuchin Archives for African History." *History in Africa* 6 (1979):341–44.

Index

COMPOSED BY WEIMER TYPESETTING COMPANY, INC.
INDIANAPOLIS, INDIANA
MANUFACTURED BY CUSHING-MALLOY, INC.
ANN ARBOR, MICHIGAN
TEXT IS SET IN CALEDONIA, DISPLAY LINES IN OPTIMA

Library of Congress Cataloging in Publication Data
Thornton, John Kelly, 1949–
The Kingdom of Kongo.
Bibliography: pp. 179–188.
Includes index.
1. Congo (Kingdom)—History.   I. Title.
DT654.T56   1983   967'.2401   82-70549
ISBN 0-299-09290-9